D1105232

Twentieth Century Architecture 3

THE TWENTIETH CENTURY CHURCH

The Twentieth Century Society
1998

TWENTIETH CENTURY ARCHITECTURE
is published by the Twentieth Century Society
70 Cowcross Street, London ECIM 6BP
© The authors 1998

NUMBER 3 · 1998
ISBN 0 9529755 2 1
ISSN 1353–1964

Twentieth Century Architecture Editorial Committee:
Jill Lever, Alan Powers, Gavin Stamp.
Guest Editor: Roland Jeffery.

Designed and typeset by Dalrymple
in Quadraat and Eric Gill's Golden Cockerel type
Printed by BAS Printers Ltd

This issue of Twentieth Century Architecture is made
possible by the generous financial support of:
English Heritage
The Marc Fitch Fund
The Paul Mellon Centre for Studies in British Art,
generous assistance with photographs of Andrew
Mead at Emap Construct Ltd., and picture research by
Alan Powers.

The Twentieth Century Society gratefully acknowledges its
debt to the following generous Benefactors of the Society
who have enabled its work to continue and develop:
Baylight Properties plc., Mr Geoffrey Wilson, Lord
Palumbo, The Berkeley Group plc., The Edington
Charitable Trust, St George plc., Craignish Charitable
Trust, Mr Brian Knox, Mr Mike Davies and The Lyndhurst
Settlement. The Society gratefully acknowledges a grant
from the Department of Culture Heritage and Sport for
part of the costs of its casework.

Contents

1 Sacred Architecture in a Secular Century

GAVIN STAMP

Sacred Architecture in a Secular Century

GAVIN STAMP

'What is this great romantic pile with its long, incised vertical lines and hidden windows?' wondered C.H. Reilly in his annual review of new British architecture in 1934. 'Is it a new cathedral by that interesting church fellow up in the north, F.X. Velarde? There is certainly something of his at Blackburn rather like it. No, it cannot be that. There is a faint plume of steam from one of the towers which can hardly be incense ...'[1]

In fact, it was the new Battersea Power Station that Reilly was admiring, but the wilful journalistic confusion was understandable. The treatment of the vast planes of brickwork on the generating station with 'jazz modern' fluting and other expressive devices represented a form of modernity which was also to be seen on many new church buildings. And, indeed, Velarde – that interesting fellow up in Liverpool – had recently designed an Anglican church in Blackburn – St Gabriel's – whose exterior was a chunky brick box with a tall chimney-like tower reminiscent of Herbert Rowse's contemporary ventilation shafts for the Mersey Tunnel, while the interior of plastered arches was embellished with Art Deco light fittings and a cinema-style reredos of chromium-plated tubing.

British church architecture between the world wars was still (sometimes) conspicuously modern in style. Historians, however, have tended to concentrate on the achievements of the Modern Movement in public and private housing, and have rather neglected churches in any general picture. Certainly church design was not at the cutting edge of development as it had been, say, at the time of Wren and Hawksmoor or in the mid-Victorian decades. Even so, it continued to be

figure 1
Sir Giles Gilbert Scott. Liverpool Cathedral, 1903–1978. Perspective showing Scott's design for the west front, drawn by A.C. Webb, 1943. (photo Stewart Bale)

1. *The Architects' Journal*, 11th January 1934, p.65.

figure 2
F.X. Velarde. St Gabriel's, Blackburn, 1932–33.

important and some of the most impressive and rewarding of modern British buildings are churches (and cathedrals). If the 20th century has seen a dramatic decline in church attendance and in the prestige of the Established Church, it has been from a high peak at the turn of the century. Decline there has certainly been: the squalor and hypocrisy of the Great War encouraged disillusionment while the decades after the Second World War saw a seemingly irresistible tendancy towards secularism – visibly proclaimed by the wholesale abandonment of churches both rural and urban. But experiment and endeavour in church design has never ceased.

For right through the century many new churches have been built. If, on the one hand, older churches were being closed in city centres – the Bishop of London's astonishing proposal of 1919 to demolish nineteen City churches by Wren and others being the most notorious example – this was the concomitant of a continuing campaign to build new churches to serve the populations moving to new suburbs. When Dr Winnington-Ingram finally succeeded in doing away with All Hallows', Lombard Street, in 1938, its tower was re-erected next to a new church in Twickenham designed by Robert Atkinson which carefully incorporated all the 17th-century furnishings.

And church architects remained conspicuous in the profession. Basil Spence was knighted, not for his public housing and university work but for building the new Coventry Cathedral, just as Maufe got his handle for Guildford. The creator of that 'great romantic pile' by the Thames at Battersea was first and foremost a church architect: Giles Gilbert Scott, the pupil of another great church designer in the tradition of the Gothic Revival, Temple Moore. Scott had been knighted at the opening of the choir of his colossal work in Liverpool in 1924, when 'the Diocese, and indeed the whole country, suddenly woke up to the realisation that there had been growing up almost unnoticed in its midst a Cathedral, which in size and beauty was worthy to be compared with the greatest churches of the middle ages.'[2] It was a design whose triumphant success encouraged the profession in the years of doubt and uncertainty after the Great War, for here was powerful new architecture at once romantic and original, traditional and modern; no wonder commissions to design libraries and power stations followed.

Liverpool, indeed, is the best place in Britain to study the complex and intriguing history of ecclesiastical design in the 20th-century. A city of sectarian division which had seen the erection of some of the finest of Victorian churches, its skyline is dominated by two large but very different modern cathedrals. Scott's, for the Anglicans, was built over eight decades and is Gothic, although treated with a monumentality and a classicizing symmetry which distinguishes it from anything done previously. Its landmark is a great tower, a response to site, expectations and a sense of continuity which Goodhart-Rendel considered – or hoped – to be 'the venerated last resting-place' of romantic architecture.[3] This tower might have been challenged, at the other end of Hope Street, by a Classical dome bigger and more accomplished than that of St Peter's in Rome. It was intended to surmount the astonishing, brilliant, impossible cathedral designed by Lutyens for Liverpool's Roman Catholics. But it was not to be, and Scott's tower is now answered by the circular spiky lantern which tops the conical building designed by Frederick Gibberd in 1959 – a form inspired by Oskar Niemeyer's contemporary cathedral project for Brasilia.

If Scott's Gothic cathedral in Liverpool represents the continuing vitality of tradition, Gibberd's reflects a crude response to liturgical change as well as to fashionable influences from abroad. For it is possible to interpret modern British church architecture in terms of polarities, of traditionalism versus modernism in both style and in liturgical planning. The story, however, is not quite so simple, as is shown by St Mary's, Wellingborough, the masterpiece of that precious darling of the Anglo-Catholic clergy, Ninian Comper. Begun in 1904, St

2. Vere E. Cotton, *The Book of Liverpool Cathedral*, Liverpool, 1964, p.6.
3. H.S. Goodhart-Rendel, *English Architecture since the Regency*, London 1953, p.252.

Mary's is the most exquisitely beautiful of buildings in which Gothic and Classical precedents were reconciled in 'unity by inclusion.' And with its free-standing gilded baldacchino, it also responded to that demand for a closer involvement by the laity loosely categorised as the Liturgical Movement. The same is true of Comper's church of the 1930s in Cosham, in which a Classical interior was contained within a spare Gothic brick box. In contrast, Spence's parish churches in Coventry, say, or Gillespie, Kidd & Coia's inventive Roman Catholic churches of the 1960s in Glasgow are liturgically conservative.

The Gothic Revival remained a powerful force in 20th-century British architecture, even if somewhat diluted and emasculated in such tasteful expressions as Edward Maufe's Guildford Cathedral, won in competition in 1932 and finished in 1966. (That the Revival is not dead is suggested by the current Millennium proposal to complete the absent crossing tower on Stephen Dykes Bower's converted cathedral at Bury St Edmunds.) But at the beginning of this century the Gothic remained a vital creative force, symbolised, perhaps, by Giles Gilbert Scott winning Liverpool with his design for a 'Twentieth Century Cathedral'. In this first (and superseded) design, the Late Victorian tradition of a refined and abstracted Late Gothic, developed in particular by his father and G.F. Bodley, was given new life. In the Edwardian years the Gothic was interpreted with great sophistication and originality by Temple Moore, Harold Gibbons, Ernest Shearman and many others.

Not that Gothic held a monopoly. The completion of the noble shell of Bentley's Westminster Cathedral at the beginning of the century – 'beyond all doubt the finest church built for centuries' in Norman Shaw's opinion – ensured a vogue for the Byzantine, particularly with Roman Catholics.[4] And, with an increasing demand for simplicity, the Byzantine evolved into an round-arched Early Christian style favoured by Roman Catholics, Anglicans, Non-conformists and Christian Scientists alike. Charles Reilly's brick and concrete vaulted church in Dalston of 1908 – 'the building I should like to be remembered by, if any' – is one of the best examples of this taste for the austere and the sublime.[5] In such churches, contemporaries hoped for the development of a modern architecture from the refinement of tradition combined with constructional integrity.

But the Great War changed everything, replacing complacent Edwardian insularity with uncertainty and, eventually, an openness to new ideas from abroad. This was reflected as much in church architecture as in other spheres so that, just as the creative years of the Victorian Gothic Revival cannot be understood without reference to Normandy and North Italy, the churches of the 1920s and 1930s manifest a close study of new tendencies in Continental Europe. At a basic level, this is shown by the widespread employment of the parabolic arch. Then there was the influence of 'Swedish Grace', with a taste for muted colours, limed woodwork and the gentle abstraction of traditional forms encouraged by visits to such buildings as Ivar Tengbom's Högalid Church in Stockholm.

But the most dynamic models for emulation were to be found in France and Germany. Notre-Dame du Raincy by Auguste Perret was a modern Sainte-Chapelle in reinforced concrete which demonstrated how new methods of construction could satisfy more traditional expectations in both liturgical planning and in the use of vibrant coloured glass. In Germany, Dominikus Böhm and Rudolf Schwarz experimented with both novel plans and dramatic architectural forms for the Roman Catholics without ever losing sight of the need to give a modern church an ecclesiastical character. At the same time, Otto Bartning explored the possibilities of both steel and concrete for the needs of a Protestant congregation. The modish details of churches in London like St Alban's, North Harrow, by Arthur Kenyon, say, or those by Velarde and Bernard Miller near Liverpool reveal the importance of these Continental models.

This is not to suggest, however, that English – and Scottish – church archi-

4. *Architectural Review* 1901, p.170, quoted in Andrew Saint, *Richard Norman Shaw*, London & New Haven, 1976, p.364.
5. C.H. Reilly, *Scaffolding in the Sky*, London, 1938, p.113.

tecture of the inter-war years did not have a distinct character of its own. In the work of Giles Scott, for instance, the expressive use of concrete lateral arches was fused with his own personal development of Gothic precedents, while the work of one of the most innovative of church designers, Nugent Cachmaille-Day, was at once national and international in character. His church of 1937 at Wythenshawe, a new suburb of Manchester, shows the influence of Perret in its use of a reinforced concrete frame, yet the handling of the large windows and the brickwork was tempered by a sense of tradition while the remarkable centralised plan of the church – governed by the superimposition of two squares at 45° to each other – was as truly original as it was thoughtful.

Cachmaille-Day's best churches, like those of Giles Scott, also reveal another important continuity with the 19th century past, with a particular manner of building. This is what Charles Booth had characterised as the 'bare style', that appropriate emphasis on unbroken planes of unadorned brickwork in urban settings which was to be seen in the work of Street and Butterfield and Brooks. It was a taste for the sublime which can be seen notably at Cachmaille-Day's church at Gorton in Leeds and his Expressionist re-interpretation of Albi Cathedral in Eltham in south-east London. Even in what seemed to contemporaries the most modern of new churches, the bright flame of the Gothic Revival still burned. Similarly, in the remarkable centrally-planned Roman Catholic church at Gorleston designed by the celebrated architect-turned-sculptor, Eric Gill, the intersecting arches which define the central space are of Gothic profile.

Some churches of the first half of the century – Comper's at Wellingborough, perhaps, or Scott's at Terriers and Cachmaille-Day's at Wythenshawe, or even Albert Richardson's unlikely streamlined timber barn at Greenford – surely compare with the best of previous centuries. And there is one in particular in which the several tendencies were fused in one triumphant masterpiece. Oddly enough, it is not in Britain but thousands of miles away in India: St Martin's Garrison Church in New Delhi designed by Lutyens' pupil, A.G. Shoosmith. This monumental pile of brickwork in Lutyens' 'Elemental Mode' can be interpreted as an abstraction of a traditional Gothic church yet, with its stepped profile, it also manifests the contemporary interest in the sublime monuments of the ancient world. Penelope Chetwode recalled that it was known as 'the Cubist Church.' Yet the tall, cool interior, vaulted in concrete, is austerely Classical in style.

figure 3
A.G. Shoosmith. St Martin's Church, New Delhi, 1930. (photo Marjorie Shoosmith)

Reviewing it in 1931, Christopher Hussey wrote how, 'elemental as the conception is, it none the less has very definite style, appropriate both to the climate and the building's purpose. Had this church been the work of a French or German architect, Europe would be flabbergasted by the magnificently simple and direct design. But since it is the work of an Englishman, it will probably never be heard of abroad.'[6]

The Second World War, even more than the First, had a profound effect on the development of church architecture. Bombs destroyed St Catherine's, Hammersmith, by Robert Atkinson – one of the most admired of modern churches – while also providing many opportunities for new ones. In the changed conditions of post-1945 Britain, with the Modern Movement now in the ascendant and in a climate of economic austerity, new churches began to look rather different. But before these could be built, there was the problem of old churches to be addressed. Here, the British record is not impressive. On the whole, war-damaged churches were neither restored correctly nor rebuilt to a modern design with conviction, while many Victorian buildings of high quality, like St Agnes', Kennington, which could and should have been restored, were replaced by smaller buildings of the utmost feebleness and mediocrity. Given the reverence for the work of Sir Christopher Wren, it now seems extraordinary that most of his City churches damaged in the Blitz were not carefully rebuilt to the original design. Instead, owing, perhaps, to a convenient (mis?)interpretation of the principles of the Society for the Protection of Ancient Buildings, they were altered, with new work done vaguely in the spirit of Wren.

There are few examples in Britain of the remains of bomb-damaged churches dramatically juxtaposed with bold new structures of high quality, like the church at Valognes in Normandy by Yves-Marie Froidevaux or the rebuilt Kaiser-Wilhelm-Gedächtnis-kirche by Egon Eiermann. Perhaps the nearest equivalent is the new church economically and cleverly built within the walls of Hawksmoor's St George's-in-the-East by Arthur Bailey. Bernard Miller's rebuilding of the parish church of Tettenhall near Wolverhampton demonstrated an imaginative reinterpretation of Gothic which seamlessly incorporates the old tower, but in this case the church had been destroyed by accidental fire rather than by enemy action.

As for new churches, inspiration from the Continent remained important as ever, with Finland joining Sweden and Germany as a source of influence and Le Corbusier's maverick performance at Ronchamp suggesting further possibilities and encouraging a much greater determination amongst younger architects to escape from inhibiting tradition. 'With the new materials, particularly steel and reinforced concrete, enabling the architect to break away from the narrow nave dictated by stone and wood, and with liturgical evolution developing in strong opposition to the Latin Cross plan, new and exciting concepts of ecclesiastical space are inevitably emerging,' argued the American, G.E. Kidder Smith in 1964.[7] What is impressive is how much thought was now going into reconciling the imperatives of the Liturgical Movement with the expectations of the Modern Movement. 'The first essential for church builders today is a radical approach,' argued Peter Hammond in 1956, 'an approach which, paradoxical as this may seem, involves forgetting all about architecture – at any rate in the early stages of the design process. The second essential is architectural seriousness... *In other words, we should be heading towards rather plain brick boxes with no tricks.*'[8]

The seriousness of St Paul's, Bow Common, by Robert Maguire & Keith Murray, or of the remarkable series of Roman Catholic churches in and around Glasgow built by Gillespie, Kidd & Coia – that is, by Isi Metzstein and Andrew MacMillan – cannot be denied. Yet somehow – in Britain – on the whole, the built results do not quite live up to the possibilities suggested by the considerable contemporary literature on the problems of church design. For Edward Mills, writ-

6. *Country Life*, 9th May, 1931, p.577.
7. G.E. Kidder Smith, *The New Churches of Europe*, London & New York 1964.
8. Peter Hammond, ed., *Towards a Church Architecture*, London 1962, p.10 (author's italics).

ing in 1956, the main problem was the past. 'If the churchmen in this country still display a tendency to conservatism in the matter of religious architecture it is because the church building of the first half of the twentieth century has inherited this legacy of pseudo-Gothic romanticism in a modified form amongst nearly all denominations. To post-war England, however, it has already become evident that the financial aspect of church building is now the major consideration in design and planning... A new type of church is envisaged which should not only be the architectural expression of a centre of worship but also provide for the social needs.'[9] Yet for all the concern with making new churches as part of the community, with treating them architecturally as part of a social centre, the results – at least in visual terms – seem to express the growing estrangement of all the Christian churches from an increasingly secular society.

This was not for want of trying. 'It is odd to reflect that we are living in one of the great ages of church-building,' wrote one commentator in 1957. 'Not so much, perhaps, on account of our piety, as because of the last war and the shift in population to new areas. Not for five hundred years have we seen so many new churches going up, and never, one imagines, in such extreme divergence of design.'[10] As Peter Hammond complained, 'Churches are built to 'express' this and to 'symbolize' that. We have churches which look like hands folded in prayer; churches which symbolize aspiration or the anchor of the industrial pilgrim's life; churches which express the kingship of Christ; churches shaped like fishes, flames, and passion-flowers. There are still very few churches which show signs of anything comparable to the radical functional analysis that informs the best secular architecture of our time.'[11]

The buildings illustrated in, say, the Incorporated Church Building Society's little book of 1957 on *Sixty Post-War Churches* seem mean and mediocre compared with those covered in the society's earlier books: *Fifty Modern Churches* of 1947, covering those built 1930–45, and *New Churches Illustrated* of 1936. Even at a distance, the overall picture of church architecture of the post-war decades in Britain remains confused. And the conservatism of Christian congregations – at least in England – cannot easily be dismissed. Perhaps the architect who was most successful in reconciling this with the use of a conspicuously modern and personal new aesthetic was George Pace, whose best work was probably his first: the transformation of Llandaff Cathedral. At Worth Abbey in the 1960s, a supreme synthesis was achieved by Francis Pollen: a great circular space under a concrete dome which represents a truly architectural response to the Liturgical Movement, defined by massive brick walls which echo the work of Lutyens as much as that of Le Corbusier.

But it is important to recognise that fine churches in historical styles and on traditional plans continued to be built and that some were of real quality. Most of H.S. Goodhart-Rendel's best churches, for instance, in which he played on the themes of his Victorian heroes, were built after 1945, while Giles and his brother Adrian Scott continued building until their deaths in 1960 and 1963. Despite their own committment to the Modern Movement, Maguire and Murray realised that style is not everything and that 'liturgy and architecture have a functional relationship.' Writing in their 1965 book of a modern church in Germany with thick masonry walls and round arches, they observed that it, 'though apparently traditional in style, is more essentially a product of the Modern Movement than a great number of new churches which are decked out with 'exciting' modern forms, but are not fundamentally concerned with the needs of the developing liturgical life of a Christian community.'[12]

In England, perhaps, a compromise between tradition and modernity is essential – at least in the design of sacred buildings – and that is why the new Coventry Cathedral was such a popular success. After much controversy, its architect, Basil Spence, managed to establish a satisfactory relationship between

9. Edward D. Mills, *The Modern Church*, London 1956, p.26.

10. Editorial in *The London Churchman*, quoted by Nigel Melhuish, 'Modern Architectural Theory and the Liturgy' in Peter Hammond, ed., *Towards a Church Architecture*, London 1962, p.39.

11. Hammond, *op. cit.*, p.24.

12. Robert Maguire & Keith Murray, *Modern Churches of the World*, London 1965, p.14.

figure 4
Gillespie, Kidd & Coia. St Benedict's, Drumchapel, Glasgow, 1964–70. (demolished)
(photo RCAHMS © Crown Copyright)

figure 5
Francis Pollen. Abbey Church of Our
Lady Help of Christians, Worth,
E. Sussex, 1965–75.
(photo Dennis Gilbert)

13. John Thomas, *Coventry Cathedral*, London
& Sydney, 1987, p.112.
14. Kidder Smith, *op. cit.* p.38.

the ruins of the old church and his new creation. More important, he succeeded in satisfying the expectations of traditionally minded Anglicans while designing a building which was conspicuously modern in style. Spence conceived his build-ing as a 'casket' containing many 'jewels,' and so he orchestrated what can now be seen as the last significant creation of the Arts and Crafts movement.[13] Even so, he was much criticised both by architects and by progressive churchmen for the essential conservatism of the plan of the new Cathedral, the sentimentality of the conception, and for such deceits as the false vault supported by structur-ally redundant columns.

Yet, when the new cathedral opened in 1962 and for several years afterwards, huge numbers of visitors came to see it. Possibly this was partly owing to the emotional and polemical significance of the wartime destruction of the old cathedral and city centre, but the new pilgrims were nevertheless impressed. As Kidder Smith observed, 'the new Coventry Cathedral has done more to revitalize the hitherto almost totally reactionary architecture of the Church of England than was ever dreamed possible.'[14] Coventry Cathedral was, in fact, the last modern building in Britain *of any type* that ordinary people have queued to see inside. That was quite an achievement.

16

2 Unity by Inclusion: Sir Ninian Comper and the Planning of a Modern Church

ANTHONY SYMONDSON SJ

Unity by Inclusion:
Sir Ninian Comper and the
Planning of a Modern Church

ANTHONY SYMONDSON SJ

On 12 October, 1932, J.N. Comper read a long paper to the St Paul's Ecclesiological Society entitled *Further Thoughts on the English Altar: or Practical Considerations on the Planning of a Modern Church*.[1] He was sixty-eight, past the height of his professional life, and associated with an expression of church architecture and planning that would have surprised his early patrons. The paper was the fruit of forty years' consideration and experience gained since he had given the first of his liturgical papers, *Practical Considerations on the Gothic or English Altar and Certain Dependent Ornaments*, at the age of twenty-nine, to the same Society in 1893.

Further Thoughts was illustrated by the developments in his work demonstrated at St Cyprian's, Clarence Gate, St Marylebone (1902–3), and St Mary's, Wellingborough, Northamptonshire (1904–31). It was an explanation of the reasons why he had abandoned late-medievalism for an accretive expression of architecture, combining the Gothic, Classic and Moorish styles into a statement of architectural unity. These developments had perplexed, even antagonised, many of his admirers who saw in them evidence of idiosyncrasy, obscurantism and decline. Yet they engaged others who discerned lasting qualities in the combination of magnificence and simplicity, the cosmopolitan mastery of European precedent, and recognised in the clarity of Comper's planning a new understanding of worship in which the congregation was involved in a fuller visual participation. How had these developments come into being and what was their underlying motive?

BEAUTY, MEDIEVALISM AND THE ORNAMENTS RUBRIC

Fundamental to Comper's understanding of art and architecture was a primary appeal to beauty and reason mediated in eucharistic terms. He was an Anglo-Catholic, motivated on a profound level by faith and religion. The Mass was the heart and centre of worship; churches were built to contain the altar and to provide shelter for the worshippers; their plan was dictated by the liturgical ceremonies that surrounded the eucharistic offering; church architecture revealed and embodied beauty within the context of the highest activity of man: worship. It was the appeal to beauty that led Comper to discover its purest form in the religious art of the late Middle Ages, exemplified by the Flemish Primitive panel painters, and in the English Perpendicular architecture of the fifteenth-century churches of East Anglia. The search for beauty became a life-long quest.

Comper's appeal to the late Middle Ages was informed by history as much as aesthetics. He believed that this period fulfilled what was ordered by the Ornaments Rubric of the *Book of Common Prayer*. Few these days know of the rubric. It loomed large in Anglo-Catholic developments in Anglican worship in the nineteenth century because it authenticated sacramentals and gave them lawful authority.[2]

The rubric was first inserted in the Prayer Book of 1549 at the beginning of the Order for Morning Prayer; it was re-enacted by Parliament in 1604 and retained in the Prayer Book of 1662. The rubric states that 'chancels shall remain as they have been in times past' and continues: 'Such ornaments of the church and of the

figure 1
The Cappella Palatina, Palermo, c.1132–40. (Photo A.F. Kersting)

1. *Further Thoughts on the English Altar, or Practical Considerations on the Planning of a Modern Church*, 1932, (Being a continuation of a paper read before the Society in 1893). SPES Transactions, X, 2, 1933.
2. Anthony Symondson, 'Theology, Worship and the late-Victorian church', in Chris Brooks and Andrew Saint, eds, *The Victorian church: Architecture and Society*, Manchester 1995, pp.196–8, 212–18.

ministers thereof, at all times of their ministration, shall be retained and be in use in this Church of England by authority of parliament, in the second year of the reign of King Edward the sixth.' Late-Medieval art and architecture synchronised with the dates 1548–9 and reinforced Comper's preferences. English churches were then scarcely touched by the Renaissance. The years immediately preceding King Henry VIII's excommunication by Pope Clement VII in 1533 became of all-consuming interest to him and his patrons in terms of reviving what was lost in the subsequent onslaught of royal and Protestant iconoclasm.

The results are well known. Informed by contemporary inventories, Comper's early restorations of medieval churches changed stripped, barn-like shells into unified works of art. This was accomplished by furniture, embroidery, exquisite painted decoration and glass. Nineteenth-century churches were changed in the same way. Between 1890–1900 Comper's work at Cantley and Egmanton, for instance, at Downside Abbey, in the crypt of St Mary Magdalene's, Paddington, and at St Barnabas, Pimlico, introduced an interpretation of English church art and liturgical worship unattempted on scientific principles since the work of A.W.N. Pugin and Gilbert Scott the Younger, both of whom, in terms of authenticity, Comper surpassed. Comper's early work was intended to fulfil the rubrical provisions of the modern age. What appeared to some to be retrogressive antiquarianism was essentially radical in the aim to restore to the National Church continuity with the medieval past and make it one with the historic faith. It was Comper's artistry and knowledge which made his experiments acceptable to the educated.

Closely associated with him was J. Wickham Legg (1843–1921), a retired surgeon turned liturgiologist and paleographer. Legg was as much concerned with tracing the origins of Christian worship as medievalism and fidelity to the *Book of Common Prayer*. He was opposed to Romanising tendencies in Anglo-Catholicism and marshalled liturgical scholarship by founding a series of learned societies. The most significant for medievalising influence was the Alcuin Club, founded in 1897 to 'encourage and assist in the practical study of ceremonial, and the arrangement of churches their furniture and ornaments, in accordance with the rubrics of the Book of Common Prayer, strict obedience to which is the guiding principle of the Club.'

Legg was, however, quarrelsome and acidulous. Within six months he had resigned form the Alcuin Club, partly because of the unwelcome influence of Dr Percy Dearmer, the future vicar of St Mary's, Primrose Hill. Dearmer was the author of *The Parson's Handbook*, published in 1899 as a popularist manual of medieval ceremonial and church furnishing. In reaction, Legg continued to campaign independently by starting in the same year the *English Churchman's Kalendar*. He edited the *Kalendar* until 1910.

On the front page he illustrated Comper's work, notably his late-Gothic altars; and inside he provided descriptive explanations of their principles. 'It was Dr Legg's intention to popularise the movement by these Kalendars and he urged against their author's objections the unanswerable argument that photographs of modern work would appeal to people who would not understand medieval pictures; and at that time other modern examples were not to be had. To anyone who knows these photographs and the altars which have followed, there is no doubt about the influence of these first Kalendars.'[3]

3. *Further Thoughts*, p.30.

PRIMITIVE WORSHIP, MEDIEVALISM AND THE ANGLICAN IDEAL

Of equal importance to Legg was the Church of England's appeal to the authority of the Primitive Church. In the *Kalendar* for 1907 the leaf for September contained a surprising note, 'The "New High Altar"'. It referred to an essay 'On the History of the Christian Altar', published by Edmund Bishop (1846–1917), the leading English Roman Catholic liturgiologist, in the *Downside Review*, for July, 1905. The subject had preoccupied Bishop for many years. He took as his ideal the early basilican model of the fourth century, found at the time of Constantine the Great (d337) and the triumph of orthodoxy at the Council of Nicea (325). 'With the fourth century the Church stands out in the face of the world, free in a new and sovereign manner to fashion her outward adornment in accordance with her own spirit and under external influences from which ... she has at no time been free.'[4]

'Of the early altar Mr Bishop first speaks of "the prominence and respect given to the holy Table, as the place of sacrifice. It was in form not oblong as now in the West but a cube; and stood as a table in the utmost simplicity. The LORD's board was too holy (too 'awful' is another view) to bear anything else but the Mystic Oblation itself. ... The rich coverings may be taken (I conceive) as an integral part of the altar itself. Everything of the nature of ornamental accessory was around, above but apart from the altar." With the ciborium or baldequin added to its surroundings, the altar of this period may be considered, says Mr Bishop, the ideal altar.'[5]

In 1909 the leaf for July illustrated the Cowley Fathers' church of the Holy Name, Poona. This is a neo-Classical work completed in 1905, which 'shows the adaptability of the fourth century basilica to the service of the Church in the present age in a hot climate, like that of India. Though extraordinarily simple, the building is wonderfully dignified, and must give pleasure to all beholders.' The only offending feature was the high altar. 'It might have been wished, perhaps, that the architect had provided a fourth or fifth century altar instead of a seventeenth or eighteenth century altar. This latter seems incongruous with the surroundings. To suit the building, the altar should have been foursquare, with a ciborium or baldequin, as it was called later, on four columns, such as may still be seen in the more ancient basilicas of Rome.'[6]

Legg only once attempted to put these primitive ideals into practice but he was anxious to see built a church which would embody his liturgical principles. This was accomplished at St Margaret's, Braemar, founded in 1898 and consecrated by the Bishop of Aberdeen in 1907. The Scottish Episcopal Church and Deeside are an obscure setting and place to build a model church with a didactic intention. Braemar's proximity to Balmoral made it popular with English visitors, for whom it was mainly intended; Legg himself had a house there and he was active in commending it as an example of what should be done in England.

The Gothic high altar was illustrated in the *Kalendar* for 1908 and described in the leaf for July. It had four riddel posts painted and decorated with the Scottish lion rampant, hung with curtains suspended by silk cords looped in split rings supporting gilded figures of kneeling angels holding tapers. There are no gradines, or shelves, for a crucifix and six candlesticks, only a low halpas (or upper frontal) of blue silk embroidered with St Margaret's cross in gold thread between the orphreys embroidered with thistles, of the same design as the altar frontal below. It embodied the principles found in medieval illuminations. 'Mr Comper's work is always excellent but this church has been pronounced to be one of the best, if not the very best of his buildings. ... He says it "follows the style of the parish church, which the middle ages developed to suit our northern climate, and later times have continued and handed down to us by a tradition never entirely broken."'[7] Braemar was not, however, London. In 1902, Comper was given the commission for St Cyprian's, Clarence Gate, St Marylebone. The foundation stone was laid on 7 July; the building progressed rapidly and it was consecrated on 31 July of the following year. Here was the opportunity Legg and Comper had been seeking.

St Cyprian's was built as a memorial to Charles Gutch, the founder of the parish in 1866. He was an Anglo-Catholic pioneer.[8] His successor, G.F. Forbes,

4. Edmund Bishop, 'On the History of the Christian Altar', reprinted from *Downside Review*, July 1905, p.4, later reprinted in *Liturgica Historica*, Oxford, 1918. Another work of significance in recovering liturgical origins was E.G. Cuthbert F. Atchley, *Ordo Romanus Primus*, The Library of Liturgiology & Ecclesiology for English Readers, ed Vernon Staley, 1905.

5. J. Wickham Legg, ed, *The English Churchman's Kalendar*, 1907, September.

6. ibid, 1909, July. Comper was to provide a ciborium for the Holy Name in 1934–7.

7. ibid, 1908, July.

8. Gutch had wanted Street to design St Cyprian's. He was opposed by Lord Portman, the ground landlord, who disliked his churchmanship.

figure 2
St Cyprian's, Clarence Gate, St
Marylebone, 1901–3, shortly after
consecration. (Photo Cyril Ellis)

9. Ivy F. Frith, *A History of St Cyprian's, Clarence Gate*, nd, p.23.

10. Letter to the Revd L.W. Comper, 1 November 1901. Comper's private papers.

11. The Revd John Comper had newly retired from being Rector of St Margaret's, Aberdeen.

was appointed in 1897; he was committed to English models of worship and had known Comper's work at the Convent of the Epiphany when he was vicar of St Paul's, Truro. The wool churches of East Anglia informed the plan, design and liturgical canons. At the consecration the rite was based on the pontifical of Egbert, Archbishop of York (d.766), because it embodied the 'real, true ceremonial of the old Church of England.'[9] That was Legg's choice. The pontifical is of great value as an early source of the history of the liturgy and of the English coronation rite. The nave was strewn with rushes and the sanctuary with flowers; and magnificent vestments designed by Comper and worked by the School of Embroidery of the Sisters of Bethany, Clerkenwell, were borrowed for the occasion. Yet the church was barely furnished apart from the long high altar beneath the low cill of the east window with its hangings of gilded and painted leather. A perspective drawing hung in the Royal Academy in 1903 showed what was intended: an unremitting statement of what superficially appeared to be late-medieval perfection.

With the building of St Cyprian's three strands were brought together: artistry, liturgical scholarship and pastoral application. The church opened a new understanding of liturgical worship for being designed as a consistent whole on rational principles. The sober piety and learning of the founders made Dearmer's experiments at St Mary's, Primrose Hill, look shallow and half-informed. The ideals of the Oxford Movement were maintained, worship was eucharistic and the practice was rooted in the sacramental system. This group regarded St Cyprian's as the quintessential Anglican church of the twentieth century. For Comper and Legg medievalism was equated with the new century. 'By medieval architecture I mean the best developments of our national English architecture which is no less medieval than is Shakespeare. Both were developments of the middle ages, but both usher in the modern world.'[10]

ST MARY'S WELLINGBOROUGH, ITALY AND THE DISCOVERY OF SOURCES

In 1900 Comper had for the first time reluctantly visited Rome. He had no desire to go but filially accompanied his father, John Comper, who wanted to see the city again before he died.[11] They went in a stiff clerical party forming a Lunn's tour. His mind was invaded by the North. He disliked the Baroque churches but was softened by the beauty of Michelangelo's lavender blue dome. It was Classical Rome that appealed to him, the primitive basilicas, and Mediterranean colour in the compartments of aquamarine set in the solidly gilded coffered ceilings of St John Lateran, juxtaposed with the splendour of the Blessed Sacrament chapel and the cathedral's rose-red hangings. Pope Leo XIII had declared 1900 a Holy Year. Comper went to the canonisation of St John Baptist de la Salle and St Rita of Cascia and saw the darkened, rose-hung interior of St Peter's illuminated by candle light for the last time. The world had converged on Rome, including Oscar Wilde who had also obtained a seat for the canonisation.

On the final day he visited the Vatican and saw the Sistine chapel and the Borgia apartments; and in the afternoon the National Museum. It was there that he discovered in Classical figure sculpture 'the same forms of folds in the draperies of the statues and the identical lines of decoration as in East Anglia.'[12] In his letters home Comper only mentioned these details in passing. In later life he described their effect in dramatic terms. 'It was ... a lesson like that of the vision of St Peter on the house-top at Joppa: "What God hath cleansed, that call not thou common." [Acts 10:15]. All beauty inspired by the Creator Spirit is one, as all goodness is one and all truth is one. It is this which Dante and the spirit of the Renaissance and the Schoolmen saw when they claimed Greece for Christ.'[13]

The Roman journey prepared the ground and sowed the seed for an aesthetic revision that would take Comper from exclusive Northern European precedents to others of diverse and far-ranging influence. It emancipated him from insularity. New impressions usually took four years to germinate in Comper's mind. The commission for St Mary's, Wellingborough, in 1904, brought them to fruition.[14]

St Mary's, as we know it today, is not what the founders expected. Henrietta, Gertrude and Harriet Sharman, the donors, were much travelled, Anglo-Catholic maiden ladies, the daughters of John Wood Sharman, a local solicitor and landowner. The motivating force behind it was Dr Salisbury Price, Comper's friend and patron, a man of means who was vicar of St Ives in Huntingdonshire. Price continued Comper's sumptuous restoration of the church in 1894–1900 which had been started by Arthur Stapylton Barnes, his predecessor. He was responsible for recommending T.J. Watts, the first vicar, a native of St Ives who had come, at an early age, under his influence.

Price was an ultra-sacerdotalist medievalist. He told Comper that should he ever ask him to design a church, he would stipulate that he did not go beyond the fourteenth and fifteenth centuries. Watts imbibed these views. Both were confident that St Mary's would be in the Perpendicular style, designed for late-medieval worship. It would, they hoped, be run as a collegiate church staffed by a small body of priests. Neither were prepared for Comper's architectural development and the emergence of his mature style. Indeed, they were dismayed by it and were carried only by Comper's artistry. His powers of persuasion on the foundresses enabled St Mary's to progress as it did.

On a personal level, St Mary's was the fruit of a crisis. '17 April 1904. 2nd Sunday after Easter', Comper recorded in his diary, 'sat in 177 Knight's Hill garden & designed St Mary's, Wellingborough, & got the chill which ended in pneumonia.' These words disguised a more serious reality. The chill led to a nervous breakdown, brought on by the troubled dissolution of Comper's partnership with William Bucknall. This was formed in 1888 but from the start was unequal. Differences of opinion were compounded by the fact that Bucknall was Comper's brother-in-law, uncle to Arthur Bucknall, his favoured assistant, and had taken to drink. It was a painful rupture. Comper was sent to a nursing home at Ventnor, on the Isle of Wight, and on 20 April of the following year set off with Arthur Bucknall to Rome on the way to Palermo. They went in high spirits, Comper aged forty, Bucknall twenty-nine; it was Comper's third visit to Italy, Bucknall's first.

12. *Further Thoughts*, p.33.
13. *Development in New Buildings*, unpublished ms. Comper's private papers.
14. Anthony Symondson, *St Mary the Virgin, Wellingborough, (1904–1931): An appreciation and Guide*, nd. This was printed from notes hurriedly written for a visit of the Victorian Society in 1989. It was published without the author's knowledge and is far from being a full and considered statement.

15. 1905, unfinished memorandum written in 1930. Comper's private papers.
16. In 1900 Mrs McClure had brought from Sicily some rose-red silk to help Comper find the authentic medieval colour. She had enormous influence on the development of his work. J.N. Comper, *Of the Christian Altar and the Buildings which Contain It*, 1950, n.9, pp.67–8.
17. 1905, op cit.
18. Quoted in *Further Thoughts*, p.35.
19. ibid.

They wore yachting caps to resist the wind and sea and were surprised that they 'laid us open to invitations which betrayed how simply and naturally pagan is the Italian, particularly in the South.'[15]

Comper had been persuaded to go to Sicily for the antiquity of the mosaic churches by Legg and his friends Canon and Mrs Edmund McClure.[16] It seemed a high-minded choice, informed by architecture and liturgiology more than pleasure. Few knew the rapture and sense of freedom the Continent induced in Comper and the effect this had on his perception of beauty. In a rare memorandum written in 1930 describing the journey he expressed his inner feelings inspired by a second visit to Rome.

Comper and Bucknall had attended the Easter Mass at St Peter's celebrated by Cardinal Rampolla, 'Our way back was through the great amphitheatre and the Forum and that, particularly the Coliseum, completed the spell of Rome for A. But is it any one of these things and not rather in the atmosphere which the sum of them creates, added to a something in the air and the light, and the richness of the flowers, and the bigness of the rain drops, which awakes a sense as of never having lived before? Something which drove me on my first day in Rome [in 1900] to wander solitary as much outside of it as I could beyond the Porta del Popolo ... It is, or was, an over-built and deserted quarter far from impressive, but in that May afternoon and sunset all was seen literally in *couleur de rose* and the impression which it brought of absorption into the Eternal City has never left.'[17]

Educated late-Victorians saw Sicily through the eyes of John Addington Symonds, the historian of the Italian Renaissance. He wrote with deep feeling about Italian art and for many of his readers replaced Ruskin as an *arbiter elegantiarum*. In 1898 he had published a third series of *Sketches and Studies in Italy and Greece*. In it he wrote lyrically of Palermo under the Norman kings of the twelfth century, of the cathedral of Monreale, of which he said that no church 'can excel it in richness and glory, in the gorgeousness of a thousand decorative elements subservient to one controlling thought', of the beauty of the Sicilian landscape and people, of the colour of the Mediterranean sea and sky.[18] The reality of what Comper himself saw far exceeded the descriptions of his friends, Symonds's jewelled prose and even the inherent magnetism of Rome.

The Palermitan mosaic churches are the most complete survivals of the cultural legacy of the Hautville dynasty. Between 1130–90 their policy of tolerance towards their subjects, Latin, Orthodox and Muslim, encouraged a cosmopolitan civilization composed of heterogeneous elements which reached its fullest expression in art and architecture. Art was controlled by the court. In the royal palaces and churches architectural styles were combined to produce a composite form, embracing mosaic, sculpture and woodwork, harmonious and altogether attractive. 'The Court of Palermo embraced not only Western Christendom but the Eastern Church and even stretched out hands to Persia and the highest culture of Islam; and of all this its churches bear the impress.'[19] For Comper the religious factor was of supreme importance; he understood the theological and liturgical significance of iconography and planning; and discovered in both the fulfilment of his spiritual longings.

Comper was not merely an aesthete. He was intoxicated by breathing Catholic air and entering the devotional life of the people and through his work wanted to open the same experience to others. 'What wins the heart abroad is the ... silent prayer in the churches and the bending of the knee in the street as the priest takes Communion to the sick. It is not the Benediction service and ceremonial procession. The English laity does not want these, but he wants the assurance of the Church's belief in the Supernatural and the Presence of her Lord, which it finds abroad in Communions made on a weekday at 4 o'clock in the morning, or at earliest daybreak, and in the sight of men and women kneeling in a church very early and very late in so great a silence that you may hear a pin drop, and in the crowds that make a thoroughfare of it in the bustle and toil of the day, and find even a moment for prayer.'[20]

Three churches demonstrate the Sicilian amalgam: the Cappella Palatina (c.1132–40), La Martorana (c.1140) and Monreale Cathedral (1174–83). Comper and Bucknall arrived in Palermo, after breaking their journey in Naples, on the evening of 27 April. The situation of Palermo was then wonderfully beautiful. The town was surrounded by a vast garden of lemon, orange and olive trees which filled the Conca d'Oro, the shell-like plain bounded by the red crags of Monte Pellegrino, the wooded Capo Zefferana and Monte Griffone. 'It is here in Sicily', he wrote to his wife, Grace, in the palm-shaded garden of the cloister of S Giovanni degli Eremiti, fragrant with the scent of roses, geranium and lemon, 'that our greatest pleasure seems to begin.' It was not only the blaze of ranunculas of every shade and larkspur and nemophila outside the cathedral, nor the aromatic pepper trees and their feathery leaves that embowered the royal palace that delighted him. They were a prelude to the visit on their first morning, a Friday, to the Cappella Palatina.

'There we have spent all the morning and heard many masses, one sung by a mitred canon. Exquisite music of silvery bells outside the Chapel and delicate playing of an (also invisible) organ of good tone, and wonderful singing from two boys, a choir in themselves, and tho' an almost laughable noise, not altogether unpleasant. But pleasant enough as the sound was, and the smell of incense, the pleasure to the eye exceeded anything I have met with in colour and simple elegance in architecture. It is small and light. Walls, arches and floor are of mosaic. The roof Moorish in honeycomb pendant work, and gilded and painted.

The story of Creation to Jacob's wrestling with the angel is told above the arches of the nave. The most beautiful image of Our Lord I have ever seen, and all in blue, fills the West wall. Again He is portrayed E. of the S. aisle, in the upper half-dome of the choir, in the summit of the dome and always in blue. Our Lady in blue and bluish purple receives the angelic message eastwards below the dome, holding her distaff. A colossal bust of St Paul beneath Our Lord, E. of S. aisle; of St Andrew E. of N. aisle. Besides, an entry to Jerusalem, Transfiguration and other Gospel stories.

For the first time too, I liked the inlaid mosaic in screens and pulpit and the mosaic work of purple and green porphyry in the floor, already most beautiful in Rome, here surpasses. The reveals of the windows are treated in gold and diaper in mosaic, much as I have done in plain gilding. Most of the windows give a borrowed light only and are better so.

Here all is pigmy compared with Pagan and Renaissance Rome: the human figure, as shewn in the Creation, or where the disciples strip to strew their garments before the Redeemer, is ill-formed; but the breath of the Holy Spirit is here as it is in the flowers. The colours of Pompeii fade both in frescoes and in the mosaic, before the Christian work. Yet its pillars and capitals are Pagan and there, as in the human form, Greece at any rate will hold its own, for the work of the Spirit is there also.'[21]

Comper wrote this description fresh from seeing the Cappella in the interval before going on to Monreale in the afternoon. It is given unabbreviated because it contains the strands – religious, aesthetic, architectural, historical, natural – that composed his thought, heightened his perception and motivated his work. Nature was as important to Comper as art and the historic faith; all were inspired by, and subsumed in, the work of the Holy Spirit. These early impressions were crystallised on the journey and arrival at Monreale. Once more the attraction of nature was combined with art and religion. Comper and Bucknall travelled from Palermo by tram to the summit of the hill on which the town stands.

'From it the view out of the gardens adjoining the cloisters is indeed beauti-

20. *All Saints, Margaret Street, Church and Parish Paper*, September 1918, XXXII, pp.157–8.
21. Letter to Grace Comper, 28 April 1905. Comper's private papers.

figure 3
The Cappella Palatina, Palermo, looking west. (Photo P.G. Meli)

22. ibid.
23. ibid, 12 May 1905.
24. 1905, op cit.
25. Sketchbook, 'XXIV Tunisia and Algeria 1924'. Comper's private papers.

ful; but the hazy clouds still follow us and sea and mountain are dim. The Conca d'Oro lies thick inlaid with patinas of bright gold: the pale gold, like the mosaics within the church, of countless lemons; the air heavy with the scent of their blossom and of the stocks and roses and box of the garden. Lemon trees all the way: aloes with flowers like our "red hot pokers". Huge cactus like (as A says) the pantomime!

The wide cloisters with their graceful colonnades like, but larger than, those of St John Lateran in Rome, and the half-Moorish fountain in one corner. The bare uninviting church outside and then the amazement of mosaics within and on so great a scale. Less delicate, less perfect and unspoilt than the Cappella but far surpassing it in size. The same subjects but more of the life, and in particular the miracles, of Our Lord who is always in a blue cloak and gold under-dress, shaded with a purple brown, and always the conspicuous figure. While his bust in the apse above the high altar must have a head some five feet high.'[22]

On Low Sunday they went on to Girgenti and embarked upon a precarious tour by train and mule to Syracuse, Taormina (where Comper bought figure studies from the Baron Von Gloëden, the photographer of the Sicilian people), Messina, Stromboli, and Cefalù (where the bust of Christ above the high altar of the cathedral was 'even finer than that of Monreale.') They returned to Palermo on 6 May and at last, on their final day, they saw La Martorana.

'The next day, Sunday, at Palermo we succeeded in getting into La Martorana twice, as well as again visiting the Cappella Palatina. ... I think the Martorana is the best lighted of all the mosaic churches. But certainly it is the Martorana that I liked best of all. I was able to note the scheme of colour on the back of my photographs of it bought at Taormina and I was disappointed not to have time to do the same to the Palatina and Monreale mosaics; but the first was closed in the afternoon and Monreale was too far off before 7.30 when the boat left. So we went to the Ziza, where there is a Moorish fountain and some mosaics of peacocks and men shooting birds. But, as I said, the scheme of colour is the same in all, but the fullest and freshest-looking at the Martorana; and there the roofs are, when not domed, vaulted in star spangled, grey toned blue, and the masses of blue are of great value. A later altar-piece, or tabernacle, is all of the most splendid lapis-lazuli and gold (there is some likewise in the Duomo) and though the mosaic blue is somewhat softer and purpler it all blends. Beside it some blue mosaic at Pompei seemed harsh and crude. The Pompei colour is harsh and turbulent; fine enough some of it but these Christian mosaics are again like the plain-chant, delicate, aspiring heavenwards.'[23]

Twenty-five years later Comper wrote dismissively of these letters. 'My letters home form a most disjointed diary from which facts can be verified; but while in 1930 they are still vivid and fresh in my mind I would fain arrest some illusive and haunting memories of a beauty and attraction which only a first visit in youth could bring, and which the new world has, besides, actually swept away.'[24]

No foreign journey had a more profound influence on Comper's mature work than his first visit to Sicily. He and Bucknall returned twice: in 1921 (their first journey abroad after the Great War) and 1924, at the conclusion of a long visit to French North Africa to see the Graeco-Roman ruins and the remains of the fourth century basilican churches for their planning. Yet the mosaic churches grew, if anything, in attraction. 'They are more beautiful these three churches and nowhere have I seen anything like them, or their equal in effect of colour. Nor is it colour only; for, in spite of much strangeness and even barbarism, they remain a model too for proportion and a, to me, inexplicable quality of spaciousness. This is our third visit to them and now I do not expect to see them again and, so entirely spoilt is Palermo when you get there, that, but for these churches, I should never wish to renew the discomforts of the journey. I prefer to remember it as I first saw it in 1905.'[25]

figure 4
Church of La Martorana, Palermo, 1140.
(Photo P.G. Meli)

Comper returned to England with his mind in a turmoil. Since his visit to Rome in 1900 he had been preoccupied by discovering the tradition behind tradition, pushing his investigations back to the early Christian centuries. This was not done in a spirit of narrow antiquarianism. It was a quest in which he sought the source from which had developed the accretive legacy of the Christian centuries as it had evolved from Greece and Rome and had been conveyed by a living tradition. Like Gilbert Scott the younger[26] and Edmund Bishop he recognised the fourth century as the consummation of the development from the birth of the Church at Pentecost. He discovered in Sicily, in the centre of the Mediterranean, the meeting place and battle ground of the races that had contributed to civilize the West and had effected its genesis. From this time his cry was *respondere natalibus*: return to your birthright.

In 1908 the church of Wimborne St Giles, in Dorsetshire, was destroyed by fire. It was an eighteenth-century building designed by one of the brothers Bastard of Blandford and had been gothicised and richly furnished by Bodley. Comper was asked by the Earl of Shaftesbury to rebuild it. It was here that he met 'the challenge to the first ideal of unity by inclusion.' The restoration of St Giles' was the first experiment in the fusion of architectural styles. It is indebted to the French Renaissance and, in the furniture, has affinities with the English, early seventeenth-century amalgam of Classic and Gothic.[27]

For the consecration on 1 September 1910 Comper was invited to a house party at St Giles's House. It was a very small party composed of Dr Christopher Wordsworth, the Bishop of Salisbury; George Wyndham, a politician, his wife Sibell, Countess Grosvenor; Fr Philip Waggett SSJE, a Cowley Father; Dr Wallis Budge, Keeper of Egyptian and Assyrian Antiquities at the British Museum, a translator of the Desert Fathers and a noted raconteur; and Lord and Lady Shaftesbury, their hosts. It was a meeting of the higher levels – social and intellectual – of Anglo-Catholicism and Conservative politics.[28]

Comper's work was conspicuous for clarity of conception and planning but he was not a clear thinker and writer; his conversation was discursive and circular. The meeting with Wyndham enabled him to put his thoughts in order. Wyndham was preparing a lecture, *The Springs of Romance in the Literature of Europe*, to be given as the inaugural address as Rector of the University of Edinburgh. The thesis proposed that Romantic literature was composed of syncretistic strands and was one with architecture and politics. He was as interested in the literary and philosophical syncretism of Palermitan civilisation as Comper was in the architecture. 'Literature is transfigured into Romance by the twilight of the West, the mirage of the East, and the uncouth strength of the North, in direct proportion to the commingling of East and West and North in the politics of the eleventh and twelfth centuries.' Furthermore, 'Romance revives and, extending her welcome to the strange, discovers in it something which has always been latent in men's minds, although starved by convention.'[29]

Wyndham was at the heart of a small, aristocratic group known as the Souls, all of whom were in polite revolt against the Victorianism of the older generation. Comper had worked for his mother, Mrs Percy Wyndham, and sister, Lady Elcho; and he was closely associated with Wyndham's cousin-in-law, Geraldine, Countess of Mayo, in the Royal Irish School of Art Needlework.[30]

Wyndham had great personal charm and was considered by his friends to be the handsomest man in England: noble, chivalrous and true. He shared with Comper a keen appreciation of beauty in nature, art and literature; he had a passion for ideas, loved talking and was an inspired conversationalist. In 1906 Comper had spent a month in Greece and in the spring of 1910 he had visited central and southern Spain. These visits added further strength to his theory that all beauty was one. The ideal of unity by inclusion was analogous to Wyndham's theory of literature and captivated him.

figure 5
Perspective of Wimborne St Giles, Dorset, 1910, drawn by E.T. Jago.

26. Comper thought Scott's *Essay on the History of English Church Architecture Prior to the Separation from the Roman Obedience*, 1881, 'the best book on architecture written.' It helped him to return to early-Christian sources and apply them to the design of St Mary's, Wellingborough. Letter from John Betjeman to Gavin Stamp, 16 August 1978. Candida Lycett Green, ed. *John Betjeman Letters*, Volume Two: 1951 to 1984, 1995, p.549.

27. *Further Thoughts*, n.1, p.33.

28. Comper's diary, 31 August 1910.

29. *Further Thoughts*, ibid.

30. Anthony Symondson, *The Life and Work of Sir Ninian Comper (1864–1960)*, RIBA Heinz Gallery monograph, 1988, p.18; 'Art Needlework in Ireland', *Irish Arts Review Year Book*, 10, 1994, pp.126–35.

31. In 1913 Comper designed the east window
of the church at East Knoyle, Wiltshire,
erected as a memorial to Wyndham by Lady
Grosvenor and both Houses of Parliament.

Wyndham and Lady Grosvenor were enchanted by Comper's work.[31] He was, in turn, invited to stay with them at Saighton Grange, in Cheshire, the dower house of Eaton Hall, to continue the conversation they had started at Wimborne St Giles. Saighton was originally the principal country house of the Abbots of Chester. It is noted for the gatehouse, built in 1490, and its oriel with a figure of Our Lady in the merlon above. It was there, in the prophet's chamber, that Wyndham had his study and in it he and Comper talked till the early hours of an October morning, elucidating the principles of Comper's theory. It was one of the most valuable conversations of his life and was sealed by the subsequent presentation of a copy of Wyndham's lecture bound in vellum.

EARLY APPLICATION OF UNITY BY INCLUSION

The fruits of these influences were manifested not only in architecture but in iconography and in a transformation of colour. The Majestas, the figure of the Pantokrator, the Almighty, the Creator and Maker of all things, represented in the Palermitan mosaics became in Comper's work an essential iconographical member. It was translated into painted glass, murals, sculpture and embroidery. And Mediterranean colour, notably lemon gold and the masses of blue observed in La Martorana, replaced the harder late-medieval primary tones of the North. They were displayed in St Mary's, Rochdale (1908–12), the Grosvenor Chapel, South Audley Street, London (1912), the chapel of St Helena's Home, Ealing (1913), in the altar screen of Wymondham Abbey, Norfolk (1913), and in the evolving development of St Mary's, Wellingborough, which continued until Comper's death in 1960.

St Mary's, Rochdale took the place of a very poor eighteenth-century church whose dumpy pillars were heightened and incorporated in the new church. They formed the starting point of the synthesis of Classic and Gothic. The belfry represented the old one; but the balustrade outside and the arches within – which have the fine coffering measured by Comper in the temple of Bassae near Phygalia, 4,000 feet above the sea in Arcadia, said by Pausanias to have been designed by Ictinus – were invented to carry them off. The main arcade followed St Mary's, Wellingborough, except for some differences in detail. The east window faced the only open space between high buildings.

From the restrictions of the site this necessitated placing both aisles on the north side, the aisle containing the Classical elements being sufficiently low to

figure 6
St Mary's, Rochdale, Lancashire,
1908–12. (Photo Derek Allen)

allow a clerestory above it. St Mary's has more obvious Greek detail than Wellingborough, but it has a more normally English rood loft. In this, and the window traceries, it resembles the re-building of the much finer eighteenth-century church of Wimborne St Giles. It is in the Grosvenor Chapel and St Helena's Home that we discover the direct result of Italy and Greece transposed to Northern Europe.

At Wimborne St Giles Comper worked within the ruins of a gothicised Classical shell. At Rochdale he re-used and refined existing Classical detail. The Grosvenor Chapel was the first Classical building in which he was invited to work. The recommendation came from W.B. Trevelyan, one of his earliest patrons, formerly vicar of St Matthew's, Westminster, for whom he had designed the first Gothic altar in 1892. Trevelyan was the Warden of Liddon House. The House had been established in Thurloe Square, South Kensington, to undertake work among young men of education, similar to that of Pusey House, at Oxford. He had been approached by the vicar of St George's, Hanover Square, to establish it at the Chapel.[32] Trevelyan did not accept the offer; but Comper had, through the Wyndhams, attracted the powerful support of Adeline, Duchess of Bedford, and, with her influence, he was chosen to change a small, eighteenth-century preaching box into a church of eucharistic worship.

This was accomplished by bringing the high altar forward with the intention of placing it beneath a ciborium in front of a Classical screen. The rest of the interior was to be changed into a Graeco-Roman temple by the insertion of a double arcade of giant Ionic columns supporting a monumental entablature. Above the screen, on a beam, Comper placed a late-Gothic rood with figures of St Mary and St John standing upon medieval Greek dragons, first seen in the Metropolis church at Mistra and at Karytaina in Arcadia. The point of such a radical proposal was to give direct emphasis to the high altar which was positioned, unobstructed by a choir, in direct relationship to the worshippers in the nave.

Legg, who had a house nearby in Green Street, Park Lane, took as much interest in these plans as St Cyprian's, Clarence Gate. In 1905 he had suggested that Bishop (with whom Comper was already acquainted through his work at Downside Abbey) should send him an offprint of his essay on the history of the Christian altar, in which he advocated the necessity of a ciborium. The ciborium was opposed at the Grosvenor Chapel. At a consistory court Comper defended the introduction of this feature in his design because of the Classical surroundings. In reality he was persuaded by Bishop's argument and stylistically this was reinforced by his visit to Greece. It loomed large in his mind and eventually was applied as a solution to making the high altar of St Mary's, Wellingborough, sufficiently prominent. The ciborium at the Grosvenor Chapel was declared illegal and both it and most of the arcade await completion. Even in its truncated form the chapel broke radical ground by being the first English church of the twentieth century to bring the high altar into a visual relationship with the congregation.

Development continued in the small chapel of St Helena's Home, Ealing, built for the Wantage Sisters as a penitentiary, in 1913. This was the first building designed as a composite whole after the manner of the twelfth century in Palermo. The Bath stone pillars were pure Tuscan, and the four-centred flattened arches had the same coffering from Phygalia, executed in plaster and richly decorated. The four-centred pointed vaults were finished in plaster and decorated; but they were constructed in concrete and the windows had simple Gothic tracery filled with bottle-end glass. In its present form the chapel has been so badly disfigured that little of Comper's detail remains.

The Majestas had been included above the rood in the designs for St Mary's, Rochdale. It was in 1913 at Wymondham Abbey that it came to occupy a place comparable to the elevated position in the apses of the Sicilian churches and

32. Derek Pattinson '"Rational and Devout": Henry Parry Liddon and Liddon House', in Ann Callendar (ed.), *Godly Mayfair*, 1980, p.41.

figure 7
St Helena's Home, Ealing 1913.
(Photo Sebastian Comper)

figure 8
The Grosvenor Chapel, South Audley Street, Westminster, furnished 1912.
(Photo Jeremy Whittaker)

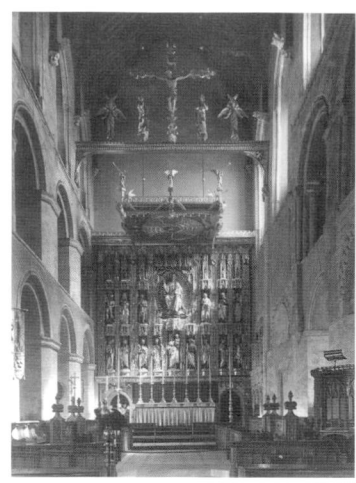

figure 9
The altar screen, Wymondham Abbey,
Norfolk, 1913.
(Photo RCHME © Crown Copyright)

33. *Development in New Buildings*, op cit.
34. Letter to Revd L.W. Comper op cit.
35. *Development in New Buildings* op cit.

figure 10
The high altar and ciborium, St Mary's,
Wellingborugh, Northamptonshire,
photograph taken in 1940 after the
decoration had been completed.
(Photo Harry Moore)

cathedrals. For the blank east wall of the nave (which was the west wall of the Abbey Church and once communicated with it by a door on each side of the altar) a great screen of tabernacle work was designed in decorated wood. It seemed consistent with tradition and with East Anglian use.

The inspiration was the high altar of Westminster Abbey as depicted in the fifteenth-century funerary role of Abbot Islip. There is a large canopy over the screen and the Majestas, on a considerably larger scale than the other figures, occupies the middle of it. Over that, upon a beam one bay of the clerestory westwards, are the rood and winged cherubim. The symbolism represents Christ in judgement as described in the book of Revelation. The design is subordinate to the Majestas which dominates the nave as the focal point and centre of the church. It is here translated from mosaic to carved wood in the same way that in 1927 it was turned into painted glass, on an even greater scale, in the east window of All Saints conventual church, London Colney, Hertfordshire. In 1934 the Wymondham screen was decorated in burnished gilding and Mediterranean colour, using the same masses of gold and blue as at La Martorana.

As Comper's travels continued so his style developed and his understanding of the nature of a Christian church matured. He became progressively impatient with the insularity encouraged by Dearmer and his followers that had grown up within the Church of England as a result of his early liturgical experiments. 'Shallow and narrow is the cry: study and copy what is only English. Why, the best and most characteristic of what is English was brought from abroad by just such English travellers and crusaders, not to mention the Italians and Frenchmen who took up their abode with us. It is the way in which it is used and made one with the England of God's creation that matters. Mere imitation of whatsoever it may be – architecture, liturgy, ceremonial: mere fashion, be it called English or be it called Roman – is worthless. It must be vitalised and made distinctive of the country of its adoption.'[33]

This explains why Comper did not follow the contemporary path of primitivism by embracing the Byzantine style, and the purely basilican plan and a literal reconstruction of fourth- and fifth-century models. He believed that the style developed in the South to suit a sunny climate was inimical to the needs of the North. Byzantine was an anachronism because, 'it was not an abiding style like the perfected Greek and Gothic of living Christianity which can never be out of date.'[34] He fiercely advocated the claims of English late-Gothic as a legitimate evolution of the primitive germ which he believed should not be confined to a primitive style.

DEVELOPMENTS IN CHURCH PLANNING

When in 1944 Comper was writing his recollections, as an old man of eighty, he recognised the significance of St Mary's, Wellingborough, in his development as a church planner for opening a second period of his work. 'The importance of St Mary's, in this story of development, is that the high altar was brought a little forward and the church planned to bring as many worshippers as possible around it. This was frustrated in part by the refusal to allow a fourth row of columns and a south chancel as open as the north.'[35] It was the protection of the high altar by a ciborium which defined the liturgical emphasis.

The Wellingborough ciborium was only allowed to be completed in 1940, although the balance of the lavish decoration of the church, both ecclesiologically and aesthetically, as may now be seen, depends upon it; for it makes the high altar what it should be, the richest detail in the whole church. But it does not take the place of the screen, as is too usual in modern churches, or where old screens have been removed ... But an English parish church without a screen may be said to have ceased to be English almost as absolutely as an Eastern church without an iconostasis. And St Mary's Wellingborough, is essentially an English church, within as well as in its exterior. Its plain tower, contrasting with a certain amount of rich masonry in the rest of the building, is characteristic and intentional, and it is East Anglia, rather than the West, that it favours.'[36]

Thus Comper explained what many saw as the ambiguity of St Mary's and the puzzle this posed for the founders and their understanding of Englishness.

It was not until 1924 that Comper discovered the primitive ideal and that was on his second visit to French North Africa, better known today as Algeria. He had made his first visit in 1922 and returned full of enthusiasm for the ruined second-century public works of the Emperor Hadrian and their architecture. Comper had been moved by two books by Louis Bertrand, *Autour de Saint Augustin* (1914) and *Sanguis Martyrum* (1918). Bertrand's themes were the Church in North Africa after the peace of Constantine, presented in vivid word paintings.[37] They fired Comper with an interest in the North African Church.

He wanted to trace the development from the Greek temple, and the scale which was found suitable for worship, to the adoption of the same principles by the Constantinian church. It was only in the Mediterranean countries that patterns from antiquity remained; and only in North Africa that the evidence could be found of churches which had not been changed by subsequent alteration. Comper recognised that they were of value in the planning of a modern church.

It was at Theveste, now know as Tebessa, in the south-east corner of Algeria, bordering on Tunisia, that his search ended. The church complex at Tebessa in its present form dates from c.400 and is imbued with Constantinian concepts. It is one of the most valuable survivals of the time. 'A broad flight of steps ascend from a forecourt (it is of a later date) towards a colonnaded propylaeum. From there, three doors lead into the church. All this recalls, if anything, Tyre, or the basilica of the Holy Sepulchre, or the first H. Sophia in Constantinople and its propylaeum. In the nave the piers ... carried arches above which appeared the openings of a gallery level by the projection of a cornice. This cornice in turn supported a second and third order of columns ascending to the roof beams. Mosaics covered the floors in nave and aisles. The sculptured ornament is – an exception in North Africa – remarkably fine. From the right aisle, a broad staircase descended to the trefoil martyrium built about thirty years before the main church and replacing a yet earlier memorial. A chancel barrier in the last bays of the nave enclosed the altar, and a second "chancel" was laid out near the entrance. The slightly raised apse is flanked by side chambers, both of which communicate through doors with the aisles as well as the apse.'[38]

Comper noticed parallels with the Roman basilicas in the placing of the high altar and it was this and their liturgical implications that sealed the precedent. 'What the earliest churches, then, establish in the position of the altar in the nave is direct contact with the people. The celebrant and clergy face east towards the doors and the people are facing west. This is still the use of the great basilicas of Rome ...'[39]

In his diary Comper wrote of Tebessa, 'It is, by a long way, the most complete and most magnificent church of the 4th century which we have seen.'[40] And in his recollections he described his mature conclusions. 'The plans of the churches which we measured of the fourth century, untouched as some of them are, and none since the seventh century, completed the lesson that it is from these examples of earlier times that we should draw for our parochially-used churches today, rather than from the plans of the middle ages when the larger parish churches were influenced by the example of the monastic choirs. Also fresh impetus was given to the love of Greek architecture by such exquisitely small temples as Sbeïtla and Dougga which were evidently the models for the church of the fourth century at Tebessa.'[41] These he had seen on his first visit to North Africa in 1922.

36. *ibid.*

37. *Further Thoughts*, p.70.

38. Richard Krautheimer, *Early Christian and Byzantine Architecture*, Pelican History of Art, fourth edition 1986, p.193.

39. *Further Thoughts*, p.70. I do not know if Comper realised that in these Constantinian churches the congregation also faced east at the consecration. He did not favour Mass celebrated *versum populi*.

40. Sketchbook, 'XXIV Tunisia and Algeria 1924', entry 2 April. Comper's private papers.

41. *Development in New Buildings* op cit.

42. ibid.
43. ibid.

figure 12 · left
Plan of the Constantinian church at
Tebessa, Algeria, c.400.

figure 13 · right
Plan of Aberdeen Cathedral, 1928.

It was in 1924 that these principles were partly realised in the conventual church of All Saints, London Colney, Hertfordshire. They were more fully applied in 1928 in the unexecuted plan for Aberdeen Cathedral, and in 1937 in the design for St Philip's, Cosham, at Portsmouth.

All Saints convent had an orphanage and hospital. The church was designed to be strictly conventual, primarily to give privacy to a large quire; but it was also made to meet the need of visual participation in the worship at the high altar of other residents of the convent, besides the nuns and their visitors; and, in particular, of children. An ante-chapel was, Comper decided, quite unsuited to such a purpose, not least because it involved the need of seculars passing through the quire to receive Holy Communion.

Low transepts, or chapels, were provided. The south transept was connected with an ante-chapel by a small cloister, opening upon a fountain in the chapel of St John Baptist. The high altar was placed beneath a ciborium (with a crown of eight arches) at the crossing, so that worshippers on all sides could see it. At the consecration by the Bishop of St Albans in 1927 those in the Lady Chapel faced west, so that all present were able to join with him in the elevation of the Host.

While North Africa contributed to the plan, the Chartreuse du Val de Bénédiction, at Villeneuve-les-Avignon, Provence, inspired the whole building, although it is completely English in character. As St Helena's Home, Ealing, was reminiscent of the blending of the Greek and Gothic of Palermo; so All Saints conventual church is of 'that essence of Gothic in the blending of France, England and Italy in the Avignon of the papal captivity.'[42] Avignon seemed to Comper after many visits 'a culmination of Gothic architecture, like that of Greek under Pericles, in which all mannerism of style and nationality are purged and the fine gold of pure form remains.'[43] It gave, notably in the Chartreuse, an ideal of what a conventual church should be.

The dimensions of All Saints are roughly those of the nave of the Chartreuse, though a little higher. In 1926, when the vaulting ribs were ready for their mouldings, Comper went again to Avignon and measured all that were accessible; and arrived closely at those which were out of reach and which were most wanted as a test for scale. The east window of seven lights was the first to be designed to contain in its tracery a more than life-size figure of the Majestas in painted glass, dominating the building in the manner of the Palermitan mosaics. Mother Mary Emily, the Superior of the Community of All Saints, was a niece of Legg and a learned religious in her own right. Her erudition and understanding of liturgical principle enabled Comper to make these radical experiments.

On 8 May 1928, Comper took the ground plan of a new cathedral to Aberdeen. Entirely unexpectedly a telegram had come on the previous Sunday morning asking him to undertake the design of a cathedral offered to Aberdeen by the Protestant Episcopal Church of the United States of America as a memorial to Samuel Seabury, its first bishop. The Anglican episcopate in America, and the former English-speaking colonies, dates from the consecration of Bishop Seabury in 1784 in Aberdeen by the bishops of the Scottish Church.

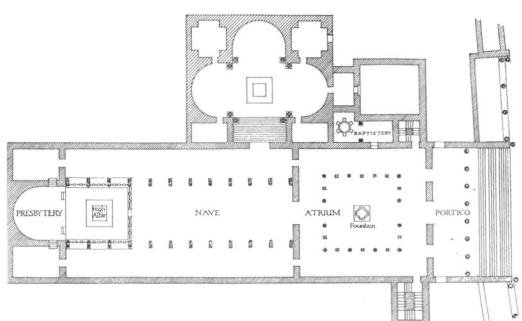

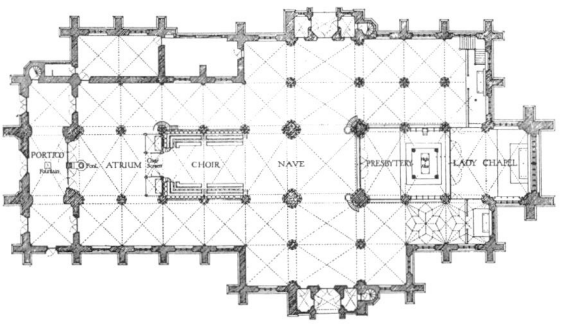

figure 14
Perspective of the east end of Aberdeen
Cathedral, 1928.

A central site was offered opposite the Marischal College, made free by slum clearance. The plan was substantially based upon Tebessa. It had an atrium, nave and presbytery; but was developed by the inclusion of side chapels and an eastern lady chapel. But the quire and presbytery had an entirely different origin and is modelled upon the developed sixteenth-century plan of Segovia Cathedral. The quire was placed west of the nave, yet beyond the atrium, with returned stalls against the screen. The high altar was to be in the presbytery to the east, with the congregation seated between them.

The lessons of Spain begun on Comper's journey in 1910 found fulfilment in the appropriateness of Spanish church planning for congregational worship.

'Now just as we have had to look to the further shores of the mediterranean for remaining patterns from antiquity, we have to look to Spain for the adaptation about the sixteenth century of Gothic churches to modern use. The churches in Spain were never so long as ours and seldom, if ever, even as long as French churches in proportion to width; but otherwise their arrangement was the same until the fifteenth and sixteenth centuries. Then it was that Spain and, it would seem, Spain alone, at least on any scale, realised, or had the wealth and willingness to realise in practise and in the Gothic style of architecture, that the medieval plan was unsuited to modern needs of worship. It is the land of tradition which knew neither reformation nor revolution in any lasting degree that returned in principle, whether consciously or unconsciously, to the primitive relation of the altar to the people.'[44]

Just as the contract for the first part of the cathedral in Aberdeen was ready to sign and the invitations were sent out to the laying of the stone on 14 August 1930 by the American bishops at the Lambeth Conference, there came the conse-

44. *Further Thoughts*, p.73. This was written before the Spanish Civil War.

quences of the Wall Street Crash and the whole scheme was abandoned. In 1938 Joseph Kennedy, the American Ambassador, laid the stone of the additions to the chancel of St Andrew's Church, to which all that remained of the funds was applied to make it worthy of a cathedral. The ciborium, gleaming in burnished gold and colour, is all that remains of Comper's original plan. If Aberdeen Cathedral had been built it would have been one of the most advanced statements of liturgical planning in Britain.

On 2 October 1937 St Philip's, Cosham, at Portsmouth, was consecrated. It was a memorial church designed at first to meet more lavish funds than in fact became available. A vicarage and parish hall, forming three sides of a quadrangle, as well as the complete furnishing of the church, including the organ, had to be included in the sum originally intended for the church alone. But the result

figure 15 · right
Plan of St Philip's, Cosham,
Portsmouth, 1937.

figure 16 · above left
St Philip's, Cosham, Portsmouth,
1937. (Photo John Bucknall)

figure 17 · above right
St Philip's, Cosham, Portsmouth,
1937, looking west. (Photo John
Bucknall)

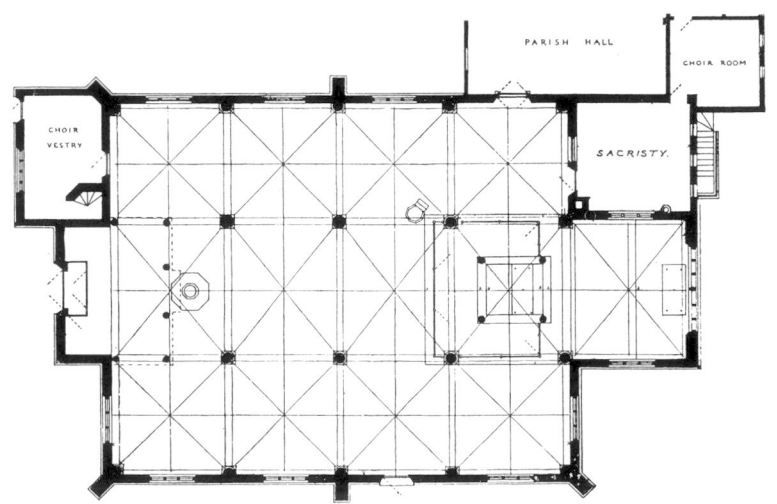

was better than it might have been; it enabled Comper to concentrate upon the essentials of liturgical planning and construction.

In plan St Philip's has a nave and two aisles of four bays in which the altar stands under a ciborium in the fourth bay in direct axial relationship to the font in the first bay at the west end. It shares the breadth rather than the length characteristic of the North African and Spanish churches. Behind the high altar is a fifth and higher central bay for the lady chapel; and a lesser proportion at the west end provides a gallery for the choir and organ.

The ciborium is decorated in burnished gold and complete in its imagery; with the figure of the risen Saviour surmounting it between four eagles at the corners from whose beaks lamps are suspended. A small metal tabernacle was provided in one of the pillars facing the high altar; in the hope that eventually it would be replaced by a suspended tabernacle, or pyx, against the ceiling of the ciborium immediately above the altar. A silver crucifix with figures of St Mary and St John stood upon the altar between four candlesticks. Comper himself gave the Majestas in painted glass in the tracery of the east window above the ciborium and on three sides of the lady chapel beneath the windows the walls were hung with rose-red silk. The font cover was decorated in burnished gold and colour, like the organ case. The walls, Classical columns with their severe and beautiful Corinthian capitals modelled on North African examples, and plaster vaults were lime-washed. The sanctuary is surrounded on three sides by oak communicants' rails. They were a prelude to open wrought iron screens, in the manner of Spanish rejas, which would have enclosed the sanctuary and were never executed. The altar is in every sense the central and richest part of the building.

St Philip's realised all that Comper had advocated in *Further Thoughts on the English Altar*. It was the fulfilment of his quest for beauty and liturgical planning on rational principles; a church that was essentially modern yet indebted to the unfolding richness of the Catholic tradition as it had evolved from Constantine to the twentieth century in which the heart and purpose of worship was the gathering of the baptised in the offering of the Mass.

'St Philip's is the most complete and perhaps the most obvious blending of the Greek and Gothic which concerns us here. And, as in all of these buildings, there is no claim of the invention of a new style; for, as has been shown, a similar combination can be found in past centuries. But, in so far as I am aware, there is nothing exactly like St Philip's; and that is because there is nothing exactly like the age and conditions which produced it.'[45]

ST JOHN OF JERUSALEM, CLERKENWELL

Comper was seventy-three when St Philip's, Cosham, was finished. It was the last church he built and thereafter his work was confined to completing existing buildings, planning unfruitful post-war reconstructions, furniture, decoration, embroidery and painted glass in a progressively attenuating practice. But he did not discontinue designing new churches and it is with the last of these that we must conclude. The second design for rebuilding the church of St John of Jerusalem, Clerkenwell, made in 1943, not only summed up the ultimate expression of Comper's theory of unity by inclusion but broke new ground in his evolution as a liturgical planner.

'As you probably know, the last big raid was a knock-out as regards church architecture' wrote John Summerson from the National Buildings Record to John Betjeman in Dublin in the early summer of 1941. 'St George's-in-the-East (well photographed by us a day or two before), St Alban's, Holborn, St John, Kennington, St John, Red Lion Square, St George's Cathedral, Southwark, and, I fear, many others – Chelsea, St Olave, Hart Street, St Mildred, Bread Street. O Lor' what a massacre!'[46] He did not include the medieval priory church of St John of Jerusalem, Clerkenwell, another fatality.

45. *Development in New Buildings* op cit.

46. Letter from Summerson to Betjeman, 7 May 1941. Betjeman papers, University of Victoria, British Columbia.

47. Quoted in letter to Betjeman, Lady Day
1943. Betjeman papers ibid.
48. Sketchbook 'xxvii Spain and Portugal
1929', entry 24 September. Comper's private
papers.
49. Letter to Betjeman ibid.
50. Letter to Betjeman, 4 October 1943.
51. ibid.

Lord Shaftesbury, Comper's old friend and patron, was Bailiff Grand Cross and Almoner of the Order of St John of Jerusalem. He was eager for him to re-build St John's. Comper had stayed at St Giles's House in 1940 in order to see his newly-completed font cover at Wimborne St Giles. Shaftesbury was aware of his continuing powers. He was appointed chairman of the Church Committee and in 1943 approached Comper to make plans of reconstruction and a large addition. Comper had two private meetings with Shaftesbury in Clerkenwell and accompanied him to Wimborne St Giles for a night where the plans could be discussed in peace. 'I think they are perfect', Shaftesbury subsequently wrote to him, 'and that you have excelled yourself in the beauty of their conception. Let us hope and pray that they may be carried out in their entirety and that no insurmountable obstacles may present themselves.'[47]

In 1929 Comper had visited the round church of the Knights Templar at the Convento de Christo at Thomar, in Portugal. He thought it 'very impressive, if a little theatrical.'[48] The church gave him the hint of how the needs of the Order of St John of Jerusalem could be met on something of the old lines, though on a much smaller scale. Comper described the evolution of the design in letters to Betjeman.

'To build on the circular plan, which was recovered and marked out on the site, is an impossibility. Some of it is already built over. But I can get in a western rectangular choir, such as Thomar has, the width of my All SS Convent choir (26ft) nr St Albans, of 2 slightly shorter bays with a third wider bay carried up higher and forming an open tower, in the middle of which the altar stands in an enclosure (reminiscent of the Holy Sepulchre) again as at Thomar but more open, being much smaller and composed of pillars only – in short like an elaborate ciborium with 8 pillars on the plan of the 8-pointed cross of the Order set diagonally ... These are the main problems on which many lesser ones depend which have now all been solved on paper ... I have had to design to a half inch scale every detail of the stalls – the most elaborate I have ever designed – and the most original, if "original" can be applied to a result which has taken ideas from so many places in Christendom.'[49]

These proposals were treated with caution by the Church Committee and were referred by them to the General Chapter with a recommendation that they should consult the Ecclesiastical Commissioners. Comper himself was, in any case, not altogether happy with the designs, they were ingenious but unsatisfactory. Later in the year 'there came unbidden the idea of building again a circular church within the present four walls; and when I suggested it to Lord S he jumped at it and got me to go down to St Giles's House with the plans.'[50]

The design was remarkable and is best described in Comper's own words. 'It removes a difficulty of which much might be made, and makes the strong appeal of being not merely reminiscent of a church of the Order; but actually resuscitates the original church which was the largest of its kind in England, and not much short of the remaining one at Thomar, in Portugal. For I find I can get it the size of the outside of the foundations marked upon the pavement, ie abt 60ft diam within. This, as I need not tell you, means enlisting the aid of modern construction; but I have gone over it with Mowlem, and by strange good fortune, the 8 necessary foundations (for actually my interior is octagonal; considerably bigger in diameter than Westminster Chapter House), come exactly where they can be obtained by under-pinning the crypt at points where no trace of it will show in its vaulted parts when done. The central octagon containing the high altar has 8 pillars of the size of the main pillars of St Mary's, Wellingborough, carrying a lantern, after the manner of Ely on a smaller scale.'[51]

St John's caused Comper enormous effort, not only in the mental exertion of working out the complications of applying a problematical design to a difficult site, but in the preparation of drawings. 'I have been hopelessly struggling with a perspective drawing for my octagonal interior – for I have, amongst all my losses, not a soul left who has even made a perspective – ie architectural perspective – drawing, or knows how to set one up. I can manage the altar itself and my particular brand of Corinthian capitals; but the unusual plan of the vaulting baffles me to draw. I want the plain honeycomb of the Bp West Chantry at Ely – but how to express its application to the irregular severies of my spacious arches is a problem.'[52]

The drawing was executed jointly by Comper, Arthur and John Bucknall and E.J. Lucas, Comper's glass painter who had worked for him since 1889; Comper himself added the tinted washes. The perspective turned out to be a drawing of considerable accomplishment and enabled Shaftesbury to persuade the Committee to launch an appeal in 1944. But the scheme was far too ambitious, far too magnificent to be considered seriously in post-war conditions restricted by planning regulations, building licences, shortages, war damage compensation and little independent money. The Order's failure to persevere with it was a severe blow for Comper and Shaftesbury. It was a lost opportunity that meant the death of early twentieth-century Romantic aspiration. Comper was, thereafter, never again able so unremittingly to concentrate on church design. St John's was the final gleam of brilliance before the fire of creative genius was put out.

The design for a circular church within a square marked the most developed expression of Comper's architectural theories and liturgical planning. It was the fruit of a life-time of study and travel in a quest for beauty. The lierne vaults ran

52. ibid. Severy: a space or compartment in a vaulted ceiling.

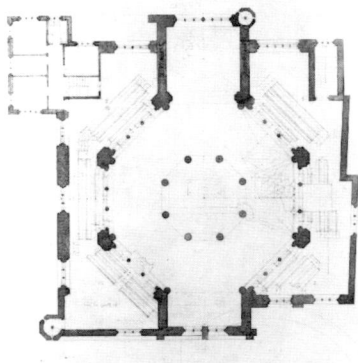

figure 18
Plan of unexecuted proposals for Order of St John of Jerusalem, Clerkenwell, 1943.

figure 19
Perspective of proposals for Order of St John of Jerusalem, Clerkenwell, 1943, drawn by J.N. Comper, Arthur and John Bucknall and E.J. Lucas.

round a circular processional path, whose walls were lined with canopied stalls for members of the order. A lady chapel was placed east of the sanctuary, creating an axial system. The altar was enclosed within an octagon, composed of a double arcade of two storeys with fluted columns, illuminated from above by a lantern. Within the vesica of the east window was the Majestas. The altar was as much the flame in a lantern as it was forty years previously at St Cyprian's, Clarence Gate.

After Comper had been dismissed St John of Jerusalem was blandly rebuilt by Seely and Paget. When Comper was knighted in 1950 the perspective was widely illustrated in the architectural and national press as an example of his recent work. It sowed a seed in the mind of Frederick Gibberd. His indebtedness to it in the design for the Metropolitan Cathedral of Christ the King, Liverpool, in 1960 is there for all to see. The difference lies in Gibberd's execution of Comper's plan and general disposition of parts in the International Modern Style, destitute of beauty and architectural tradition.

CONCLUSION

In 1937 Peter Anson published an article, 'The Work of John Ninian Comper: Pioneer of the Modern Liturgical Revival', in *Pax*, a Benedictine monthly published by Prinknash Abbey. It had previously been offered to *L'Artisan Liturgique*, the leading Belgian liturgical periodical published by the Benedictines of St André-les-Bruges; but had been summarily rejected because the editor thought Comper's work was *trop classique*. 'Perhaps what chiefly distinguished him from most other architects is his approach to his subject: in other words he is more concerned with the functional purpose of a church than with its aesthetic appearance,' Anson wrote. 'What this amounts to is that he works out the design of every church more from the practical than from the aesthetic point of view, just as if he were designing a factory, a motor car, or a battleship, although it is not obvious at first sight owing to the traditional forms he employs.'[53]

Two years later, in 1939, Betjeman published 'A Note on J.N. Comper: Heir to Butterfield and Bodley' in the *Architectural Review*. He recognised that the reason why a church designed by Comper hangs together is because 'it is clearly planned, and the plan, but not the beauty, unfolds itself at once, ... Everything in the design and every colour takes its heightening from the altar.' He later came to regard Comper as the most daring English church planner of the twentieth century.[54] Anson and Betjeman both responded to the beauty of Comper's work but identified the essential qualities which distinguished it from mere furnishing and decoration. They recognised him as the most influential church architect of his generation.

In this essay I have tried to demonstrate the validity of these claims for Comper as a pioneer of the Liturgical Movement and a radical church planner by using as much as possible his own words. Comper was conservative in religion, politics and life. He resented progress and the modern world, abhorred the secularising tendencies in the Church of England after the First and Second World Wars and was dismayed by what he saw of the 'cult of the hideous' in liturgical reform in France during his final visit in 1949; he could not reconcile this with the 'innate good taste of the French.' Ugliness was for him equivalent to blasphemy. The majority of his admirers tend to share these attitudes, to the extent that some deliberately ignore the implications of his theories and their application to modern church design as it has been practised since the Second Vatican Council.

Comper discovered that the more familiar he became with Church art the better grasp he had of tradition. This was accomplished as a gradual process of unconscious assimilation. He moved from seeing the late Middle Ages as a golden age in comparison with which other centuries were either immature or

53. Peter F. Anson 'The Work of John Ninian Comper: A Pioneer of the Modern Liturgical Revival', *Pax*, 27, 1937, p.177.
54. Anthony Symondson 'John Betjeman and the Cult of J.N. Comper', *The Thirties Society Journal*, VIII, 1991, pp.3–4.

decadent; to concluding that the Christian centuries and their Classical inheritance had a valid application to an understanding of tradition as a vital, rather than static, force. Comper's thought was analagous to the central features of the twentieth-century French Catholic theological revival characterised in the work of the Jesuit, Henri de Lubac, and the Dominicans, M.D. Chenu and Yves Congar. Their theory of *ressourcement* looked back to tradition, expressed in the patristic age, and forward to the social and cultural future. The object of theology and liturgy was to reveal the mystery of Christ, his life, death and resurrection, diversely expressed through the different ages of the Church. The mystery is not approached in a spirit of antiquarianism but in such a way that we can, through tradition, discover Christ in the world of the present time.

This essential element of Comper's thought was recognised by Peter Hammond in his influential book, *Liturgy And Architecture*, published in 1960 to encourage modern church design on functional principles consistent with the Continental Liturgical Movement. He declared that of all recent churches of whatever style, St Philip's, Cosham, was unprecedented in its advanced understanding of liturgical planning. Hammond recognised that for Comper 'architecture was essentially the handmaid of the liturgy, and Christian tradition something far more vital than a storehouse of precedent and detail.'[55]

Comper discovered that there is a special significance attached to the art and architecture of the first Christian centuries. From the fragmentary remains of the basilicas of the fourth century he distinguished the plans on which all subsequent developments of church building varied. The basilica, by the interrelation of its composite elements – nave and apse, bishop's cathedra, reading desk and altar, with the baptistery by its side – expressed in architectural form the priorities of patristic Christianity in the doctrine of the Church and defined constant liturgical polarities. The Church, inferred from the evidence of architecture, is the assembly of the faithful who become initiates through baptism; a body taught by the bishop who expounds the Scriptures and an assembly of worshippers that, as ministers and people, celebrate the Mass as the central act of worship.

The fruits of nineteenth-century liturgiology, the rediscovery of the primitive prototype, were universally applied in the liturgical reforms after the Second Vatican Council. Pope Paul VI defended them in the name of tradition. 'Not only have we maintained everything of the past but we have rediscovered the most ancient and primitive tradition, the one closest to the origins. This tradition has been obscured during the course of the centuries, particularly by the Council of Trent.'[56] The reforms led to a greater simplicity of expression in an attempt to make liturgy more corporate and intelligible to worshippers. Idealistic and soundly based in scholarship though they were, they led to a Puritan rage which, like Ocam's razor brutally wielded, swept out and left bleak the household of the Catholic imagination.

In new church architecture governed by liturgical principles two mutually exclusive theories were inimically united: primitivism and Modernism. Comper's canons of church planning were applied by Robert Maguire in 1958–60 at St Paul's, Bow Common, Stepney, in a style as robbed of beauty as the Metropolitan Cathedral at Liverpool. George Pace attempted to apply Comper's ideas of unity by inclusion and planning but distorted them by wilful individualism and perverse artistry. The Majestas would not have been chosen as the subject for Jacob Epstein's sculpture in Llandaff Cathedral, nor for Graham Sutherland's tapestry in Coventry Cathedral, if Comper had not insisted in his writings on its iconographical application. The spectre of Comper's precedents is seen employed by Buttress Fuller Alsop Williams *en travesti*, like crudely applied cosmetics, in the recent rebuilding of Tonbridge School Chapel. The only mid-twentieth century church architect who understood and put to use Comper's theories on their own terms was Stephen Dykes Bower whose work consistently demon-

55. Symondson, *Life and Work*, op cit, p.25.
56. Peter Hebblethwaite, *Paul VI: The First Modern Pope*, 1993, p.673.

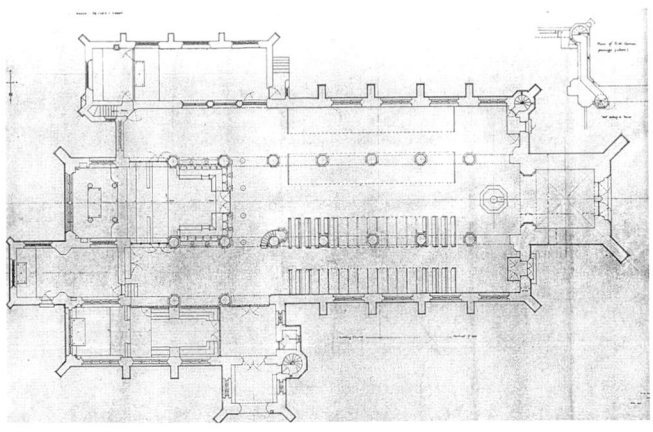

strated the concerns of *Further Thoughts on the English Altar*. Above all, he shared with Comper the recognition of the supremacy of beauty in architecture. This cardinal quality is an attribute of God and gave to Comper's work and intentions their transcendent property. Comper believed that to stir the soul by beauty is to remind it of the source of all loveliness, God, and what we love we become.

Running through this essay are many references to Comper's masterpiece, St Mary's, Wellingborough, the most beautiful church built in England in the twentieth century. St Mary's provides a framework for all that has been described. Let Comper describe it in the words he used in his lecture to the St Paul's Ecclesiological Society in 1932:

'The main ceiling has the unbroken fan and pendants of the latest English vaults and which, so far as I am aware, have not been combined before. The octagonal pillars (again I believe unlike all medieval examples), have the Greek entasis and they have the same details of flutes as the Parthenon, while the capitals and bases are of new design. A ciborium stands in advance of the east wall and in front of the large window. The high chancel screen has mouldings and acanthus straight from Classic Greece and a general design which is as much Italian as English, or English as Italian. The dragons on the rood loft are borrowed from medieval Greece, while the ironwork owes most to Spain. It may be added that the main part of the eastern plan of the church has its origins in France. Only to its contemporaries does the church owe nothing.'[57]

Comper, more than any other English architect of the twentieth century, endeavoured with passionate conviction to penetrate to the very core of Western civilization by studying the Church art and architecture of Europe to find there spiritual values applicable to his own time. Therein lies a lesson for the present and future. The ideological *impasse* in which modern Church architecture finds itself could be broken without compromising the integrity of its liturgical principles by applying Comper's unique understanding of the indispensability of beauty and the crucial legacy of Christian tradition. The social conditions of his generation, the learned and cultivated world of the English upper-classes, the perfectionist expression of their spiritual aspirations in early twentieth century Anglo-Catholicism are gone for ever. But beauty and tradition, as Comper discovered, never dies; threads of continuity may be concealed, but are never broken.

The threads could re-emerge in church architecture new born, made one with the Christian centuries. Titus Burckhardt reminds us that the altar is for the church what the heart is for the body; and through the presence of God in the sacrifice of the Mass the church changes from a lifeless heap of stone into a living organism.[58] Nothing more fully expresses this truth than Comper's design for St John of Jerusalem, Clerkenwell. The drawings exist. They could be executed elsewhere in the next Christian millennium and would make a more positive statement of faith than a vacuous fabrication of 'sacred space' with no objective purpose.

ACKNOWLEDGMENTS

I am indebted to Peter Howell and Alan Powers for reading this article and making helpful suggestions and corrections.

57. *Further Thoughts*, p.32.
58. Titus Burckhardt, *Chartres and the Birth of the Cathedral*, 1995, p.114.

3 Peter Anson: A Personal Memoir

PATRICK NUTTGENS

S. SAVIOUR, ELTHAM (Cachmaille-Day and Lander, 1931)
The streamlined furnishings represent similar fashions in domestic *décor*
and clothes

Peter Anson: A Personal Memoir

PATRICK NUTTGENS

In the middle of the 1950s, exploring the North East Lowlands of Scotland and studying its villages and vernacular architecture, I found myself one evening in Macduff on the Moray Firth and called on Peter Anson at his house in Shore Street. I had met him before, when I was a schoolboy. Most years he came to talk with Eric Gill, first at Ditchling and later at Llanthony or Pigotts. At the latter I found him talking to Gill and my father. I was puzzled by this man who looked like a sailor but had for fourteen years been a monk. Now in Macduff I met him again and made a new friendship. Peter was endlessly hospitable. I slept in a 'bun-in' bed (box bed) under the stairs and set off each morning on my explorations.

One afternoon he shouted down from his study and asked me to check if there was anyone at the front door; he had been disturbed by a loud hammering on his window. There was no-one there. 'Don't worry,' said Peter, 'it must have been Aelred on his way to heaven; he promised to call again before he died.' The next day there was a telegram saying that Aelred Carlyle had died – at exactly the time Peter had heard the hammering on the window. Peter went back to his typewriter and began the book *Abbot Extraordinary* that was published to considerable acclaim three years later.

Aelred Carlyle, said Rose Macaulay in her Foreword to the book, 'had immense character and dash ... What went on in his strangely split mind? He seemed to live from boyhood in a romantic dream. His charm was almost (though never quite) all conquering. Of this charming and questionable eccentric, Mr. Anson has made a fascinating study, at once amusing, analytic and affectionate.'

Peter loved Aelred but was under no illusions. He joined the Anglican Benedictine community which Aelred had founded on Caldey Island and became a Catholic when the whole community joined the church of Rome. Within three years, Aelred (ordained and consecrated as a Catholic abbot with unseemly haste) had to leave after various visitations and rumours concerning boy oblates and appalling debts. He went abroad, travelled in South America and Canada and found a new life as 'Father Carlyle' and chaplain to old people and sailors, ending as the prison chaplain in Vancouver. He accompanied prisoners to their execution. 'Just look at me' he said to a terrified young man and helped him to die in some sort of peace. When he left Vancouver he was given the Freedom of the city. After a lifetime of absurd and grandiose monastic schemes he had found his true vocation.

Peter kept all Aelred's letters. He had stayed at Caldey until 1924, visiting other communities from time to time and testing his vocation in other monastic orders. He spent some months as a Carthusian, stayed at the Benedictine abbey at Fort Augustus and eventually became a member of the Tertiary order of the Franciscans, changing his name from Dick to Peter. In 1921 he founded the Apostleship of the Sea, to give shelter and spiritual help to seamen.

Before he joined the monks at Caldey, Peter was already a compulsive artist.

figure 1
Peter Anson, illustration from *Fashions in Church Furnishings*, 1960

45

CALDEY ABBEY AND VILLAGE.

PONTIFICAL HIGH MASS, CALDEY ABBEY.

figures 2 and 3
Peter Anson, two illustrations from
A Roving Recluse, 1946

He spent two years at the Architectural Association school in London, made sketches all his life and spent several months in Chipping Campden learning from the great topographical artist and engraver, F.L. Griggs. Most of his many hundreds of sketches were pen and ink drawings, with occasional water colour. His accuracy was phenomenal and appreciated, notably by the many fishermen whose boats he drew and who (I know from experience) would never fail to spot an error, however small. He drew the boats, the tackle, the nets, and the men. And he wrote books and articles. Of his many books (there are said to be about forty), many are about the sea and ships. One of the best is *Fishing Boats and Fisher Folk on the East Coast of Scotland* (1930), one of the most personal *Life on Low Shore* (1969), the most successful and running to many editions was *How to Draw Ships* (1941).

Drawing and writing (his typewriter seemed always to be in action) by no means filled the whole of his life. When he first came to Macduff he acquired a low white house on the end of the harbour and made it a centre of social and religious life. He called it *Harbour Head* (and wrote a book under that title) and opened its doors to all, eventually creating a chapel in the attic. Fishermen and boys, old and young, especially those suffering from some form of disability (like Alec John Mackay who had had polio), crowded into the cottage so that it was always full of life and laughter. The kettle was always boiling and ready for tea. It was a simple life, austere and unpretentious.

But for me the most compulsive conversations were about the church and monasticism and the bewildering oddities of clerical life. Aelred Carlyle, for example, despite having no money except what he borrowed, had built an absurdly romantic abbey with towers and turrets; he visualised an even greater abbey, with a church more than 300 feet long. When a tower fell down he rebuilt it still

JOHN KEBLE CHURCH, MILL HILL (D. Martin Smith, 1936)
'English' altar in contemporary setting

THE HOLY HOUSE, WALSINGHAM (1931)
This Anglican shrine in Norfolk recreates the atmosphere of the *Santa Casa* at Loreto

figures 4, 5, 6 and 7
Peter Anson, illustrations from *Fashions in Church Furnishings*, 1960

COMPTON BEAUCHAMP, BERKS
Baroque furnishings by Martin Travers, 1928

higher. And he lived well, travelling first class and staying only in the best hotels.

Peter's speech was impaired; he stammered at the beginning of every sentence. That and the twinkle in his eye meant that I was never quite sure whether he, was serious or joking. It might be, I occasionally thought, that he found it all fundamentally absurd. When I drove him one day to Pluscarden, the ruinous abbey restored and occupied by the white Benedictines who had left Caldey for

Prinknash in Gloucestershire, old friends whisked him away and indiscreetly gossiped even though they must have known that he would gossip to all of us in the evening. Or it may be that they valued his fantastic erudition; he knew more about churches than anyone else I had encountered.

If I had ever doubted that, I would have been completely convinced by his *magnum opus* on ecclesiastical buildings, *Fashions in Church Furnishings 1840–1950* published in 1960. The title is precisely correct. He saw the changes as fashions – and his basic theme was announced in the Foreword 'Plus ça change, plus c'est la même chose' with some superb photographs of the most unlikely as well as brilliant exercises in ecclesiastical décor and over one hundred of his own drawings, sedate, elaborate or witty. He analysed and explained places with which he was obviously familiar. Not only architecture and furniture; he put in people – mainly women – in fashionable clothes that precisely reflected the fashions in furnishings.

Who were his heroes? He started with A.W.N. Pugin, the architectural and literary phenomenon who died at the age of 40 having re-established Gothic as the right style for churches and carried out as much as five ordinary men. He ended with Eric Gill and Gill's discovery that the altar should be in the centre of the church. 'The altar must be brought back again into the middle of our churches, in the middle of the congregation, surrounded by the people.' Gill's own chapel at Pigotts was like that; I remember it well, having served mass there for many years.

In between, he describes as many scenes and as many changes, delighting in materials as well as design. 'The Exeter Cathedral high altar and reredos (1876) were an astounding mixture of marble, alabaster, malachite, amethyst, cornelian, jasper, onyx, garnet, bloodstone and lapis lazuli.' As for fashions in clothes, he notes that at St George's Lancaster, 'The older men still sport standing collars and cravats, but the younger ones prefer neckties. A few more dashing gentlemen may sport a cloak instead of a coat. Rather tight striped trousers are regarded as suitable wear with Second Pointed ecclesiastical architecture.'

As for the women, 'Fully to appreciate a typical Gilbert Scott church, designed at the peak of his middle period, one must visualise it filled with well-to-do ladies dressed in enormous crinolines. By 1860 a fashionable skirt was ten yards round. As much as 1,100 yards of material was needed for tulle dresses worn in summer … The crinoline did away with the many petticoats of the eighteen-forties, which went with the 'First' and 'Second Pointed' churches of that decade.'

Was he being serious, or, as he often was when reminiscing about Carlyle and his church, wicked or just naughty? His basic theme was clear: 'Between 1840 and 1940 the circle had been completed. Today we have gone back to the 'auditory church' of Sir Christopher Wren and his followers. The reasons for this change of fashion can be found in various factors – social and economic as well as liturgical.'

For me the story of Peter Anson continued as bizarre as it started. I had hardly finished reading *Fashions in Church Furnishing* when George Howard, the owner of Castle Howard, saw it on my desk and asked if he could borrow it briefly. That was in 1962. When I started to write this memoir I thought I should get it back and recovered it from the Castle Howard library 33 years after lending it to him. Peter, your jokes are not over – and I *still* don't know whether or not you were serious.

4 Liturgy and Architecture: Liturgical Reform and the Development of the Centralised Eucharistic Space

ELAIN HARWOOD

Liturgy and Architecture: The Development of the Centralised Eucharistic Space

ELAIN HARWOOD

THE LITURGICAL 'NEW LOOK' OF THE 1950S

'We all know the purpose of a church, which is a simple one in that it is fixed and unalterable and therefore does not involve the architect in a search for improvements in the programme he is initially set, as a factory often does, or a hospital.' So claimed J.M. Richards, when writing of the new Roman Catholic church of St Basil by Burles, Newton and Partners at Basildon, in March 1957.[1] But it was not a good year to make so sweeping a statement. Having evolved in a continuous process from about 1870, there were at last signs of change in the design of churches of all denominations. The refined, abstracted Perpendicular style evolved then by G.F. Bodley and George Gilbert Scott junior had informed church architecture for the next ninety years. In part this was due to its universality and adaptability, in part it was because of the longevity of leading practitioners such as Sir Ninian Comper and Sir Giles Gilbert Scott – both of whom died only in 1960. Long-term projects like Liverpool and Guildford Cathedrals confirmed the supremacy of this tasteful tradition. With hindsight a subtle evolution can be seen in the planning of churches by Comper, Scott, H.S. Goodhart-Rendel, N.F. Cachemaille-Day and others, but by 1957 a younger generation was chafing to revolutionise church architecture just as they had other forms of building since the war. This revolution was not merely one of style. The new generation of church architects explored the fundamentals of what the denominations required, at a time when these were being questioned by the clergy and their commentators. Though the architecture parallels the development of the New Brutalism in secular work, the fundamental changes made to the religious

figure 1
Gerard Goalen, Church of the Good Shepherd, Woodthorpe, Notts. 1961–4. (Hank Snoek photographer, lent by Martin Goalen)

1. J.M. Richards, 'Church at Basildon New Town', in *Architects' Journal*, vol.125, No.3239, 28 March 1957, p.459.

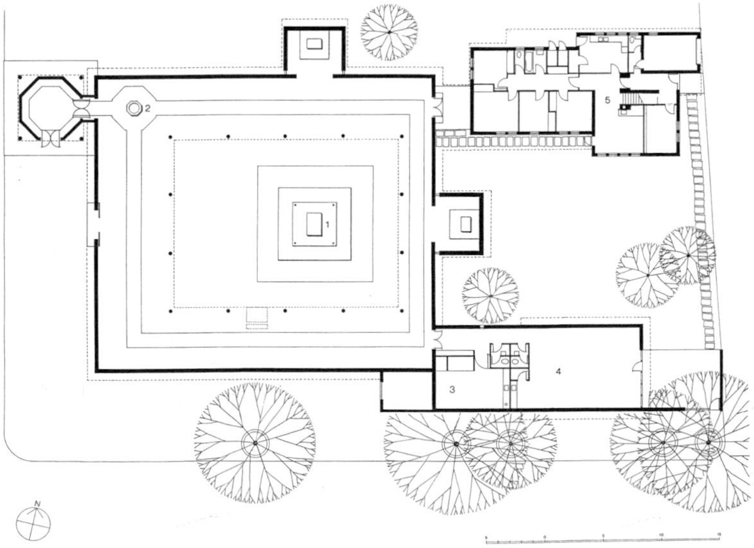

figure 2
Robert Maguire with Keith Murray, St Paul, Bow Common, Tower Hamlets. 1958–60. Plan (photo Robert Maguire)

2. Robert Maguire and Keith Fendall, letter to the Architects' Journal, vol.125, no.3241, 11 April 1957, p.532.

3. Peter Hammond, 'The Rediscovery of Eastern Christendom', in The Listener, vol.LVIII, nos.1494 and 1495, 14 November 1957, p.789, and 21 November 1957, p.839. The second part is a criticism of the western tradition from a liturgical viewpoint.

4. David Bishop, introduction to New Churches, Council for the Care of Churches exhibition catalogue, April-May 1969.

5. Many post-war churches were brought to my attention by Diane Kay, who compiled English Heritage's selection for listing. I am particularly grateful to Andrew Mead for his help with photos.

service gives churches an underlying discipline which makes their study most rewarding. This was the Liturgical Movement.

Richards's piece prompted the first appearance of the Liturgical Movement in the architectural press. This was a retort from Robert Maguire, a young architect then working for Richards on the Architects' Journal, and Keith Fendall, a pseudonym of the designer Keith Murray with whom Maguire went into partnership in 1959. 'The purpose of a church is not simple, ... Requirements have changed in the past and are still changing.'[2] In October 1957 there was a broadcast on the Third Programme by Peter Hammond, which was subsequently published in The Listener, and the New Churches Research Group was founded.[3] Within five years the Liturgical Movement had brought about an entire rethink on church planning in Britain, most vocally in the Church of England, most profoundly in the Catholic Church, and with some of its effects imparted also to the Free churches. By 1969 the Council for the Care of Churches could claim that all the denominations were searching for a 'common liturgical expression'.[4] The result was that the late 1950s and early 1960s were an exceptionally inventive time for church architecture.[5]

In the middle years of the twentieth century the Liturgical Movement was a major international movement aimed at popularising Christian worship. Though it centred on the Eucharist, it embodied within the Catholic tradition a nascent evangelism that has been far reaching. The word 'liturgical' is a product of the Greek 'laos' (people) and 'ergon' (work). In origin it meant any kind of public duty, and it must be stressed that the Liturgical Movement is concerned not just with the form of the Eucharist, but is about the relationship of the congregation or 'brethren' individually and collectively, to each other and to God. This essay looks at the history of the Liturgical Movement, and then at its influence on British church design.

THE ORIGINS OF THE LITURGICAL MOVEMENT

The Liturgical Movement began in France. In 1832 Dom Prosper Guéranger refounded the Benedictine Abbey of Solesmes as a monastery dedicated to the study and rediscovery of early Christian worship and especially to the authentic Gregorian Chant. Solesmes spawned a publication, L'Année Liturgique, which first appeared in 1841. It coincided with the medieval-inspired Oxford Movement and Gothic Revival in England, but its preoccupation with the earliest years of Christianity were to put France and Belgium into the vanguard of Catholic thinking in the early twentieth century.

In 1903 Pope Pius X issued a Motu Proprio on church music, which proclaimed that the active public participation in worship was the primary and indispensable source of a true Christian spirit. This change in values coincided with the arrival of general literacy, and the discovery in the late nineteenth century of a number of early Christian texts. A key point was a speech by Dom Lambert Beauduin at a Catholic conference in 1909 at Malines, Belgium. For him liturgy was something in which everyone should actively participate, bringing the whole Christian community before God. He believed that a better understanding of the incarnation and its meaning would lead to a deeper appreciation of the dignity of human life, and that an understanding of the nature of the church as the body of Christ through the Eucharist would enable the development of a deeper sense of community in both worship and life. This vision was taken up at the Benedictine Abbey of Maria Laach in Rhineland Germany, where Dom Ildefons Herwegen and, especially, Dom Odo Casel studied the origins of early Christian worship in the Graeco-Roman world and its debt to the older Jewish and Greek traditions.

This re-evaluation of the roots of Christian worship was widely disseminated in the inter-war period. The Austrian monk Pius Parsch of Klosterneuburg sought to apply the ideas of the Liturgical Movement to the parish situation, important for what was conceived as a pastoral movement. In the United States the Benedictine Abbey of St John, Collegeville, Minnesota, founded the magazine *Olate Fratres* in 1925, later renamed *Worship*, and encouraged the 'ministry of the laity'. The movement was also influential in the Lutheran church. In Sweden Archbishop Brilioth published *Eucharistic Faith and Practice* in 1930, and in Germany Friedrich Heiler, an ex-Catholic, emphasised the link between the liturgical and ecumenical movements. The Anglican Church of South India and the Protestant Taizé community in Burgundy were among the first non-Catholics to adopt liturgical thinking.[6] But it was the Catholic church that was most profoundly transformed, leading to a series of promulgations and decrees by Pope Pius XII from 1947 (*Mediator Dei et Hominum*) and an encyclical, *De musica sacra*, in 1955 which laid down guidelines for the increased participation of the laity in the rites of the church. The culmination of this papal acceptance of the Movement came between 22 October and 13 November 1962, when the Vatican Council devoted fifteen sessions to debate on the proposed constitution, and eventually passed *De sacra liturgica* by an overwhelming majority in 1963. Its effect was to unleash the liturgy to become the 'living service' of the Christian community, introducing vernacular language to the rite and becoming part of a wider missionary phenomenon. In England the rule that in new Catholic churches the altar must stand proud of the eastern wall was enacted in September 1964.

The liturgical development within the Catholic church in the 1950s coincided with increasing tension in the English Anglican church, symbolised by the debate over the reform of the 1662 *Book of Common Prayer*. Disagreements over its revision between the Anglo-Catholic and traditional arms of the church in 1928 perhaps gave the Liturgical Movement in England its spur. In 1955 the Archbishops of Canterbury and York set up a Liturgical Commission to prepare new services. In the meantime Father A.G. Herbert published *Liturgy and Society: the Function of the Church in the Modern World* in 1935, which Peter Hammond acknowledges as a formative influence on his generation, and Dom Gregory Dix produced *The Shape of the Liturgy* in 1945.[7] Both stress the importance of the Eucharist as a corporate action of the community, looking especially to the practice of the early church. Their ideas found a receptive audience at Queen's College, Birmingham, under J.O. Cobham, which hosted liturgical conferences in 1949 and 1950. In the 1930s and 1940s Birmingham was to become England's centre of liturgical renewal, based at Holland Hobbiss's Queen's College Chapel of 1938–46.[8]

In the Congregational Church a growing interest in liturgy was demonstrated by a symposium, *Christian Worship*, in 1936, and the publication in 1948 of a service book, *A Book of Public Worship*. The Presbyterian Church produced its *Book of Common Order* in 1940, while William Maxwell's careful reassessment of early Christianity, *An Outline of Christian Worship*, was published as early as 1936. A nascent interest in liturgy among the Baptists can be seen in the writings of Neville Clark and Ian Gilmore. In the Methodist Church this interest was coupled with a re-evaluation of John Wesley's origins in the High Church Anglicism of the early eighteenth-century non-jurors. Wesley's own commitment to regular communion, though admittedly as a means of conversion as well as a reverence, was forgotten in the diaspora of Methodism into various branches during the nineteenth century. The movement was reunited in 1932, when it published its first *Book of Offices*.[9] The equal importance given to the pulpit and table was born out in a guide to church building, *The Methodist Church Builder's Decalogue*, which planned for 'the total experience of worship, and to welcome outsiders in'. Though the concept of communion as a means of proselytisation is indicative of the heart of Methodism, in practice the bid for Church Unity in the 1950s and 1960s saw a greater conservatism in its liturgical arrangement, which led to the Lord's table being set back against the wall and communion rails introduced.[10]

6. H. Ellsworth Chandlee, 'The Liturgical Movement', in J.G. Davies, ed. *Dictionary of Liturgy and Worship*, London, SCM Press, 1972.

7. Peter Hammond, *Liturgy and Architecture*, London, Barrie and Rockcliff, 1960, p.67.

8. Andy Foster has identified a movement in Birmingham interested in liturgical planning before the First World War. Edwin Reynolds won the RIBA Soane medallion in 1903 with a church design whose free-standing altar had the choir to the sides and priests behind.

9. Raymond J Billington, *The Liturgical Movement and Methodism*, Epworth Press, London, 1969, p.37; 139–77.

10. Trevor Dearing, *Wesleyan and Tractarian Worship*, Epworth Press, London, 1966. Oliver Phillipson, *The Methodist Church Builder's Decalogue*, Methodist Church, Manchester, 1966, pp.6–7. Martin S. Briggs, *Puritan Architecture and its Future*, Lutterworth Press, London, 1946.

Everywhere the preoccupation with the worship of the early church can be interpreted as a yearning for a period before Christianity became divided within itself, firstly between the eastern and western traditions and more recently between Catholics and Protestants. The upshot was a widespread movement towards greater church unity. As a line of historical enquiry it was exactly contemporary with the investigations being made into the Elizabethan staging of Shakespeare, and the results for theatre and church planning were to be remarkably similar.

Peter Hammond, the rector of Bagendon, Gloucestershire, had studied art before his ordination. He was likened by Peter Anson to John the Baptist for bringing liturgical ideas to an architectural audience. In April 1958 he published a provocative article on new church planning in the *Architectural Review*, which was followed by a book, *Liturgy and Architecture* (1960), a powerful, even intemperate, manifesto.[11] Hammond contrasted English churches unfavourably with those built in France, Germany and Switzerland since the 1920s.

THE DEVELOPMENT OF A MODERN CHURCH ARCHITECTURE

Auguste Perret's Notre-Dame du Raincy, east of Paris, of 1922–3, was (and is) taken as a starting point for the new church architecture.[12] In part this is for the honesty of its exposed concrete construction and absence of Gothic detail, but also because its nave and sanctuary occupy a single space, with the altar separated from the east end by an ambulatory. Its long, basilican plan set the pattern for many of the most advanced churches of the inter-war period.[13] St Antoniuskirche, Basle, designed by Karl Moser and built in 1926–7, repeated many features of the design on a more monumental scale. It is an early demonstration of the importance of Swiss architects and commissions to changing liturgical fashions.

Like France, Germany underwent a religious revival, albeit a patchy one, during and immediately after the First World War. Most of the major commissions were from the Catholic church, since a few progressive dioceses controlled a large number of commissions, whereas each Lutheran church was handled by an individual community. Nevertheless, the Protestant tradition of centralised planning was significant. Otto Bartning had designed an octagonal Lutheran church at Schenkenhahn in 1909, and in 1922 he produced a widely published project called the 'Star Church'. In 1929–30 he built an entirely circular church, the Auferstehungkirche (Church of the Resurrection) at Essen-Ost, with four radially placed segments which can be closed off separately if required. He followed this

11. *Church Buildings Today*, No.1, October 1960, p.15; Peter Hammond, 'A Liturgical Brief', in *Architectural Review*, vol.123, no.735, April 1958, pp.240–55; Hammond, *Liturgy and Architecture*, ibid.

12. ibid, pp.52–3. See also Anton Henze and Theodor Filthaut, *Contemporary Church Art*, New York, Sheed and Ward, 1956; Robert Maguire and Keith Murray, *Modern Churches of the World*, London, Studio Vista, 1965; Reinhard Gieselmann, *Contemporary Church Architecture*, London, Thames and Hudson, 1972.

13. Andrew Saint, 'Notre-Dame du Raincy, in *Architects' Journal*, vol.193, no.7, 13 February 1991, pp.26–45.

with an exploration of fan-shaped plans, which were dynamic in their construction, with concrete trusses radiating from the altar, as well as liturgically.

A series of Catholic Congresses of Christian Art was held from 1922, which brought together Abbot Herwegen of Maria Laach and architects including Dominikus Böhm, Martin Weber and Rudolf Schwarz. The writings of Johannes van Acken on theology and architecture were influential, particularly on Böhm and Weber. 'What we want is in a word: the altar as the "Mystical Christ" shall be the point of departure and the artistic focal point of the church building and furnishings.'[14] Many of their more radically planned churches were never built, including virtually all those designed after 1933.

Dominikus Böhm's first centralising plan was made in 1915–17 for a church at Neu-Ulm, and it was in another design for the same town, the war memorial church of St Johann Baptist, that he was to evolve an interest in concrete construction as a means of liberating design. More dramatic was his Frielingsdorf church, built using parabolic concrete trusses in 1926–7. Something of this tech-

14. Johannes van Acken, *Christozentrische Kirchenkunst, Ein Eintwurf zum liturgischen Gesamtkunstwerk (Christocentric Church Art – towards the Total Work of Liturgical Art)*, pamphlet, 1922, quoted in translation in Hugo Schnell, *Twentieth Century Church Art in Germany*, Munich, Verlag Schnell and Steiner, 1974, p.45.

15. Hugo Schnell, ibid. p.46. See also August Hoff et al, *Dominicus Böhm*, Munich, Verlag Schnell and Steiner, 1962.

left to right:

figure 3
Auguste Perret, Notre Dame de Raincy, Paris. 1922–3. View of the sanctuary. (photo Architectural Press)

figure 4
Karl Moser, St Antoniuskirche, Basle. 1926–7. (photo Basle Museum)

figure 5
Otto Bartning, Gustav Adolf Kirche, Berlin-Charlottenburg. 1932–4. (photo Author)

figure 6
Dominikus Böhm, St Apollinaris, Frelingsdorf, Germany. 1926–7. (photo Architectural Press)

figure 7
Rudolf Schwarz, Fronleichnamskirche (Corpus Christi), Aachen, Germany. 1928–30. (photo Author)

nical virtuosity was seen also at his circular Immaculata-Kapelle at the international press exhibition (the Pressa) at Cologne in 1928; made of plate glass set between deep-cut piers, it showed an austerity that was to dominate his designs of the 1930s. Though most of his built churches had plans with long naves and high altars set only slightly forward of the east end, Böhm's St Englebert, Köln-Riehl, (1932) placed the congregation in an entirely circular nave. As funds and materials for new churches declined, so his planning also became simpler and his naves shorter; his last work of the 1930s, St Wolfgang, Regensberg (1937–9) was almost square, with the congregation set in a 'U'-formation around a forward altar and with the organ set in an apse behind. 'As almost no other architect he reflected from work to work on the meaning and position of the altar and the much-discussed tabernacle, the sites for the font, ambo, confessional, choir and organ, the workday church, as well as on the purely artistic problems of conscious handling of interior and light, and finally on questions of ornamental and abstract art.'[15]

Böhm's onetime collaborator and closest follower was Martin Weber, who produced designs for a series of churches in Frankfurt that clearly demonstrate the development of liturgical planning in Germany in the years 1924–33. Weber himself produced a drawing of the four plans to show how they were intended to evolve from an extended rectangle in the manner of Le Raincy to a contracted, squarer plan. At the Heliggeist church, Riederwald, Frankfurt (1930–1) he planned a central altar, though as built the church has a forward altar set under a

figure 8
Various plans by Martin Weber for his Frankfurt churches. (Verlag Schnell)

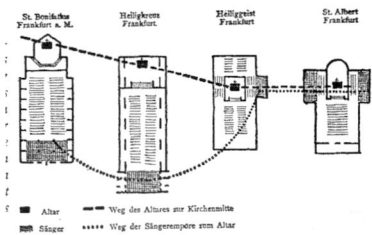

figure 9
G.F. Bodley and Thomas Garner, St
Michael, Camden Town. 1879–93.
(photo English Heritage)

figure 10
Sir Giles Gilbert Scott, Our Lady and St
Alphege, Bath. 1925–54. (photo RIBA / BAL)

figure 11
N.F. Cachemaille-Day, St Michael and
All Angels, Wythenshawe, Manchester.
1937. (photo RIBA / BAL)

broad chancel tower, as had his earlier and more monumental St Bonifatius, Sachsenhausen, of 1926–7.

Weber was also the initiator of the 'Study Circle for Church Art', which also included Rudolf Schwarz, designer of Fronleichnamskirche (Corpus Christi), Aachen, built with Hans Schwippert in 1928–30. Though its basic form was the long plan used by Perret at Le Raincy, this was a white box of sensational purity, its architecture and space left equally unencumbered by traditional fittings and its materials nakedly expressed. Hammond commented that 'it is sobering to reflect that, so far as church architecture in this country nearly thirty years later is concerned, the lesson embodied in Schwarz's fine church has still to be learned. We are still fighting for the basic honesties'.[16]

CHANGES IN CHURCH PLANNING IN 1930s ENGLAND

Hammond crucially underestimated the development of the single, rectangular space as a common church plan in England. The notion of setting chancel and nave within a single space undivided by a formal chancel arch goes back to the work of G.F. Bodley. His St Augustine, Pendlebury, of 1871–4, is a good example: the roof line and space are continuous, even if there are screens to closely define the nave, choir and sanctuary at ground level. St Michael, Camden Town, designed by Bodley in two stages in 1879 and 1893, is a more refined and still more open version, as is Edmund Scott's St Bartholomew, Brighton. In the 1950s only Goodhart-Rendel and George Pace recognised Bodley's honesty of purpose. 'Bodley would have argued that religion and Gothic went together and he was able to add this new quality as it grew out of the demands of nineteenth-century Anglo-Catholicism.'[17] Hammond and his contemporaries particularly reviled architects of the inter-war period for their associations with the nineteenth century high Anglican movement. They were virulent in their distaste for Victorian churches, as a fixed and archaic product of a worship where the congregation was largely passive. To them the Anglican revival had 'failed', because it had perpetuated the hieratic division between clergy and laity, and they opposed its personal, not collective, nature. For Keith Murray, 'The Gothic Revival gained its power from the attempt to recapture the richness of worship, but its popular appeal was fed by the Romantic Movement: a literary rather than an architectural phenomenon. It created a popularly accepted image of a church, imposing a general pattern on the buildings of most denominations'.[18]

Yet the earliest years of the twentieth century saw the further simplification of English church design. The Roman Catholic Church of Our Lady of the Assumption, Northfleet, Kent, built by Sir Giles Gilbert Scott in 1913–16 is remarkable for its minimalisation of Gothic detailing within a plan that is almost completely rectangular, with only the most vestigial and rectangular chancel arch under a flat ceiling. Scott took these ideas further at his Church of Our Lady and St Alphege, Bath, commissioned in 1925 and completed in phases between 1929 and 1954. Photographs show this church to have had a forward altar from the first, with chairs for the congregation right up to the sanctuary steps.[19] More remarkable was the style chosen by Scott as appropriate to such a basilica plan, for St Alphege's is thoroughly Romanesque and based largely on the church of St Maria in Cosmedin, Rome. Such a conscious historicism was, however, to be vilified by the younger generation as architectural pastiche. 'It is a popular misconception to think that the Liturgical Movement seeks to re-establish the liturgy of the Primitive Church or to imitate fourth-century buildings, as Sir Giles Gilbert Scott has in the Roman Catholic Church of St Alphege, Bath. Nothing could be further from the truth.'[20]

One way of bringing the congregation closer to the service was widely recommended by the mid-century. Both Goodhart-Rendel and his one-time assistant Cachemaille-Day made a feature of placing their choirs in rear galleries, when they were permitted by clients – as at the former's St Wilfred, Brighton (1932–4), and the latter's St Saviour, Eltham (1932–3). Goodhart-Rendel considered that 'it is bad that we should hide altars behind screens, push pulpits round corners, obstruct seating space with pillars, confine organs in close chambers, and give to mere singing men and boys the prominence and vesture rightful only to collegiate choirs.'[21] Cachemaille-Day wrote persuasively on the importance of not separating the altar and the congregation, and in 1960 claimed that 'fashions and change are just as necessary to keep church planning alive, as they are to keep anything else alive. There must be movement, as was understood by the medieval church builders'.[22]

Hammond, however, was only interested in the most centralised English plans. The John Keble Church, Mill Hill, of 1934–7 by D.F. Martin-Smith, with its broad nave wrapping round the centrally placed choir, was commissioned by the Rev. O.H. Gibbs-Smith, first incumbent of the new parish. It was he who chose the distinctive dedication, and this appreciation of the pioneer of the Oxford Movement was coupled with an emphasis on ceremonials, music and new liturgies also. It was one church suggested as a model for new churches by A.B. Knapp-Fisher in 1951.[23] The star-shaped St Michael's and All Angels, Wythenshawe, by N.F. Cachemaille-Day and also completed in 1937, was intended to be still more radical. It was originally to have had a forward altar, but this was pushed further back into the sanctuary at the insistence of the Bishop of Manchester who wanted more room for choir stalls between it and the congregation. Hammond also rated an obscure work by Cachemaille-Day, the tiny mission church of the Good Shepherd built in Sunderland in 1938, which with its broad, stark sanctuary and apsidal east end anticipates some of his 1950s' churches. More widely admired was Comper's St Philip, Cosham, built in 1936–8. Though complex in the ideas surrounding its decoration, the planning of this small rectangular church with its altar set on a single step under a ciborium and the choir committed to a west end gallery was simplicity itself. It, rather than the John Keble Church, was to prove the role model for the advanced church architects of the 1950s. Perhaps the most exceptional Anglican chapel, however, was that built by the Society of the Sacred Mission as an addition to Sir George Gilbert Scott's Kelham Hall, which it acquired in 1919. Begun in 1927–8 to the designs of the Derby architect Charles Clayton Thompson but never completed, its brick and concrete interior is powerful and stark, the more so since its fittings (many by C. S. Jagger) were dispersed when the Society moved to Milton Keynes.

Two truly innovative Catholic churches were built in England in the 1930s. First, at Bradford, is an octagonal church in a neo-Norman style, the Church of the First Martyrs, designed by the local architect J.H. Langtry Langton for Father John O'Connor, who wanted a central altar so that his congregation could be closely involved in the eucharist. It is an outstanding church for 1935, and particularly impressed Eric Gill. 'The altar is right in the middle, and the result is very remarkable. The sacrifice is offered not only for the people, but by and in the middle of them'.[24] Gill's interest in the liturgy is shown by the second important Catholic church of the period, the centrally-planned St Peter, Gorleston, built to his own design in 1938–9.

Hammond reserves particular venom for the work of Edward Maufe and for his book, *Modern Church Architecture* (1948), where he looks at the spiritual or symbolic ideas which can be evoked by spatial planning and new materials, rather than looking first at functional needs.[25] Similarly, Pace wrote contemptuously of architects who 'like to be given churches as it gives them opportunities to evolve strange shapes.'[26] In the early 1950s the temptation to treat a church simply as a sculptural space was great, particularly as it became easier to bridge large spans with lightweight materials, and the liturgists' views can be seen as a reaction to this initial freedom.

figure 12
D.F. Martin-Smith, John Keble Church, Mill Hill, L.B. Barnet. 1934–7. (photo Author)

16. Hammond, *Liturgy and Architecture*, op. cit. p.57.

17. George Pace, 'Architecture and Architect in the Service of the Church', in William Lockett, ed. *The Modern Architectural Setting of the Liturgy*, September 1962, SPCK, p.89 (with thanks to Edward Mills).

18. Keith Murray, 'Material Fabric and Symbolic Pattern', in Peter Hammond, ed. *Towards a Church Architecture*, London, Architectural Press, 1962, p.89.

19. This arrangement remains, though sanctuary walls have been removed. At Ampleforth, derived from the Romanesque brick tradition of south-western France, Scott placed the altar in the central crossing.

20. William Lockett, 'A Lesson from Anglican History', in Lockett, ed. op. cit. p.45.

21. H.S. Goodhart-Rendel, *Commonsense Churchplanning*, Incorporated Church Building Society, 1947, p.1.

22. N.F. Cachemaille-Day, 'Church and Community', in Ernest Short, ed. *Post-War Church Building*, London, Hollis and Carter, 1947, esp. p.36. *Church Buildings Today*, No.1, October 1960, p.5.

23. A.B. Knapp-Fisher, *The Future of Church Building*, Incorporated Church Building Society, 1951.

24. Letters of Eric Gill, ed. Walter Shewring. London, 1947, p.351. Quoted in Hammond, *Liturgy and Architecture*, op. cit. p.69.

25. Edward Maufe, ed. *Modern Church Architecture*, ICBS, London, 1948. Hammond, *Liturgy and Architecture*, op. cit. esp. pp.76–8.

26. George Pace, 'Architecture and Architect in the Service of the Church', in William Lockett, ed. op. cit, p.78.

figure 13
J.H. Langtry Langton, Church of the First Martyrs, Bradford. 1935. (photo Peter Smith)

figure 14
Eric Gill, St Peter, Gorleston, Norfolk.
1938–9. (photo Author)

27. Public Record Office IR 34 657. War Damage Commission records. Repairs to ecclesiastical properties.

28. For the full story see Louise Campbell, *Coventry Cathedral: Art and Architecture in Post-War Britain*, Oxford, 1996.

29. John Summerson, introduction to Trevor Dannatt, *Modern Architecture in Britain*, London, Batsford, 1959, pp.26–7.

30. Rayner Banham, 'The Church Stimulant', in *New Statesman*, vol.LX, no.1532, 23 July 1960, pp.116–8.

Over 250 Anglican churches were built in England and Wales during the inter-war period. At the end of the war a great many more were needed, not only to replace those bombed but also to supply the needs of the very large numbers of people who had moved to new settlements before, during and since the war. By December 1942 283 churches of all denominations had been lost, and the damage from flying bombs was to be as great.[27] The control of scarce materials by means of Building Licences meant that only 41 Anglican churches were consecrated in the period 1945–56, and this was one reason why so much attention was given to the flagship of the church's revival, the rebuilding of Coventry Cathedral. Won in competition by Basil Spence in 1951 and dedicated in 1962, its building thus straddles the advent of centralised planning. Yet Bishop Gorton, appointed to the see of Coventry in 1942, initially obtained a centrally planned design from Giles Scott, who had been appointed to rebuild the cathedral earlier the same year. It was a dispute over the architectural style that caused Gorton to engineer Scott's withdrawal from the scheme in 1947. Gorton was not to have so free a hand thereafter. The brief for the subsequent competition, and the evolution thereafter of Spence's winning design, was compromised by being the work of a

figure 15 a & b
Sir Basil Spence, Cathedral Church of
St Michael and All Angels, Coventry.
1951–62. (photo Architectural Press)

above View towards high altar

right Narthex and west end

committee, including more conservative thinkers who defeated Gorton when he attempted to bring the altar forward again in 1952. Spence's more traditional concept for the main space was largely worked out between 1951 and 1954, and is significant as the mightiest of the buildings of the era conceived as an amalgam of all the arts or *gesamkunstwerk*.[28] By 1959 John Summerson was asking 'whether Basil Spence's new cathedral … will turn out to be a religious building or only the most striking pavilion of religious art of the century'.[29] 'It will assuredly be the biggest consecrated Odeon in the Anglican communion', Reyner Banham jibed.[30] 'The new Anglican cathedral at Coventry, for example, illustrates no less clearly than its revivalist predecessors at New York, Liverpool and Guildford the isolation of ecclesiastical architecture from any kind of theological or social context, the subordination of function to visual effect' complained Hammond.[31] The sanctuary at Coventry was particularly criticised, as a two-dimensional backdrop to be seen from a distance by a passive laity who had no place in the worship save that of personal contemplation amid so many beautiful objects.

POST-WAR CHURCH PLANNING OVERSEAS

In the timing and extent of their rebuilding programmes Britain and Germany greatly differed. In Germany the destruction of church buildings had been greater, but so too was the pace of rebuilding with Marshall Aid funding from the United States. In the bishopric of Aachen only 43 of the 498 Catholic churches survived undamaged while 142 had been completely destroyed. But 123 had been rebuilt by 1960. 323 churches were built in the diocese of Cologne alone by 1955, and 240 more were at the planning stage. It has been estimated that about 8,000 churches were built or restored by the Catholics and Lutherans between 1945 and 1960.[32] No wonder then, that after an initial period of uncertainty so many interesting new buildings were produced.

Many of these churches were radical reconstructions of bombed churches, or salvaged such fragments as remained. There is little differentiation between old and new works; both served for experimentation into the technical possibilities of steel, concrete and glass. Schwarz reordered bombed out churches like the Liebfrauenkirche, Trier (1950–2), with central crossing altars. Yet there were constraints too. Despite such extraordinary works as the aeroplane-shaped St Michaelis, Frankfurt-am-Main (1954), Schwarz himself never accepted the concept of the priest facing the congregation, and the authorities, too, resisted the logic of a central altar.[33] However, Canon 802 of the Cologne diocesan synod of 1954 directed that everything should be avoided which accentuated the separation of congregation and altar, and Canon 803 welcomed the placing of the congregation round three sides.[34]

Architects responded to this liturgical uncertainty with an obsessive variety of cleverly-engineered roof structures, with square, circular and egg-shaped plans. Innovation took two basic forms: the evolution of a semi-circular layout for the congregation, and of a three-sided arrangement that leant itself to a more square or apsidal plan. The first semi-circular plan was that devised by Richard Jörg for the Heilig-Kreuz-Kirche at Mainz-Zahlbach, built in 1951–4. It was followed by the even more impressive St Albert, Saarbrücken, by Dominikus Böhm's son Gottfried (1952–4), its altar set on a circular stand surrounded by columns within a elliptical hall. The effect is reversed in Horst Linde's University Clinic chapel at Freiburg, Switzerland, with an oval sanctuary set in a segment of a circular church. Fritz Metzger's SS Felix and Regula in Zurich was a larger version, whose plan was widely published, while Giefer and Mäckler's Heiliggeist, Würzburg-Dürrbachau (1957) is almost triangular. Emil Steffann's St Elisabeth's, Opladen (1957), is arranged like an amphitheatre, a form which was widely adopted. The placing of the sanctuary in the corner of a square space

31. Peter Hammond, 'A Radical Approach to Church Architecture', in Hammond, ed. *Towards a Church Architecture*, op. cit, p.26.

32. Hugo Schnell, op. cit. p.75.

33. Gilbert Cope and Giles Blomfield, 'A Survey of Continental Churches', in *Church Buildings Today*, No. 5, January 1962, p.17. Anton Henze and Theodor Filthaut, op. cit.

34. Hugo Schnell, op.cit. p.77. Peter Hammond, 'A Liturgical Brief', op.cit., p.242.

figure 16
Gottfried Böhm, Wallfahrtskirche (Pilgrim's Church), Neviges, Germany. 1966–8. (photo Architectural Press)

figure 17
Reinhard Riemerschmid, Dreifaltig-keitskirche (Trinity Church), Hamburg, Germany, 1956–7. The 'alpha and omega' plan of Schwarz's St Michaelis, Frankfurt, here used for a Lutheran church. (photo Architectural Press)

35. Edward D. Mills, *The Modern Church*, London, Architectural Press, 1956, p.167.

36. Karin Becker, *Rudolf Schwarz 1897–1961*, Bielesfeld, Kramer-Druck, 1981.

37. At the church's dedication in August 1951, Wright gave an address from the pulpit on 'Architecture as Religion'.

38. Brendan Gill, *Many Masks, A Life of Frank Lloyd Wright*, New York, 1987, pp.418–20; Reinhard Gieselmann, *op. cit.*, p.16; Aline B. Saarinen, ed., *Eero Saarinen on his Work*, 1962, p.36.

39. Hammond, ed. *Towards a Church Architecture*, op. cit. pp.11, 172–5.

40. Ernest Benjamin Koenker, *The Liturgical Renaissance in the Roman Catholic Church*, University of Chicago Press, 1954, pp.130–33.

grew out of institutional churches, where altars were placed at the junction between the main body of the interior and a weekday chapel; Steffann's St Bonifatius, Dortmund (1951–4) is an early example, as is Schwarz's St Anna, Düren (1951–6) and Henri Matisse's refurnishing of the Dominican Chapel of the Rosary at Vence, France (1951, with M. de Peillon).[35] Relatively few churches were built which placed the congregation on three sides of the altar, for this proved to be wasteful of space and split the congregation into separate blocks. Exceptions included Steffann's church of Maria in den Benden, at Düsseldorf-Wersten (1956–9, with N. Rosiny); the soaring Maria Königin, Saarbrücken, by Rudolf and Maria Schwarz with Hubert Friedl (1954–7); and Hans Schädel's pilgrimage church of Maria von rauhen Wind at Kälberau in Franconia.[36] Yet the wholly circular plans were no more successful in bringing the congregation together. Most remarkable of all is the church of St Rochus, Düsseldorf, by Paul Scheider-Esleben of 1955, its plan taking the form of three inter-connecting circles and built up as a series of inter-penetrating ellipses. In all these churches a strong geometry and sense of structure remained, and it was only with Hans Schilling's Allerheiligen, Wesel (1952–8), that a profoundly irregular, organic form was attempted.

But German church architecture was not the dominant force it had been in the 1920s, and other other countries were producing more experimental designs. Work in America demonstrates the variety of 1950s' churches well. Not all were

figure 18 · above left
Rudolf Schwarz, St Anna, Düren, Germany. 1951–6, tower 1964. (photo Author)

figure 19 · above right
Frank Lloyd Wright, Unitarian Church, Shorewood Hills, Madison, Wisconsin, USA. 1947–51. (photo Ezra Stoller)

figure 20 · right
Aarno Ruusuvuori, Hyvinkään Kirkko, Finland. 1958–61. (photo Architectural Press)

based on liturgical premises, and they ranged from the personal response of Frank Lloyd Wright's Unitarian church of 1947–51 at Shorewood Hills, Madison, Wisconsin, to the more central arrangements of Saarinen's chapel for private contemplation at the Massachusetts Institute of Technology (1950–5) and Marcel Breuer's Benedictine abbey church of St John at Collegeville, Minnesota (1953–61). Few churches could be less liturgical than Wright's, for its triangular section, formed of a great copper welted roof said by him to be symbolic of 'hands joined in prayer', raised questions about the Holy Trinity, of which Unitarians are sceptical.[37] Saarinen himself later considered his MIT chapel to be 'too egocentric'. Mies van der Rohe's chapel of St Saviour at the Illinois Institute of Technology (1952) offered the ultimate in simplicity.[38] Yet though they reflected the personal inspiration of their architects rather than some greater purpose, all these churches were widely imitated.

Inspiring churches were produced by the Lutheran church in Sweden and Finland, usually as part of a larger complex. Aarno Ruusuvuori's village church at Hyvinkää (1961), formed of two unequal pyramids, has a free-standing altar bathed in concealed light. Hammond admired the chapel at Otaniemi Technical University by Heikki and Kaija Siren (1958–61), a simple hall with wooden trusses whose great glass window gives on to a symbolically charged view of ancient woodland.[39] Sigurd Lewerentz showed that a church could be incorporated into a community complex yet retain the architectural interest and the sense of timelessness associated with places of worship – as best seen at his Markuskyrkan at Björkhaven, Stockholm (1958–60).

But by the late 1950s the most stimulating churches were being built in France. The seating at the Pontifical Pavilion of the 1937 Paris Exhibition had been arranged in a circle round a central altar, and the same year Cardinal Pacelli, later Pope Pius XII, had celebrated mass facing the people at Notre Dame de Paris. A more profound and radical religious revival began with the publication of La France, Pays de Missions? in 1940, an account of 25 'worker priests' who celebrated Mass in the factories and dockyards where they worked as labourers. Likened to the medieval Friars, their roots religion prospered in the camps of the Nazi occupation, and subsequently led to a revival of church building.[40] Auguste Perret's last church, St Joseph du Havre, built between 1952 and 1955, was as remarkable as his first – again of concrete and panel construction, it has a 350ft tower above a central altar. A feature of Perret's work is the piercing of his concrete panels with areas of coloured glass, developed as dalle de verre, in more abstracted form a feature of Hermann Baur's St Thérèse at Hem, Roubaix (1958), and of Robert Faraut's Notre Dame de Grace at Marsang-sur-Orge, whose openings Hammond likened to those of a columbarium. Artists of the highest rank began to work in churches, encouraged by the journal L'Art sacré and its influential editor, Marie-Alain Couturier. These included Matisse at Vence, and Fernand Léger at Maurice Novarina's Le Sacré Coeur, Audincourt (1950–2), with its abstract scheme of glass, mosaic and tapestry by Léger and Jean Bazaine. From Perret, too, evolved a powerful use of concrete, manifested by Guillaume Gillet at his raw and expressive Notre Dame du Royan, of 1954–8, which thrusts an oval of thin, tall concrete blades out of a flat landscape.

The two elements of tough concrete and thick, pierced glazing are brought together most famously and organically by Le Corbusier at Notre Dame du Haut, Ronchamp. As he grew older Le Corbusier drew more upon ideas of spirituality and symbolism which were none the less profound for being agnostic, arguing that he who searches for harmony has a sense of the sacred. His interest in ancient Greece and in classical systems of proportion were part of this evolution, resulting in 1947 in the exposition of his Modulor, based on Fibonacci's twelfth-century system of proportion. Le Corbusier was announced as the architect for Ronchamp in October 1951, and the chapel was completed in 1955. A pilgrim-

figure 21
Sigurd Lewerentz, Markuskyrkan, Björkhaven, Stockholm. 1958–60. (photo Martin Charles)

figure 22
Auguste Perret, St Joseph du Havre, France (model). 1952.

figure 23
Le Corbusier, Notre Dame du Haut, Ronchamp. 1951–5. (photo Architectural Press)

age chapel and not a parish church, at Ronchamp Le Corbusier was freed from normal liturgical needs to produce an integration of masses and works of art that remains unique. 'The free, flowing lines of an open plan design have made the altar the supreme pivotal point of the whole interior'.[41]

THE IMPACT OF THE LITURGICAL MOVEMENT IN ENGLAND

Some British churches were clearly influenced by these foreign sources. Peter Bosanquet's St John, Hatfield (1958–60), shelters its single space under a vast roof reminiscent of Wright's Madison chapel. It did, however, group the altar, pulpit, lectern and font into the sanctuary, as one strand of liturgical thought suggested. Yet critics found it 'restless and confused', symbolising all the modernist imagery against which many in the Movement revolted.[42] Louise Campbell has shown that just as Spence was evolving his designs for Coventry Cathedral and for three little churches in the city outskirts in May 1956, he visited Hermann Baur's All Saints, Basle (1950), Ronchamp, and probably Audincourt.[43] Baur's basilican form, with its simple bay construction, and openwork campanile directly inspired Spence's smaller churches, while the top-quality art in the French churches impressed him. Spence's portal-frame churches in Coventry, Sheffield and Manchester gave him the opportunity to experiment with totally glazing one or both ends, just as he was proposing for the (liturgical) west end of the Cathedral.

Older architects also continued to be experimental. Many of Cachemaille-Day's preliminary drawings were more radical than the final built design; for example, his initial sketches for St Edmund, Northwood Hills, Middlesex (1957), show a square plan and forward altar which were superseded by a traditional rectilinear design. At St Richard of Chichester, Crawley (1954–5, demolished) he placed a free-standing sanctuary at the junction of a long basilica church and a church hall set at right angles which could be opened up for special services. The position of the font was a controversial issue to liturgists, and here Cachemaille-Day showed himself at the forefront of contemporary thinking by placing it in a shallow, glazed apse to the side of the altar, distinct but not separate from the main focus of worship. At All Saints, Hanworth, where the main church space was designed in 1955–6 and built in 1957, a forward altar was placed in a broad apse, serving a square church. The choir was originally placed in a central position resembling that used at the John Keble Church, but was soon moved to the west end.

41. Henze and Filthaut, *op. cit.* Tim Benton, 'The Sacred and the Search for Myths', in *Le Corbusier, Architect of the Century*, London, Arts Council, 1987, pp.238–49.

42. E.D. Mills and W.E.A. Lockett, 'Plans of Churches', in *Church Buildings Today*, no.1, October 1960, pp.11.

43. Campbell, *op.cit.* p.152.

figure 24 · left
Peter Bosanquet, St John, Hatfield, Herts. 1958–60. (photo Author)

figure 25 · right
N.F. Cachemaille-Day, All Saints, Hanworth, Hounslow. 1952, 1955–7. (photo English Heritage)

When Hammond came to write *Liturgy and Architecture* he could point to few completed English churches that were liturgically innovative. He illustrated 31 Anglican plans, of which only eighteen had been built. Most of these are basilican forms, finished in a variety of styles from the Georgian of All Saints, Bawdeswell, Norfolk, by J. Fletcher Watson in 1955, to the simple, stripped Scandinavian modernism of D.F. Martin-Smith's St Mary, Southgate, Crawley, of 1958. Robert Potter, a pupil of W.H. Randoll Blacking, admits that he was much inspired by the latter's master, Ninian Comper. The influence of St Philip's, Cosham, is striking in two of Potter's designs which combine traditional and modern materials to create dramatic, light spaces with forward altars in a basilica plan. These are the Church of the Ascension, Crown Hill, Plymouth, built in 1956, and St George, Oakdale, Poole (1959–60), a project taken over from the Mothers' Union which in consequence incorporated a large Lady chapel within the single space. Both churches have western galleries for the choir, which are open behind because Potter believes this increases the flow of sound; these spaces also make impressive full-height west end baptistries.[44]

Hammond also admired George Pace, an architect often identified with the continuing arts and crafts traditions of church architecture, but who could also find inspiration in modern continental work. His search for an organic architecture which looked fresh and yet was timeless in its spirit drew him towards an assimilation of vernacular and nineteenth-century sources, that met in a curious fusion of Lethaby with modern French elements. He, too, considered St Philip, Cosham, the most significant church of its day, and its influence can be seen in his early adoption of free-standing, square sanctuaries – often, as at the Scargill and Keele University Chapels, set forward of the long wall of the enclosure. Though in 1956 he was still writing in support of 'a traditional Anglican east end',

figure 26
J. Fletcher Watson, All Saints, Bawdeswell, Norfolk. 1955. (photo English Heritage)

figure 27
Potter & Hare, Church of the Ascension, Crownhill, Plymouth. 1956. (photo English Heritage)

a series of churches for the Diocese of Sheffield show that he was not afraid to bring the altar forward, as in his single space halls like that of SS Leonard and Jude, Doncaster (1959), which grouped the altar, font and pulpit.[45] This was 'intended to show that the ministry of both the word and the sacraments are of equal importance, and all take place in view of the people, who themselves are participants in them all', as he wrote of another church, Holy Redeemer, Acomb, York (1959–65), where he incorporated an aisle and masonry from a demolished medieval church into a rectangular hall lit by small openings.[46] His most modern works are small buildings like St Michael's College Chapel, Llandaff, of 1957–9, another mix of natural stone and Corbusian pierced glazing in a simple stone building that is a particularly sculptural, plastic volume.

A church so organic in form as to be leaf-shaped is the Holy Family at Blackbird Leys, Oxford, designed by Colin Shewring and built in 1964–5. It has a hyperbolic-paraboloid, hanging timber roof by Hugh Tottenham, engineer of

figure 28 · left
George G. Pace, Holy Redeemer, Acomb, York. 1959–65. (photo English Heritage)

figure 29 · right
George G. Pace, St Michael's College Chapel, Llandaff, Wales. 1957–9. (photo Author)

44. Author's interview with Robert Potter, 6 August 1996.

45. George G. Pace, 'On Designing New Churches', in Central Council for the Care of Churches, *Post-War Church Buildings*, exhibition catalogue 1956–7.

46. Peter G. Pace, *The Architecture of George Pace*, London, Batsford, 1990, p.195.

figure 30
Colin Shewring, Holy Family, Blackbird
Leys, Oxford. 1964–5.
(photo Architectural Press)

47. Charles MacCallum, 'Gillespie Kidd and
Coia, the History of the Firm', in *Mac Journal
One*, Glasgow, 1994, p.12.
48. Kenneth Nugent, 'Churches and Liturgy',
in *Mac Journal*, ibid. p.31.
49. The campanile of St Bride, East Kilbride,
was demolished in 1983. St Benedict,
Drumchapel, was demolished after a
Twentieth Century Society visit in 1991, as it
was about to be listed. St Joseph, Faifley, was
destroyed by fire in 1993. St Peter's Seminary,
Cardross, is currently derelict.

Manchester's Oxford Road railway station. Churches lent themselves to the
sculptural possibilities of imaginative engineering. The hyperbolic paraboloid,
in concrete, was first used for foundry and manufacturing buildings for Alfa
Romeo, in Milan, by Giorgio Baroni in 1934 and 1937 respectively. It was brought
to church builders' attention by the Smithsons' Coventry Cathedral design in
1951, but became fashionable only in the late 1950s. St John, Ermine, Lincoln,
designed in 1961 by Sam Scorer of Denis Clarke Hall, Scorer and Bright, was one
of the first Anglican churches developed on a fan-shaped plan, with the altar set
towards one end of a hexagon. Scorer had already been experimenting with concrete hyperbolic paraboloid roofs and had designed a similar church for Welwyn
Garden City that was never built. At Lincoln two elevations are filled with glass,
with the roof descending to ground-level between them, and with two upward
sweeping points which he truncated to facilitate future expansion. These intended extensions and a campanile were never built, but perhaps the building is
more forceful without them.

The adoption of liturgical plan forms came more suddenly and completely to
Roman Catholic architecture, where in the years 1959–60 Britain came to the
forefront. Hammond mentions only the Most Holy Redeemer and SS Wulstan
and Eadburgha, Pershore, by Hugh Bankart (1959) and St Paul, Glenrothes, by
Isi Metzstein and Andy MacMillan of Gillespie Kidd and Coia (1956–7). In the
1930s Jack Coia had built a handful of brick basilica churches modestly inspired
by northern European sources. With St Paul, Glenrothes, Metzstein and Mac-
Millan revitalised the firm. Wedge-shaped and with a forward altar under a taller
and top-lit east end, St Paul's is remarkable, too, for the vitality of its facades, in
which the glazing pattern of the west wall is the chief source of decoration. 'A
radically different piece of architecture, modest in scale but of iconic clarity, and
above all derived from a rigorous consideration and an inventive exploration of

a hierarchically ordered problem.'[47] For Kenneth Nugent, it had 'a lapidary quality in the whole concept. It was contemporary, it was minimalist; small and beautiful, it encapsulated the gathering of priest and people; it was a homage to architecture liberating function.'[48] With their use of hidden light sources to give natural form and chiaroscuro to their unashamed brickwork and concrete, there is an exceptional organic quality to Metzstein and MacMillan's work that comes out of an individual response to each site coupled with a broad awareness of contemporary architecture abroad. The larger Catholic dioceses gave large numbers of commissions to one or two favoured firms, and over some fifteen years the firm produced about twenty churches for the Archdiocese of Glasgow. The most ambitious have high, deep choir balconies that turn square halls into rectangles, and give a greater complexity to what may already be an intricate sculptural form. The loss of the square St Joseph, Faifley (1961–4) and diamond-shaped St Benedict, Drumchapel (1965–7) have made St Bride, East Kilbride (1963–4), St Patrick's, Kilsyth (1961–5), and Our Lady of Good Counsel, Dennistoun (1964–6) the more precious.[49] Theirs is the finest body of post-war church building in Britain.

In England the Roman Catholic Church had the greatest need for new churches, for wartime bombing and post-war dispersement had exacerbated an existing shortage, to which Irish and especially Polish immigration subsequently added. A rapid building programme began around 1953 and lasted until the mid-1960s, and became steadily more adventurous. Goodhart-Rendel built his best surviving churches, still in an Arts and Crafts manner, and Giles Scott continued his rarefied Gothic approach. His brother Adrian rebuilt one church in the plan

figure 31
Gillespie, Kidd & Coia, St Patrick, Kilsyth, Dumbarton, Scotland. 1961–5 (photo Author)

figure 32
Gillespie, Kidd & Coia, St Paul, Glenrothes, Fife, Scotland. 1956–7 (photo Architectural Press)

figure 33
Adrian Gilbert Scott, St Mary and St
Joseph, Lansbury, Tower Hamlets.
1950–4. (photo RCHME © Crown copyright)

figure 34
Weightman and Bullen, St Mary,
Leyland, Lancashire. 1959–64.
(photo English Heritage)

50. Marian Curd, 'Why build a Church in the
Round', in *Catholic Herald*, 29 June 1962, p.6.

51. *Architect and Building News*, vol.231, no.22,
1967, p.938; *Churchbuilding*, no.7, October
1962, supplement p.1; *Churchbuilding*, no.9,
April 1963, p.31.

52. Bryan Little, *Catholic Churches since 1623*,
London, Robert Hale, 1966, pp.219–220.

53. I am grateful to Martin Goalen for a copy
of his father's slide notes. Joseph Pichard, *Les
Églises Nouvelles à Travers le Monde*, Paris,
Diffusion Française, 1960, p.60–62; Barbara
Kahle, *Deutsche Kirchenbaukunst des 20
Jahrhunderts*, Darmstadt, Wissenschaftliche
Buchgesellschaft, 1990, p.148.

of a Greek Cross, SS Mary and Joseph, Lansbury, East London (1950–2, as part of the Festival of Britain 'live architecture' exhibition) which has adapted to liturgical requirements particularly well. F.X. Velarde continued to design basilica churches of brick, such as St Alexander, Bootle (demolished) and St Luke, Pinner (1957). Meanwhile in every diocese one or two specialist firms produced a large body of work: Burles, Newton and Partners, F.G. Broadbent and Partners, Tomei and Maxwell, and Justin Alleyn in the south; Harrison and Cox in the West Midlands; Ivor Day and O'Brien, and F.R. Bates, Son and Price in the South West and Wales; and Weightman and Bullen in the North West. Most of these firms produced at least one new church with a polygonal plan. As early as 1962 the *Catholic Herald* could point to more than a dozen churches which had been built in the round – far more than the number of Anglican examples.[50] One early oddity was Hector Corfiato's Notre Dame de France, Leicester Place, London (1953–5), so planned because it was on the site of Robert Barker's Diorama of 1793, into which Louis Auguste Boileau had in 1868 inserted an earlier church, bombed in 1940. More typical was St Catherine, Horsefair, Birmingham, built with a circular auditorium by B.V. James of Harrison and Cox in 1962–4. Other examples included Walter Stirrup and Son's St Mary, Denton (1961–3), with a shell concrete roof, and St Mary, Walsall, by Jennings, Homer and Lynch (1962–3) with laminated timber crucks.[51]

In a large body of undistinguished work two churches by Weightman and Bullen stand out. One is their octagonal St Catherine, Lowton, built as early as 1957–9 and with a campanile filled with jangly concrete tracery. The other is St Mary, Leyland, commissioned in 1959 by the Benedictines of Ampleforth, who carefully defined the innovative brief, and opened in 1964. The project architect was J. Faczynski, and as the church also has important ceramics by Adam Kossowski it well illustrates the considerable contribution made by Polish immigrants on Catholic church building. The High Altar stands in the centre of the nave, which has a raked floor, but as the organ console and the choir seats are behind it the congregation does not normally gather all round. The angled concrete roof, the triangular clerestory windows, and the nave's drum with its walling of warm brickwork, rest on fourteen Y-shaped concrete piers. Across the aisles the outer windows have *dalle de verre* glass by Patrick Reyntiens. The church is as important for its various works of modern art, including a tapestry designed by Faczynski, as for its basic design and construction, and this is one theme that is clearly derived from continental sources.[52]

Gerard Goalen designed the T-shaped Our Lady of Fatima, Harlow, as early as 1954 when he was employed by the New Town Development Corporation, though it was not built until 1958–60. In 1958 he set off on a continental church tour, visiting works by Dominikus and Gottfried Böhm, Rudolf Schwarz and others in Germany, Switzerland and France. As a student he had designed a Benedictine monastery similar to Notre Dame de Raincy. Now he admired Moser's St Antonius, Basle, 'the original post-Perret', but was disappointed by many of the round churches he saw. Schneider-Esleben's St Rochus, Düsseldorf, he describes as 'Round, but bad!', and he was also unimpressed by Gottfried Böhm's St Albert, Saarbrücken. While he took more slides of Le Corbusier's chapel at Ronchamp, his limited notes concentrate on the fine glass he found elsewhere. He was particularly impressed by Novarina's church at Audincourt, and by Albrecht Dietz and Bernhard Grothe's *dalle de verre* glass at St Mauritus, Saarbrücken, an early 1950s' church by Boris Kleimt.[53] This interest is significant because of the important role played by glass in Goalen's own churches. The large windows of Our Lady of Fatima, Harlow, are entirely glazed with the searing glass of Dom Charles Norris of Buckfast Abbey. The completed church was admired by Father Mooney of the Church of the Good Shepherd at Woodthorpe, Nottingham, who was looking to erect a new church for his fast-expanding

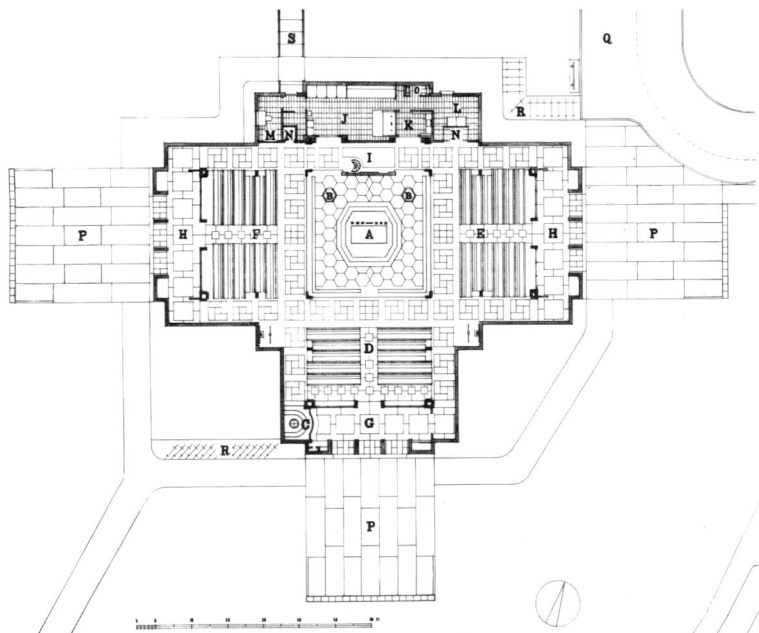

figure 35
Gerard Goalen, Our Lady of Fatima,
Harlow, Essex. 1954–60. Exterior,
interior and plan (Hank Snoek
photographer; lent by Martin Goalen)

congregation. This church, designed in 1961 and built between 1962 and 1964, has *dalle de verre* glass by Reyntiens based on the Trees of Life and Knowledge. It is also hexagonal in plan, in part because of the awkward site, and this resulted in the curious structural system whereby the roof is made up of four hexagonal shells like inward-blown umbrellas.

By the time that the Harlow church was being built, Goalen had joined Frederick Gibberd in partnership. The Nottingham commission enabled him to set up in private practice, and to build such churches as St Gregory the Great, South Ruislip (1965–7), St Gabriel's, Holloway (1966–8) and the Catholic Chap-

54. Author's interview with Lady Gibberd.
55. Frederick Gibberd, *The Metropolitan Cathedral of Christ the King, Liverpool*, London, Architectural Press, 1968, p.10.
56. ibid. p.12.

laincy in Cambridge (1977). In 1959 he had entered the competition for a new design for Liverpool Metropolitan Cathedral, which prompted Gibberd to enter too.[54] Goalen must have been cruelly disappointed when, despite having neither church building experience nor particular religious convictions, Gibberd won.

Sir Edwin Lutyens had been commissioned to design a Catholic cathedral for Liverpool in 1930, but by 1940 only the crypt was completed. Adrian Scott reduced the design, but in 1959 this too was set aside as impossibly expensive and ambitious, and a competition was held for an alternative. One of its conditions was for the congregation to be close to the High Altar. Archbishop (later Cardinal) Heenan himself wrote a prefatory letter to the competitors, which without defining the shape of the new building was a liturgical manifesto.

'The High Altar is the central feature of every Catholic church. It must be the focus of the new building. The trend of the liturgy is to associate the congregation ever more closely with the celebrant of the Mass ... The High Altar is not an ornament to embellish the cathedral building. The cathedral, on the contrary, is built to enshrine the altar of sacrifice. The attention of all who enter should be arrested and held by the altar.'[55]

Gibberd's was the winner out of 289 entries, the assessors concluding that it 'powerfully expresses the kingship of Christ', because the whole building is designed as a crown.[56] Gibberd's skill was as a planner, to roof over Lutyens's crypt as a platform for open-air worship and to design a new church – complete with underground parking – to the south. Though sixteen-sided and with a perfectly central altar, by placing the Blessed Sacrament chapel and organ directly opposite the principal entrance he was able to give his new building a strong north-south axis intended to link the two areas. The entrance evolved as a free-standing structure with a detached bell-frame similar to Breuer's at St John Collegeville in Minnesota. The High Altar itself was lit by a glazed corona, which complemented the tower of Giles Scott's nearby Anglican cathedral, then still under construction, as confidently as had Lutyens's dome. Gibberd first worked out many of these ideas at a small chapel for the De La Salle College, Hopwood Hall, near Middleton, Rochdale, built in 1963–5. The small scale of the Hopwood chapel meant that Gibberd could place the altar under its funnel-like corona, and still arrange the seating in a fan formation with three of the eight sides given over to subsidiary spaces. At Liverpool, its 194' diameter made this impossible, and

figure 36
Sir Frederick Gibberd, Metropolitan Cathedral of Christ the King, Liverpool. 1960–7. (photo RIBA BAL)

though the choir are placed behind the celebrant there is no escaping the overwhelming centrality of the design nor the possibility of witnessing an entire service from behind. Just as Spence had done at Coventry, so at Liverpool Gibberd was able to commission a large group of modern artists to design glass and fittings. Some, like Piper, Reyntiens, Margaret Traherne and Elisabeth Frink, worked on both.

One achievement at Liverpool was the speed of its construction, so that it was completed before its design were deemed 'out of date'. Nevertheless, though in 1959 it had been at the forefront of Catholic thinking, by 1967 the entirely circular form had given way to the less monumental but more practical fan-shape. This is ably demonstrated by the Catholic Cathedral of SS Peter and Paul, Clifton, Bristol, commissioned from the Percy Thomas Partnership in 1965. Ronald Weeks was the architect in charge, and the entire building was constructed between 1969 and 1973. Though from a distance Clifton Cathedral presents a strong, sculptural image redolent of the ambition of the early 1960s, internally this has given way in favour of a more humble, practical and organic form. Richard Gilbert Scott's Our Lady Help of Christians at Tile Cross, Birmingham of 1966–7, with its T-shaped plan, neon-bright glass and soaring, radiator-grille front, is one of the few churches of the late 1960s to be built with the ambition and panache of the first half of the decade.

figure 37
Percy Thomas Partnership (Ronald Weeks), Cathedral Church of SS Peter and Paul, Clifton, Bristol. 1965–73. (photo Author)

THE WORK OF MAGUIRE AND MURRAY

A greater opportunity for innovation was provided by small clergy chapels than was often possible in parish churches. One example is the chapel built by the Royal Foundation of St Katharine in Stepney, East London, a religious community was founded in 1148 by Queen Matilda. It survived the Reformation because it was a Royal Peculiar, only for its site to be sold by Act of 1825 for the building of St Katherine's Docks. The community moved to Regent's Park, where it languished until in 1943 a campaign began to restore it to the East End.[57] In November 1948 Queen Mary granted the Foundation the site of the bombed St James, Ratcliff, with its surviving vicarage. A new chapel was designed by Roderick Enthoven, and erected under a special licence from the Festival of Britain committee in 1952. It is a simple building which reflects the shortage of money and materials in the 1950s, but in 1954 a freestanding altar was installed. The original design, won in competition, was by Keith Murray and his silversmith brother; Robert Maguire helped them draw up the scheme, and admits to being inspired by Soane. Most dramatic is the wrought iron construction set over the altar, carrying six candles and a hanging pyx. This skeletal frame was originally partially covered by fabric, making a more solid corona, but this was removed at some time between 1967 and 1974. There were to be no candles on the altar itself. It was, however, carved with a long inscription by Ralph Beyer, the son of a distinguished authority on the incised lettering and symbols found in the catacombs at Rome, Professor Oskar Beyer. Henry Cooper, Master of the Foundation, claimed proudly that this was 'perhaps the first free-standing altar in modern times'.[58] It combines many liturgical themes: it is centrally placed, its decoration comes from the earliest Christian sources, and the employment of a Jewish sculptor embodies ecumenism.[59] Beyer was to use the same symbols at Coventry, where he was introduced to Spence by Sir Nikolaus Pevsner the next year.[60]

The church of St Paul, Bow Common, was another East End church damaged beyond repair in the War, but was not rebuilt until the late 1950s. Father Gresham Kirkby was appointed vicar in 1951, and remained at St Paul's until his retirement in July 1994. Kirkby was much influenced by the ideas of Conrad Noel and his church at Thaxted, a clear-glazed Perpendicular church that Maguire says was the first to be stripped of Victorian 'clutter'. Socially committed (he marched from Aldermaston with a papier maché dinosaur), Kirkby also travelled exten-

figure 38
Roderick Enthoven, Royal Foundation of St Katharine, Radcliff, Tower Hamlets, 1952. Altar by Keith Fendall, carving by Ralph Beyer, 1954. (photo Author)

57. In 1914 Lord Chancellor Haldane restored the benefit of the foundation to the East End, funding a maternity clinic at Bromley Hall in Brunswick Road, which lasted until the introduction of the National Health Service in 1948.

58. Henry Cooper, 'Royal Chapel of St Katharine in Radcliffe', in East End Papers, vol.10, no.2, 1967, pp.125–32. The same article reappeared in Cosmos, no.2, Winter 1968, p.2.

59. East End News, 1 April 1949; 10 June 1949; 12 September 1952. The Mirror of Literature, Amusement and Instruction, no.CLIV, 6 August 1825, p.97. Olwen Headley, 'Historic Royal Foundation', in Country Life vol.CLXX, No.4395, 12 November 1981, pp.1660–2. Antony Grant, Notes on the Royal Foundation of St Katharine, May 1977, unpublished thesis held at Tower Hamlets Local Studies Library, Bancroft Road, London E1.

60. Basil Spence, Phoenix at Coventry, London, 1962, pp.74–5; John Thomas, Coventry Cathedral, London, Unwin Hyman, 1987, pp.113, 116, 146.

61. Author's conversation with Fr. Kirkby, January 1990. Reginald Groves, *Conrad Noel and the Thaxted Movement*, London, Merlin Press, 1967. *Architects' Journal*, vol.153, no.3, 20 January 1971, p.144.

62. Author's conversation with Robert Maguire, July 1996. The revised design was approved by Archdeacon Hodgins without it having to go back to the DAC, as the sympathetic Hodgins ruled that the plan had not been altered.

63. Rudolf Wittkower, *Architectural Principles in the Age of Humanism*, London, Warburg Institute, 1949, revised 1962, Academy Editions, 1988, p.25.

sively in Europe looking at new churches before discovering Murray's work for the Royal Foundation and at Queen Mary College nearby in Stepney Green. He says how disappointed he was with the new continental churches, as well as with contemporary British work.[61] Murray was not yet in partnership with Robert Maguire, who was so young that he was obliged to credit his design as 'in association' with the established firm of Carden and Godfrey. This first design was more rectangular, with a recognisable spire in its centre. Maguire says he submitted this to please Albert Richardson, Hector Corfiato and Walter Godfrey, then members of the Diocesan Advisory Committee.[62] But honed down, the final version was England's first committed liturgical design, thought through from the principles of a forward-facing celebration of the mass (from an altar placed slightly east of centre) and from the desire to incorporate regular processions into the liturgy. Unlike St Philip, Cosham, its importance was immediately recognised and it was published both in its design stages and on completion.

Yet Maguire's sources were not the new churches of Europe. He was a student at the Architectural Association between 1948 and 1953, where his tutors included Robert Furneaux Jordan, John Summerson and Rudolf Wittkower. Wittkower profoundly influenced a generation of architects not only towards the use of classical proportions but a greater formalism and thoroughness in their planning and design. The Renaissance period looked back to the earliest manifestations of man's intelligence and the simplest elements of geometry. 'With the Renaissance revival of the Greek mathematical interpretation of God and the world, and invigorated by the Christian belief that Man as the image of God embodied the harmonies of the Universe, the Vitruvian figure inscribed in a square and a circle became a symbol of the mathematical sympathy between microcosm and macrocosm. How could the relation of Man to God be better expressed, we feel now justified in asking, than by building the house of God in accordance with the fundamental geometry of square and circle'.[63] Here was the perfect architectural justification for the Liturgical Movement. The Renaissance saw a crop of centralised churches, with circular, square or Greek cross plans set under a central dome. Bramante's Tempietto (1502) in Rome was itself derived from the *martyria* of early Christians, which were nearly always centrally planned in imitation of the Pantheon – itself put to this use. Palladio's Tempietto at Maser, in Ticino and built around 1580, is a later derivative. The influence of this planning

figure 39
Robert Maguire with Keith Murray, St Paul, Bow Common, Tower Hamlets. 1958–60 (photo Robert Maguire)

can be seen in the work of Christopher Wren and in early non-conformist churches. Maguire's own inspiration came from Filippo Brunelleschi's Pazzi Chapel, a private oratory in Florence commissioned about 1430 and built c.1439–60, Santa Fosca at Torcello, and early Greek churches such as Hagia Sophia in Istanbul.

Where other architects exploited organic forms of architecture, Maguire went for a geometrical purity based on the same sources as informed early Brutalism. 'The formal clarity ... is to be seen as part of a determination to make the whole conception of the building plain and comprehensible. No mystery, no romanticism, no obscurities about function or circulation'.[64] This description of the Smithsons' celebrated school at Hunstanton, won in competition in 1949 while Maguire was at the Architectural Association, is a reminder that their early work, too, had a source in Wittkower's teachings. 'An architectural generation nourished on Professor Wittkower's studies of centrally-planned Renaissance churches was bound to respond to the Liturgical Movement's preference for arena productions, and Robert Maguire's church of St Paul, Bow Common, indicates that the Movement is going to get the architecture it deserves – and wants'.[65]

St Paul, Bow Common attracted attention well before it was built. The church was designed from the inside out, with the altar placed off-centre under a glazed lantern. The basic form is a stack of three diminishing cubes with ancillary spaces added at the sides, including the entrance porch. The lower, wavy roof defines a processional route around the sides that is picked out on the floor in brick. The congregation sits under the high brick drum, on benches that can easily be moved. The altar is raised up Maguire's preferred two steps, and set under a baldachino as well as the lantern. The centralised plan is the dominant theme but there is also a principal axis: from ceremonial doors, under the organ, through the front of the altar, and into the larger of the two side chapels. The Lady chapel is at right-angles to this, while the more customary entrance in the corner brings you symbolically first to the font – a Doulton's stoneware firkin, set in a concrete surround. There are thus several layers of ideas in what seems at first a simple space.

The building today is virtually unaltered. Apart from a series of mosaics, designed by Charles Lutyens – great-nephew of Sir Edwin – and paid for out of the War Damage Commission's funds for stained glass, Father Kirkby was never able to commission the rich fittings he intended. Much therefore depends on the spare, steel frame of the baldachino and hanging lights by Murray which defines the raised sanctuary space. The result is very different from the Catholic churches with their strongly hued glass. What mattered for Maguire was the concept of solid, unbroken walls and pillars defining an ambulatory, which he likens to a Greek temple; and the presence of a spatially defining light. St Paul's achievement was to define a form of modern classicism appropriate to the function of liturgical worship.[66] But in Maguire and Murray's love of a few, simple but beautiful objects, and the way that light falls on them, there is also a debt to the Arts and Crafts Movement and the ideas of W.R. Lethaby. The one playful gesture at St Paul's was Beyer's lettering around the projecting porch: TRULY THIS IS NONE OTHER BUT THE HOUSE OF GOD. THIS IS THE GATE OF HEAVEN. Banham and Nicholas Taylor felt that Beyer's work belonged to an older tradition, while it caused Andrew Saint to place the building within 'the compromise of styles worked out by Sir Basil Spence for his churches and cathedral at Coventry.'[67] But in Maguire and Murray's work it is significant that such rare mannerist touches are reserved for details which contradict but do not overwhelm the classically-inspired main body of the composition. Banham early recognised it as an ecclesiastical equivalent of a Unité d'Habitation. 'It may only be days, it may be months, before St Paul's is denounced as "only a machine for worshipping in",

64. Rayner Banham, *The New Brutalism*, London, Architectural Press, 1966, p.19.

65. Rayner Banham, *New Statesman*, op.cit. p.118. Robert Maguire made the reference absolutely clear in 'Continuity and Modernity in the Holy Place', in *Architectural History*, vol.39, 1996, pp.1–8; based on his lecture to the Society of Architectural Historians of Great Britain on 20 November 1995.

66. *Architectural Review*, vol.128, no.766, December 1960, pp.400–05.

67. Banham, *New Statesman*, op. cit.; Nicholas Taylor, 'St Paul's Bow Common, a Realistic Church for Our Time', in *East London Papers*, vol.8, no.1, July 1965, pp.41–9; Elain Harwood and Andrew Saint, *Exploring England's Heritage: London*, Norwich, HMSO, 1991, p.33.

figure 40
Maguire and Murray, St Matthew, Perry
Beeches, Birmingham. 1962–4. Interior
and plan (photo Robert Maguire)

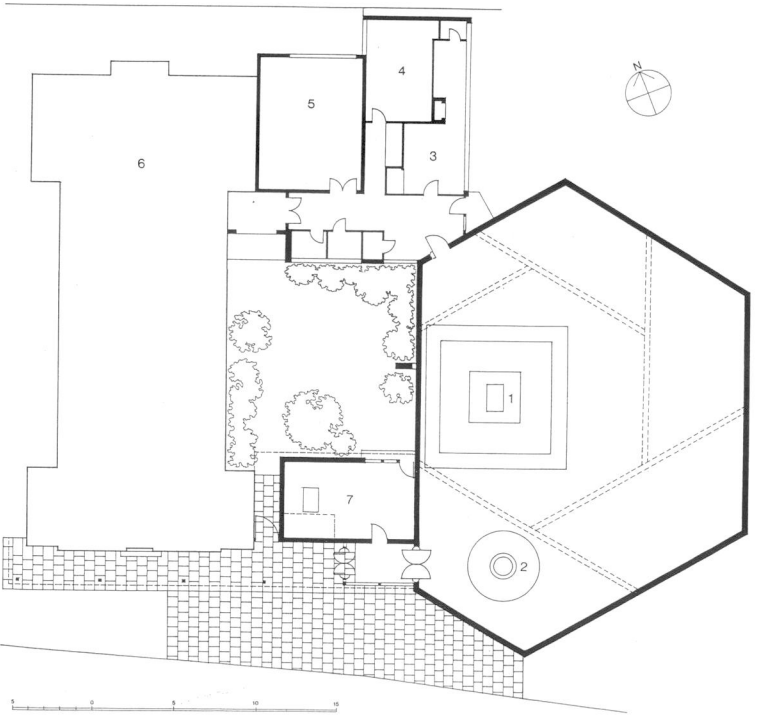

but when it is we shall know that even its detractors have admitted that it has started from essentials, and serves them properly'.[68]

Further commissions for Maguire and Murray followed from their membership of the New Churches Reform Group, which they co-founded in 1957. First came St Matthew's, Perry Beeches, built in 1962–4. It is a lone modern intrusion into a 1930s' suburb, where previously a parish hall had served for worship. The firm's most inventive and freely-planned church, Maguire there first divorced the altar from a place under a central lantern, by lighting the church from a sequence of seven stepped clerestories which rise in a circle from the low baptistry round the congregation to the sanctuary, set forward of the longest wall. This means that the sanctuary and font are physically close, as liturgists were coming to demand, yet separately defined and at opposite ends of the processional route. The original structure was devised as an Archimedes spiral swirling into infinity, and an early drawing shows an entrance porch comprising a cylinder piercing a semi-circular vault derived from Ronchamp. The present hexagonal roof structure was a revision made on grounds of cost. The cool quality of St Paul's is repeated in the bands of exposed grey brick and concrete walling, blue paviour flooring and simple bench seating, with a greater sophistication. Most bizarre is the de Stijl-like timber formwork of the pulpit-cum-lectern, admitted by the incumbent who, however, refused a baldachino. 'There are no views of the primeval forest, no glories of stained glass, no splendid images to possess empty space and force the visitor to his knees. One stands within a volume of rather formidable dimensions filled with soft light and furnished with a number of beautiful but evidently practical objects which look ready for use.'[69]

Big roofs over narrow clerestories were to become a feature of the firm's later work. At All Saints, Crewe (1964–5) where the single roof over the church, hall and vicarage gives a domestic feel. The cigar-shaped abbey church at West Malling (1964–6) is Maguire's favourite, although the daring structural system that enabled the central drum to be supported without columns was not properly built, and columns had to be inserted. St Joseph, Northolt (1967–9), described by Maguire as 'a symphony in white', is clad externally in industrial zinc, yet its interior is almost 'high tech' in the elegance of its light steel construction.[70]

The second issue of *Churchbuilding* edited by Maguire and Murray was given over to a study of the Smithsons' entry for the Coventry Cathedral competition in 1951, another building in which Wittkower's influence was strong. The design was prescient not only for its hyperbolic paraboloid roof but for its liturgical plan. The main axis of the design was across the diagonal of a square, with the altar towards its eastern end in an 'ark similar to the *scuola cantorum* of the early church'. The Smithsons hoped that the cathedral 'will finally explode the fallacy that Modern Architecture is incapable of expressing abstract ideas and will prove that *only* Modern Architecture is capable of creating a symbol of the dogmatic truths of the Christian faith.'

'Christianity ... deeply influenced the Renaissance concept of total architecture, which, is the perfect relationship of the natural order and allows Divine law to reveal itself. Modern Architecture is the heir to this great tradition and has at its disposal means of expression which would have sent Brunelleschi wild with joy. For the first time it is possible for architects to be completely aware of the forces at work in their structures and to find their exact plastic expression without arbitrariness or fear.'[71]

CONCLUSION

The Liturgical Movement came late to Britain. However, in the New Churches Reform Group collected round Hammond, Maguire and Murray, there is a consensus in building churches which are clear demonstrations of their ideals of

68. Rayner Banham, *New Statesman, op.cit.*
69. *Architects' Journal*, vol.142, no.14, 6 October 1965, pp.794–802; Robert Maguire, *Architectural History, op. cit.*
70. *Architects' Journal*, vol.148, no.36, 4 September 1968; *Concrete Quarterly*, no.80, January-March 1969, pp.31–4; *Architecture North West*, no.35, July 1969, p.17; *Architects' Journal*, vol.152, no.27, 8 July 1970, p.70–82.
71. Alison and Peter Smithson, 'Design for Coventry Cathedral', in *Churchbuilding*, no.8, January 1963, pp.3–17.

figure 41
Maguire and Murray, Church of the Resurrection of Our Lord Jesus Christ and of the Blessed Virgin Mary, West Malling Abbey, Kent. 1964–6.
(photo Robert Maguire)

figure 42
Alison and Peter Smithson, Competition design for Coventry Cathedral, 1951 (Photograph of model, taken by Nigel Henderson. Peter Smithson)

worship. But there was much else going on besides. Far greater patronage was in the hands of the Roman Catholic dioceses because of their close involvement with a few designers, and there is a remarkable similarity in many of the works commissioned. The sacrifice of detailing to a powerful total effect gives a coarseness to many works, including Liverpool Metropolitan Cathedral, which is however offset by an intelligent use of works of art including some examples of exceptional quality. Only the Archdiocese of Glasgow chose to work regularly with an inspired firm of architects. Gillespie Kidd and Coia's work is less austere than Maguire and Murray's, rougher and so fanciful as to be almost unhinged from the reality of structure. While Metzstein and MacMillan's achievement belongs with that of Pace, Goalen and others firmly in the European sphere of expressionistic modernism, the Wittkowian sources of Maguire and Murray set them in the English classical tradition. This long-time dalliance with Palladianism, not found elsewhere, sets English Brutalism apart from its contemporaries; it is an extra dimension of sources which make it harder to understand. What is confusing about the work of the Smithsons is that they soon began to incorporate many other ideas in their work. By sticking firmly to a classical inspiration, Maguire and Murray help clarify what was happening elsewhere in English architecture.

Whither the Liturgical Movement? By 1969 David Bishop could write that 'liturgical insights that appeared to be the "property" of the avant-garde are now almost universally accepted, indeed, are in danger of becoming cliché.' He found that churches were no longer 'borrowing' from secular architecture but at their best were in the vanguard of modern design.[72] But a new architectural form having been found for the post-war church, it was as quickly abandoned.

In 1960 Gerard Goalen wrote enthusiastically of 'the house of God. It should be as fine a building as we can afford, and in particular its *scale* should be generous. If we spend large sums of money on parish halls and club rooms, we may be tempted to put up mean buildings for the performance of the liturgy.' He argued for the building of community centres by the local authorities and New Towns where people of all faiths and denominations could congregate.[73] Yet the demand that churches be Church Centres became pervasive as the decade progressed. The idea of a church built round with clubrooms, meeting rooms and ancillary social accommodation goes back to the large non-conformist central missions of the late nineteenth century, and was popular, too, with churches of foreign denominations in London and the major ports. In the post-war period Handisyde and Stark's Trinity Congregational Church, built will integral halls and schoolrooms as part of the Festival of Britain in 1950–1, was a widely published model for churches of all denominations. Edward Mills's Mitcham Methodist Church (1960) was also much acclaimed. By the mid-1960s most Lutheran and Catholic churches in Europe were being built with large halls. In the Anglican church the multi-use movement was promoted by J.D. Davies's *The Secular Use of Church Buildings* in 1968, and its flagship church of St Philip and St James, Hodge Hill, Birmingham, opened the same year. This church is important not for its architecture, but because it aimed to be totally multi-functional, with the main worship space being used for recreational pursuits between services. The scheme was devised by the Institute for the Study of Worship and Religious Architecture at the University of Birmingham in 1963, and carried out by the architect Martin Purdy. Open up to fourteen hours a day, Hodge Hill sought to demonstrate Christian belief by through working in the community, principally in the form of youth clubs. It is to its generation what St Paul, Bow Common, had been a few years before.[74] Perhaps it is the logical progression of the ideals of the Liturgical Movement, with its call for greater openness. But architecturally, as well as spiritually, the result has too often been divisive and a debasement of the sense of place that is as important to the religious and the agnostic alike.

72. David Bishop, *New Churches*, Council for the Care of Churches, 1969, pp.2–3.
73. *Church Buildings Today*, no.1, October 1960, p.3.
74. *Architects' Journal*, vol.150, no.15, 8 October 1969, pp.876–84.

figure 43
Martin Purdy, St Philip and St James, Hodge Hill, Birmingham. 1963–7. (photo Architectural Press)

5 F.C. Eden: Building on tradition

EDWARD HAGGER

F.C. Eden: Building on tradition

EDWARD HAGGER

During his lifetime F.C. Eden (1864–1944) commanded the highest respect of the small but influential circle of traditional ecclesiastical architects of the period. Sir Charles Nicholson (1867–1949) and Sir Walter Tapper (1861–1935) were both close friends; the latter very frequently accompanying Eden on his regular foreign travels. Sir John Betjeman championed Eden too. In an adulatory letter of 1939 to Sir Ninian Comper (1864–1960) Betjeman gushes 'There is no doubt that you have transformed church architecture in England and you stand on your own as the only creative genius in that sphere – with F.C. Eden a little lower down the scale.'

Today, Comper's flame continues to burn bright fanned by an appreciative public wider than it was during his lifetime. Eden, in contrast, is an altogether less distinct figure. True, his name has not passed into obscurity but knowledge of his work is unlikely to extend beyond the modest white-washed Italianate brick church of St George improbably built on the Berkshire Downs at Wash Common, Newbury or perhaps from a Cornish holiday memory of the glittering numinousness of the mediaeval church of St Hyacincth and St Protus, Blisland.

Ignorance of his work has given lie to the belief that he was an important architect who built very little. This simply is not so. His output was large and varied and is evident in churches throughout Britain where he added numerous chancels, chapels, screens, altars and provided embroideries and furnishings of all kinds. However his career is notable for the paucity of large or prestigious commissions. Eden built only three modest churches and their small budgets allowed him inadequate scope to do justice to his ability. His talent and connections should have ensured that the opportunities were there but 'He rarely illustrated his works ... partly because his critical sense never allowed him to feel wholly satisfied with them and partly because he abhorred any form of publicity. Genial and social in private life, he was too retiring to take a large part in professional affairs'.[1]

His relative obscurity has been compounded by the fact that much of what was executed remains unrecorded and the generation that knew the man himself and his work when new is nearly extinct. Eden did write several articles and lectured, particularly in the period up to the First World War, but was always careful to avoid reference to his own work. Like Comper he fell foul of the Pevsnerian *zeitgeist*; the historicist approach of the *Buildings of England* series giving his work scant treatment. His death during the Second World War went more or less unnoticed and his practice ceased at that time. If his two principal urban works, St Matthew's, Bethnal Green and All Saints', Clifton had survived wartime bombing Eden would be better remembered today and his reputation not so eclipsed by the ascendancy of Comper's. The consequence of this is that the literature on Eden is all but non-existent and his work poorly recorded. On the plus side the RIBA Drawings Collection has a representative, if not comprehensive, selection of the full spectrum of his work.

Frederick Charles Eden was born in 1864 the son of Frederick Morton Eden,

figure 1
St Protus and St Hyacinth, Blisland.
Screen and rood loft by F.C. Eden, 1896.
(photo Edwin Smith)

1. Stephen Dykes-Bower in his obituary of F.C. Eden in the *Journal of the* RIBA, November 1944.

figure 2
St Matthew, Bethnal Green. Screen by
F.C. Eden, c.1918 (destroyed).
(photo 1920 RCHME © Crown Copyright)

a Fellow of All Souls, Oxford and Agent of the Duke of Buccleuch. His family lived in considerable style in a wing of Boughton House, Northamptonshire which was set aside for their exclusive use. His mother had been a Hyde-Parker from Long Melford Hall, Suffolk, where from the age of eight, following the death of his mother and his father's remarriage, Charlie spent much time. Consequently he grew up with an intimate knowledge of two great houses both of which were splendidly furnished and which he acknowledged to have been a great influence on his impeccable and eclectic taste. He was educated at Wellington and Keble College, Oxford.

His architectural training gave him the grounding that enabled him to excel in both classical and gothic styles but also indicating a personal restlessness as to stylistic preference; a restlessness which he spent the whole of his life trying to resolve. Appropriately, on leaving Keble College he entered the Office of the ageing William Butterfield (1814–1906). His father arranged the introduction, deeming Butterfield to be eminent enough for his son. Never a fan of the Butterfield style it was no surprise that the position lasted only a few months and in 1887 he joined the *atelier* of Walter John Nash Millard (1855–1936).[2] Eden then moved on to another protagonist of what was to become the Edwardian *Beaux-Arts* style, Fairfax Blomfield Wade (1851–1919) who specialised in houses in Jacobean, strict classical, and Wrenaissance styles. Both practices also under-

2. Millard had set up an *atelier* with his partner Baggally along the lines of the French *Ecole des Beaux-Arts*. The Maitre de l'atelier was the red-bearded and besmocked W.G.B. Lewis of William Burges's Office.

took ecclesiastical restoration work. In 1889, in an apparent stylistic about turn he joined the office of George Frederick Bodley (1828–1907) and Thomas Garner (1839–1906) the leading church architects of the late nineteenth century who had developed and refined the gothic revival to a Late Perpendicular perfection. He seems to have been a favoured pupil and accompanied Bodley on his foreign travels acting as courier, interpreter, sketcher and secretary. Comper and Tapper were both in the Office too and the influence of Bodley and Garner on all three young architects cannot be overstated.

In 1890 'growing a little impatient of confinement to the Late Perpendicular, he left to work on his own'.[3] Cushioned by a private income Eden remained in sole practice at several addresses in London throughout his career. In 1934 he suffered a disabling stroke which resulted in the closure of his glass shop. However he recovered sufficiently to continue his architectural work only resigning as a Fellow of the RIBA in 1938. He died, aged eighty, on 15th July 1944 in Ramsbury, Wiltshire, a war evacuee from London at the home of his cousin, Rear-Admiral Edmond Hyde-Parker. 'With a love of England – and he was not ashamed to proclaim his allegiance to Church and State as that of an old-fashioned High Church Tory – Eden combined an admiration for the arts of France and Italy.... In London he lived and worked in a house in Bedford Square, which he had filled with beautiful things and in which he maintained a *régime* of frugal and somewhat meticulous bachelor comfort. He would dine by candlelight, perusing the latest detective story or reading in Latin from some antique publication of the Sacred Congregation of Rites'.[4]

If proof was needed of Eden's genius one need look no further than the exquisite restoration Eden undertook at St Protus and St Hyacinth, Blisland. This was his first important work and is truly remarkable for its early date 1894–96. Here is full-blooded 'unity by inclusion' of different styles years before Comper legitimised the concept and years before the 'back to baroque' movement espoused by the Society of St Peter and St Paul from 1911 became an established ecclesiastical fashion. His response at Blisland might be seen as a reaction to the dogma and insensitivity of much nineteenth century church restoration. But it is not as simple as this. In his teaching Eden was strict in his adherence to many of the tenets of Bodley's ideal gothic and only later in life could he morally justify the use of what he termed 'foreign' architecture. His work at Blisland suggests an aesthetic response rather than one which he could necessarily explain or justify. Fittings aside, Eden's work at Blisland is exemplary in its restoration of the fabric, which required substantial reconstruction yet seems to have lost none of its 'veneer of antiquity' in the process. Exotic, striking and 'inauthentic' though many of the fittings are they are subservient to the mood of the church which remains timelessly Cornish in character.

Blisland's great glory is the spectacular chancel screen which stretches the full width of this typical wide-aisled Cornish church. Eden was unparalleled in his knowledge of extant examples of ancient screens in England and Wales and was invariably keen to introduce them wherever possible regarding England as 'the country of screens *par excellence*'.[5] He was proprietorial towards the English screen as Comper was to the idea of an English altar and was critical of what he saw as abuses. Commenting in 1905 on C.J. Blomfield's plans for Swaffham Prior church he notes 'The vulgar error of making the rood far to small. The cross is poorly designed and the attendant figures are mere dolls' and on A. Grove's otherwise favourably received plans for St John the Divine, Richmond 'unhappily there is no screen, but only that abomination unknown to English ecclesiology, but known to reporters as a low 'screen wall.'[6]

The career of Eden has to be seen alongside that of Comper. Both architects were born in 1864; both were pupils of Bodley and staunch Anglo-Catholics; both were more concerned with ecclesiastical fittings and restorations than new

3. W.I. Croome (1963) 'Frederick Charles Eden FSA FRIBA', Journal of the British Society of Master Glass Painters, Vol XII No.4 1963.

4. Stephen Dykes-Bower (1944) ibid.

5. F.C. Eden (1908) 'English Church Furniture', The Builder 19/09/08.

6. F.C. Eden (1905) 'Architecture at the Royal Academy' Architectural Review 06/05.

buildings; and both relied as much on Continental as British precedent. Unlike Eden, Comper stood aloof from the architectural establishment and had little regard for most of his contemporary ecclesiastical architects. However he held Eden in high regard and a friendship existed albeit based more on mutual respect than intimacy. In their professional work they were indebted to each other. Comper, for instance, adopted Eden's preference for the technique of burnished gold rather than the oil based gilding he used in his earliest work and was also indebted to Eden for his example of the dramatic use of chancel screens and for the idea of 'unity by inclusion'. Eden used Comper for the three stained glass windows at Blisland and when he set up his own glass shop was clearly influenced by Comper in his own work, particularly in its translucency and the predominant use of blues and yellows.

Eden had the advantage over Comper in that as a young man he was far more extensively travelled, visiting the Continent once or twice a year from his school days and throughout his life. Eden had an intimate knowledge of Normandy and Brittany and of the district around Troyes being an authority on the region's stained glass. He also had an intimate knowledge of Italy from the Alps to Rome and as he grew older this country became his spiritual home. But in the early years of his career the churches and chapels of Brittany were the important influence on him and the similarity between the cultural and physical characteristics of the western Celtic extremities of Britain and France stood him in good stead at Blisland. Eden sketched and made careful drawings of the plans and elevations he saw and formed his ideas as to what the ideal characteristics of an English altar should be; contrasting, for instance, the undignified stumpiness of most modern altars against the generous length and depth of those he saw in France.

The French method of restoration which invariably involved a thorough scarification of the building inside and out made Eden acutely aware of the need for sensitivity in restoration. He found the typical *Monument Historique* to be 'frigid and inhuman'.[7]

Eden's next major restoration after Blisland was at Elham, Kent, which spanned most of his working career. Having taste and money in abundance, the Rev. Alard C. de Bourbel,[8] Anglo-Catholic incumbent at Elham 1900–34 was typical of the sort of patron Eden could work well with. Elham remains incomplete lacking, amongst other items, the chancel screen and rood designed by Eden to incorporate traces of the destroyed original. The restoration was notable for the inclusion of a significant number of high quality ecclesiastical antiques and old masters producing what is widely considered to be the most beautiful church in the county. As at Blisland, Elham was first and foremost a sensitive restoration of the fabric. Eden was careful not to eliminate the uneven textures of the tiled floors and the plastered walls and retained fragments of wall-painting in the whitened interior. The sanctuary was lavishly furnished in 1908 in a rich Wren style with a pavement of polished black and white marble and the walls in polished inlaid oak by Edgar Pitcher and Elham craftsmen embellished by exquisitely fine limewood carving by Colley.[9] Eden's appreciation of the art of ironwork is evident in the magnificent baroque wrought iron and oak communion rails. For all the metropolitan sophistication of Eden's fittings, Elham remains very much a country church in character.

The other restoration on a par with Blisland and Elham was at North Cerney in Gloucestershire. As at Elham it was carried out over many years, the patron being a lifelong friend of Eden's, W.I. Croome. An extensive photographic archive exists of this church at the National Monuments Record from which it is possible to observe the gradual transformation of the church and appreciate why Eden had the enviable reputation of never putting a foot wrong.

Eden's first known architectural design, exhibited at the Royal Academy in

7. F.C. Eden (1904) 'Some Breton Chapels' *The Builder* 13/08/04.

8. Fr. de Bourbel also commissioned Eden to remodel the vicarage which was transformed from an old Kentish farmhouse into something that would not look out of place in Tuscany with its white rendering, loggia and extensive use of marble. It serves as a reminder that Eden was as stylistically adept in his small *oeuvre* of domestic architecture as he was in his church work.

9. The restorer of Grinling Gibbons' work in St Paul's Cathedral, London.

figure 3 a & b
All Saints, North Cerney.
above Before restoration.
left After restoration. (photo Author)

1892, was an unexecuted scheme for St Luke's, Winnington; a conventional cruciform Perpendicular gothic church which owed much to Bodley. Eden remained a committed supporter of Bodley's later work well into the second decade of the twentieth century. Of the earlier gothic revivalists he had scant regard describing, for instance, Butterfield's Keble College as 'ungainly'.[10] As late as 1914 Eden defended the gothic revival but significantly his defence was not specific to the gothic style 'The accusation of copyism has been so often brought against the Gothic Revival that many believe it to be justified, in spite of the fact that the alleged fraudulent antiques could deceive none but the most ignorant. The art of those gifted men [Bodley and Garner], though makes avowed use of the Gothic machinery, just as Milton and Wren made use of the Classical machinery for their purposes is in no way obnoxious to this charge'.[11]

Eden's St John the Baptist, Harpenden, Hertfordshire of 1908 demonstrates much that he admired in Bodley and Garner's work. It is a simple rectangular church, the tower of which was never built. Great care has been taken in the detailing of the massively buttressed exterior by the use of brick of different sorts with occasional tile infils to heighten the texture and by the use of both stone and tile-hung copings. The east window tracery was based on a window in Dorchester Abbey. The pointed architecture of the exterior gives no clue to the elegant stone round-arched arcade running the length of the south and north walls. Eden had a loathing for interior exposed brickwork and the interior is characteristically rendered and enlivened in the side aisles by plaster relief Tu-

10. F.C. Eden (1919) Untitled lecture privately printed by All Saints', Clifton.
11. F.C. Eden (1914) 'The Work of Bodley and Garner' *The Architect's and Builder's Journal* 08/04/14.

dor roses and fleurs de lys. Whilst under construction the benefice passed from an Anglo-Catholic patron to a stern Protestant trust who had no use for Eden's beautifully designed fittings insisting that all they required was a pulpit inscribed with a sentence from Scripture. Eden obliged them choosing the pointed text 'Where there is no Vision the people perish' executed in wood marquetry.

From the standpoint of the late twentieth century it is easy to forget the importance attached a century and more ago to the writings of Ruskin and a belief in the existence of an overall architectural philosophy. Eden considered himself an architect philosopher and jokingly declared his relief that claimed inbreeding had only stunted his physical stature and not his intellectual capabilities. Throughout his life he struggled to define a rationale for architecture of the new century which had seemingly slipped into a morass of anarchy in its untrammelled stylistic diversity, and by the possibilities and economies opened up by new building methods. He maintained an allegiance to Ruskin long after this had ceased to be fashionable attempting, for instance, a Ruskinian ten point classification of mystery in architecture – albeit with a caveat that 'as in all aesthetic analysis, there is this risk: that 'we murder to dissect'.[12]

In the early part of his career Eden did reserve a special place for the gothic style but never restricted himself to it. His last important commission, the new church of King Charles the Martyr, Potters Bar, Hertfordshire of 1939 was very closely based on an alternative scheme of 1908 for St John's, Harpenden and is testament to Eden's belief in the immutability of style. If it was good enough for 1908 it was good enough for 1939. The simple suburban church is a mixture of styles; gothic detailing in the main but with round-headed arcades and owing more to secular rather than ecclesiastical precedent in its Jacobean barn-like character. There are also arts and crafts touches notably the Voyseyesque porches.

Eden was, however, no enthusiast of the arts and crafts; not so much objecting to the Movement but its manifestation in naturalistic *art nouveau* and tendency towards a 'cottage heresy' of affected rusticity. Nevertheless he admired the Movement for emphasising a more intimate relationship between material, workmanship, and design considering its influence to have been 'considerable and in the main wholesome'.[13] This is reflected in his own restorations which are characterised by a judicious mixture of specialist and local craftsmen and which where appropriate sought to avoid perfection in execution; something Comper never did.

As late as 1912 Eden had a Ruskinian aversion to the use of modern materials and methods maintaining them to be un-natural and ungenerous. Eden's own attitude to post-1920 modernity in architecture is not recorded but his work, which remained resolutely traditional, speaks for itself. History, for him, provided both a full justification of a stylistically historical approach and a warning against the folly of deliberate stylistic innovation. Furthermore, he deemed such an approach natural to human endeavour: 'All periods of intellectual activity in the arts have been periods of revival and reversion; ... markedly so in that most fertile and inventive of all epochs, the Italian Renaissance. It is, indeed, sympathetic of all healthy human endeavour that it should look to the rock whence it was hewn, rather than gaze outwards into the void. Retrospection is no reproach'.[14]

In the years immediately before the First World War the influence of Italy became increasingly important on his architectural thinking and in his work. As in France it was the smaller chapels and churches that were a particular fascination and inspiration to him. He was especially captivated by the area south of Monte Rosa and Simplon becoming a noted authority on the Sacra Monte. The attraction of these buildings were their diversity rather than their originality. 'I am not going to pretend that the architectural merits of these buildings ... are particu-

12. F.C. Eden (1905) 'Mystery as an Architectural Quality', *The Builder* 07/01/05.
13. F.C. Eden (1912) 'The Practice of Crafts in Modern Building' *The Architect's and Builder's Journal* 18/12/12.
14. F.C. Eden (1919) ibid.

larly noteworthy ... It is simply as they are, where they are'.[15] The same buildings were a profound inspiration to Geoffrey Scott at around the same time. Scott's *The Architecture of Humanism* of 1914 was the only important architectural treatise published in the first part of the present century and Scott's and Eden's views were up to a point coincident, although as characters they had little in common.

The centrally planned Florentine chapel of 1919 (destroyed) which he built for All Saints', Clifton, Bristol marks the watershed in Eden's architectural thought where he finally concluded that gothic was inadequate for his purpose. All Saints' was a fine and large gothic church by G.E. Street. Eden justified his use of an Italianate style to complete a building that was so uncompromisingly gothic by admitting that 'I have studied Gothic Art for thirty years, and with the years I grow more and more convinced of the futility of attempting to evoke the gothic spirit'. He concluded that without mediaeval forms of co-operation in construction it could never be more than a 'frigid and soulless caricature, or at best in a sort of faked antique'. In its stead he found that 'Renaissance Architecture does not lie under the same disability. It was always more or less a 'one man show'; and it can pass almost unscathed the deadening ordeal of modern methods and machinery – methods which rob the gothic of all its poetry and pathos, in fact, all that makes it truly gothic'. As a justification for using an Italian style in England Eden explained 'All styles are foreign, though of course, we have our own treatment of the various architectural manners, whether gothic or classic, that we have adopted ... Foreign, then, the style may be, in the sense that Christianity is foreign, viz., it has been imported from overseas. 'All our religion', says Dr Johnson, 'almost all our law, almost all our arts, almost all that sets us above savages, has come to us from the shores of the Mediterranean' – that means, broadly speaking, from Italy. In architecture we are all *cives Romani*'.[16]

Whilst Italianate became Eden's preferred style he never raised its use to a dogma; his aesthetic eye continued to demand an essentially eclectic approach to style. His other principal addition to All Saints' Clifton was a lead-covered wooden octagonal tower closely based on that at the *Hotel de Ville* in Calais, which was added in 1928. He did continue to build in a conventional gothic style too such as the chancel of 1932 he added to Comper's nave at Southchurch, Essex. His unsuccessful entry for the Guildford Cathedral competition of the same year was in an entirely conventional Perpendicular gothic style in brick with a vaulted stone interior.

An opportunity for a fully Italianate church came in 1930 when Eden obtained the commission for a new church at Wash Common, Newbury erected in 1933.[17] Without knowing Eden's justification for using 'foreign' architecture it might seem strange that such a design was chosen given the additional function of the church as a national memorial to England's fallen soldiery with a dedication to the nation's patron saint. The church remained incomplete until 1965 when the nave and cloister were added to the designs of a local architect John Griffin. One of the attractions of Italian architecture for Eden was the ability to use cheap materials in an effective manner and the modest budget allowed for an elegant system of plaster vaulting in the transepts and a barrel vault for the nave; all executed by an Italian firm from London. Most of the fittings were subsequently added by Stephen Dykes Bower although the rood beam was installed under Eden; the figures of which were carved in Italy by Alphonse Nofleur and decorated in London by Messrs Maurus. The rich ultramontane colouring of the rood contrasts with the pastel shades of Dykes Bower's high altar and baldachino which are faithful to Eden's designs in every respect save that of colour.

Eden's large output of stained glass – his Glass Book[18] for the period 1913–1932 lists more than two hundred windows – is testament to the continued popularity of stained glass windows as memorials in the first part of this century. Although a connoisseur of stained glass he was against the profligate installa-

15. F.C. Eden (1915) 'Varallo and its Imitations' *Journal of the* RIBA 23/11/15.

16. F.C. Eden (1919) ibid.

17. Featured in the Incorporated Church Building Society's *New Churches Illustrated*, 1936.

18. In the RIBA Library.

figure 4

F.C. Eden. St George, Wash Common, Newbury, 1933. (photo Alan Powers)

19. F.C. Eden (1931) 'Stained Glass and Architecture' *The Architect's Journal* 1931.

tion of new glass preferring it to be confined to windows over altars and at west ends with aisle windows left clear. He made his first windows about 1909 some of which are in St Margaret's Church, Oxford. Whereas Comper's glass at Blisland looked to fifteenth century English examples Eden looked to the more immediate past and to C.E. Kempe (1839–1907) in particular whom he knew from his days with Bodley and Garner. Eden's style soon matured and from around 1913 his windows became remarkably and characteristically translucent. Eden, like Comper, considered that 'The Glory of glass is its transparency and colour, not realistic modelling of form or effects of relief'.[19] In stained glass as in architecture Eden followed his oft quoted maxim to 'look to the rock whence ye were hewn' and regarded his style as neither antique nor modern but as a logical development of the continuum of the past.

Eden's style of glass with its simply modelled and translucently coloured subject matter set against a background of clear quarries spawned many imitators and set the direction of the traditional school of ecclesiastical stained glass which persists, to a degree, today as an alternative to what might be termed the 'Coventry Cathedral' style. Sadly much of the output of the traditional school has been mediocre which has done no favours to Eden's reputation as a stained glass artist since the time of his death.

Stephen Dykes Bower was the last prolific specialist ecclesiastical architect working in the traditional idiom. His death in November 1994 marked not only the end of an era but also the end of a remarkably fecund architectural lineage that stretched back to Bodley and the earliest years of the nineteenth century gothic revival. A key figure in this pedigree, whom Dykes Bower maintained was by far the most important influence on his own work, was F.C. Eden. Eden was responsible for creating some of the most beautiful country churches in England and should be better known for this achievement. But how many nineteenth and twentieth century restorers who made the country's ancient churches what they are today are given more than a passing nod in church histories? His lifelong concern to fashion an architectural philosophy out of the tattered dogmas of the nineteenth century may seem to have little relevance today. Of scarcely greater influence, with the hindsight afforded by the late twentieth century, was Eden's promotion of traditional architecture as an architectural style for the century.

Yet, in his own specialist field of ecclesiastical architecture his influence has been enduring; perhaps more so than any of his contemporaries. It is a matter of regret that Eden's *opus* is composed entirely of modest commissions. To some extent this was compensated for by his influence on others. Of his contemporaries Walter Tapper was a loyal disciple. But it was Stephen Dykes Bower, whom he first met as a young man at the Architectural Association, where Eden lunched daily, who became as near to being a pupil of Eden's as was possible without actually serving articles. Teaching Dykes Bower to seek beauty rather than originality Eden enthralled the young architect by the fertility of his imagination and his ability to do the right thing in every circumstance. Eden made a lasting impression on Dykes Bower and his architecture cannot be fully understood without reference to his mentor. Through his ability, longevity, and dwindling competition Dykes Bower came to dominate the traditional school of ecclesiastical architecture in the latter part of this century and in so doing has ensured that Eden must be seen in the pantheon of twentieth century church architects as a figure of significance not merely as a talented but obscure curiosity.

6 Buildings of endearing simplicity: The Friends Meeting Houses of Hubert Lidbetter

ELEANOR GAWNE

Buildings of endearing simplicity:
The Friends Meeting Houses
of Hubert Lidbetter

ELEANOR GAWNE

Hubert Lidbetter (1885–1966) was one of the most prolific architects of Friends meeting houses during the 20th century. He designed over a dozen new meeting houses and carried out numerous alterations and extensions to existing ones. In many ways, his career followed that of Fred Rowntree (1860–1927), whose practice he trained in[1]; in the inter-war period he became, along with Leonard Brown[2], the principal architect of Friends meeting houses. After the war Paul Mauger (d.1982)[3] and Norman Frith[4] came to the fore in the design of these buildings, though Lidbetter was less enthusiastic than they were about the new tendencies in church design brought about by changes in the pattern of church worship. In reaction to the movement, Lidbetter wrote in the early 1960s 'it is to be hoped that those responsible for the new Meeting Houses of the future will discountenance and discourage those restless eccentricities of design which mark many present day places of worship, particularly continental, and cannot be said to be conducive either to devotion or religious ardour'.[5]

Working in the Quaker tradition, Lidbetter's designs retain the traditional values of meeting house architecture, described by Frank Roscoe as 'well built, unostentatious and sensibly honest'.[6] For architects like Rowntree, working in the early 20th century, Quakerism found expression through the Arts and Crafts aesthetic; for Lidbetter and those of his generation, the insistence on simplicity was expressed through the neo-Georgian aesthetic. However, Lidbetter introduced innovative features in the planning of the buildings, which took into account the new requirements of the Quaker doctrine.

This is shown at Friends House, Euston Road, London, the headquarters of the Society of Friends completed in 1927 and for which Lidbetter is principally known today; but he also designed many local meeting houses around London. Many were built in the 1950s as a result of war damage and town centre redevelopment, and designed towards the end of his career and are perhaps naturally less innovative than his earlier work. Although specialising in meeting houses, Lidbetter's practice also designed some important office buildings, namely the National Union of Municipal & General Workers building, Endsleigh Gardens, c.1955 and the Salvation Army International Headquarters, Queen Victoria Street, in the City, completed in 1963, (designed with his son Martin, who took over the practice after his father's death). He also developed a considerable practice designing nonconformist churches for Methodists and Congregationalists, as well as private houses and housing for local authorities. His clients included a number of Quaker institutions, charities and schools, as well as Quaker individuals.

Lidbetter's designs for Friends meeting houses can be divided into two types. The first was those for large urban congregations built mainly in the inter-war period, based on early 19th century classical examples, and following the tradition of Quaker building as described in William Alexander's *Observations on the Construction and Fitting up of Meeting Houses etc. for Public Worship*, 1820. The second type, built mostly after the war, were designed for smaller suburban congrega-

figure 1
Hubert Lidbetter, c.1938
(photo BAL / RIBA)

1. Rowntree designed many Friends meeting houses between 1907 and c.1920 including those at Scarborough, Hampstead, Golders Green (Hampstead Garden Suburb) and Muswell Hill; he also designed buildings for a number of Quaker schools. See entry in *Who's Who in Architecture*, 1926.

2. Leonard Brown designed Friends meeting houses at Peterborough, New Barnet and Colchester in the 1930s.

3. Paul Mauger, later of Paul Mauger, Gavin Mathers & Mitchell, designed numerous Friends meeting houses and Methodist churches in the 1950s and 1960s.

4. Norman Frith designed Friends Meeting Houses at Harlow, Romford, Wanstead, Maidstone and Saffron Waldon in the 1960s.

5. Lidbetter papers, Friends House Library. A similar sentiment is expressed at the end of Chapter IX in Lidbetter's *The Friends Meeting House*, 1961.

6. Frank Roscoe 'Design brief to design small Meeting House for the Society of Friends', Northern Polytechnic London, Day School of Architecture, 14 May 1942, in the Lidbetter papers, Friends House Library.

tions and followed the 'domestic' tradition of the late 17th century meeting houses.

These earlier buildings rejected all forms associated with 'church' building and ornate furnishings. They differed too from other non-conformist buildings in that there was no set form of service or music and therefore no symbolic hierarchy or distinction in the plan. During the early days of Quakerism in the late 17th century meeting houses were usually converted from one or two domestic buildings. Sometimes an upper room was converted into a gallery, to be used for larger gatherings than the Sunday Meetings, such as Monthly and Quarterly Meetings or Women's Meetings. A distinctive feature of early meeting houses was the shuttered partition used to divide the large meeting house from the smaller one, or used to separate the gallery from the main room. During the 19th century large purpose-built buildings were erected, principally in towns, of a foyer portico type. Inside the meeting room galleries ran around three sides, supported on columns and banked seats under. Benches were laid in parallel rows for the 'congregation', who faced the Minister's Gallery or 'stand' where the Recorded Ministers and Elders sat and which became the principal focal point of the room.

In the early 20th century, as the hierarchical nature of Quakerism declined, Elders began to sit amongst the 'congregation', whilst Recorded Ministers ceased to exist from the 1920s as it was felt that such a distinction was undemocratic. Men and women also no longer had separate business meetings, so the need for two meeting rooms declined. As meeting houses began to function as small community centres, existing 'stands' became redundant and seating rearranged without reference to it. Benches were still required in large meeting houses but in small ones, moveable chairs in concentric circles became the norm, creating an informal and secular tone. In the 1960s this approach of centring the meeting inwards led to a number of hexagonal or octagonal plans.[7]

Perhaps not surprisingly Lidbetter disliked the new plans. In a lecture he wrote 'A Meeting House proper should be a simple rectangular room – circles and octagons are all very well in their way and though by no means unQuakerly, they hardly seem to fit in with the Quaker mode of worship...'[8]

The design of Friends meeting houses was affected by changes in the Quaker doctrine from the late 19th century when as a result of developing scientific ideas, the Quakers' fundamental faith was disturbed, the sect became less formal and a more flexible outlook prevailed. From the beginning, meeting houses were never dedicated and had always been used for secular as well as religious purposes. This idea was further encouraged at the Yearly Meeting of 1893, when Joseph Rowntree argued for a new approach that would bring Friends into contact with other Christians, and asked for a readiness to accept new social responsibilities. The Manchester Conference of 1895 also re-examined Quaker's work in the world, and stressed the need for literacy and adult education classes. This led to the buildings being used for wider social and community uses,[9] so that the balance between the meeting room and ancillary accommodation changed, and more rooms of a higher standard of comfort were required for lobbies, cloakrooms and kitchens.

More space was also required for educational uses. Although Friends were actively engaged in education from their earliest days, and classrooms were often built or added to meeting houses, the Adult School Movement and the Bedford Institute Association required further classrooms, influencing the planning of later buildings.[10]

Lidbetter conducted thorough research into the historical records of both the early and later meeting houses. Records were often to difficult to collect as properties had passed in and out of possession of the Society. In the 1940s he began to collect this information systematically in the form of photographs and writ-

7. Examples include the Meeting Houses at Stevenage, by William Barnes, c.1960; Wanstead, by Norman Frith, 1964–68; Blackheath, by Trevor Dannatt, 1972.

8. Lidbetter papers, Friends House Library.

9. Edward Mills and Paul Mauger, writing in 1955, felt that the Nonconformist church was probably developing more rapidly than other denominations in providing the church as a centre of community activities. See 'Church Design', *Architectural Association Journal*, April 1955, Vol. LXX, No. 791.

10. The Adult School Movement was founded by Joseph Sturge in 1847 in Birmingham, and later supported by William White and Joseph Rowntree, and provided adult education during evenings and Sunday mornings. The Bedford Institute Association was named after Peter Bedford (d.1864), a Spitalfields entrepreneur who established the Bedford Institute to improve the religious, social and benevolent character for the poor of Spitalfields and Bethnal Green.

ten sources. He also visited a number in person and made measured plans and occasionally elevations and sections. From this material, Lidbetter was able to study the evolution of the meeting house as a type-form, and establish dates when individual Meeting Houses were built and subsequently extended, and the original functions of rooms. This material was used in an article Lidbetter wrote for *The Wayfarer* in 1942, followed by a longer article for the *Architectural Review*, 'Quaker Meeting Houses, 1670–1850' prepared with the encouragement of the then editor Nikolaus Pevsner and published in April 1946. Lidbetter's article followed John Betjemen's 1940 essay *Nonconformist Architecture*, and should be seen in the context of the celebration of anonymous vernacular building types and reappraisal of Victorian architecture in Britain during this period.[11]

His research culminated in the first book to be written on Friends meeting houses as an architectural genre: *The Friends Meeting House* published in 1961 (subsequent editions 1979 and 1995), and containing many of Lidbetter's line-drawings.[12] Although the book is essentially a historical survey, it offers some practical advice, in part drawn from William Alexander's book of 1820, based on the building of York Meeting House in 1817, and partly based on Lidbetter's own experiences in designing meeting houses.

The Quaker religion played a central role in Hubert Lidbetter's life. Born in Dublin, he attended the Quaker schools of Ackworth and Bootham, York, before being articled to the architect Henry Higginson (1862–1922) in Carlisle, from 1902–06. He subsequently worked in the offices of Fred Rowntree (1860–1927), Arthur Heron Ryan-Tenison (1861–1930), Henry Victor Ashley (1872–1945) and Francis Winton Newman (1878–1953). His experience with Fred Rowntree was undoubtedly influential on his subsequent career[13] – Lidbetter records that he assisted in the survey and sketch plans for the new Hampstead Meeting House whilst working in Rowntree's office in 1906. This was a two-storey domestic style building with pitched roof, dormer windows and buttresses, combined with 18th century motifs such as Palladian and circular windows and semi-circular columned porch.

After the war, in 1919, Lidbetter established himself as an architect in London, working in collaboration with Gerald Warren (1881–1936) until Warren's death. Warren had been in partnership with Sydney Ernest Castle from 1908–18 and together they designed a number of houses in the Home Counties in a strong vernacular Arts and Crafts style, including an exclusive estate at St George's Hill, Weybridge, Surrey, in 1910. Warren had a thorough knowledge of domestic architecture of the 17th and 18th centuries, and was keen to use old materials, qualities that Lidbetter sympathised with.

Elected an Associate of the Royal Institute of British Architects (RIBA) in 1918 and a Fellow in 1927, Lidbetter played a prominent role in the affairs of the RIBA, serving on the Council and Executive Committee from 1938–41 and as Vice-President in 1942–43. He was also deeply committed to the education of the architect, and was chairman of the Board of Architectural Education from 1938–41, RIBA examiner, and external examiner to the schools of architecture at the Bartlett School of Architecture and Regent Street Polytechnic. During the Second World War, Lidbetter carried on his practice, working on war-damaged buildings and in 1950 his son Hubert Martin Lidbetter (1914–1992), known as Martin, joined him in practice. As Hubert approached retirement, Martin took over the principal responsibility for the work.

Lidbetter's design for Friends House, Euston Road, the headquarters of the Society of Friends, incorporates many of his design principles, launched his career and won him the RIBA London Architectural Bronze Medal in 1926. The building replaced the Society's previous headquarters, Devonshire House in Houndsditch, considered an inconvenient group of buildings. Although much fuss was made at the time over the sacrifice of the trees in Endsleigh Gardens,

11. *Architectural Review*, December 1940, pp.160–174.

12. Most of the photographs were deposited at Friends House in June 1968; others plus drawings and correspondence in February 1995. His drawings of the old Meeting Houses at Amersham, Jordans, Hammersmith, Yealand Conyers, Ackworth and Swarthmore are in the National Monuments Record.

13. *Architectural Review*, October 1927, No. 371, p.138. This was not an altogether unbiased view – J.E. Hodgkin was Chairman of the Building Sub-Committee of the Society of Friends.

figure 2
Friends House, Euston Road, London,
1925–27. Interior view of the large
meeting house showing the galleries
over the surrounding corridors.
(photo The Library Committee of Britain
Yearly Meeting of the Religious Society
of Friends)

figure 3
Friends House, Euston Road, London,
1925–27. The main entrance on the
north front. (photo The Library
Committee of Britain Yearly Meeting of
the Religious Society of Friends)

14. Kenneth Lindley, *Chapels and Meeting
Houses* John Baker, 1969, p.66.
15. David M. Butler, The Making of Meeting
Houses, *The Friends Quarterly*, July 1980, p.323.
16. Kenneth Lindley, *Chapels and Meeting
Houses* John Baker, 1969, p.66.
17. It appears from reports of addresses made
at the openings of certain Meeting Houses
designed by Lidbetter that some Friends to a
moral stand, feeling strongly that the building
should not represent the meeting.
18. David M. Butler, The Making of Meeting
Houses, *The Friends Quarterly*, July 1980, p.323.

the new building was generally written about enthusiastically in the architectural press; J.E. Hodgkin in the *Architectural Review* wrote that the building 'unites quiet common sense with just so much of relief from absolute plainness as gives pleasure to the eye without disturbing the conscience in the matter of unnecessary expenditure'.[14]

The design, a low four-storey neo-Georgian building with Doric portico and Greek Revival details, built of purple grey Luton brick and Portland stone, was designed to blend with the other 18th century buildings nearby and the Doric Euston Arch then opposite. It comprised a large meeting house around which were committee rooms, the central offices of the Society, the library and book centre. An open courtyard provided light to the corridors and a block of business premises were built at the west end, intended to be let (known as Drayton House).

For Lidbetter the first essentials of a Friends meeting house were good acoustics and sound insulation. His main innovative feature in this building was a result of the need for the large meeting house to hold approximately 1500 people to be acoustically 'perfect', so that any person could see and hear, and be seen and heard, by anyone in the room, in essence producing a debating chamber. This was achieved by using a cloister-type plan, in which the upper galleries of the meeting house were placed over the corridors surrounding the square hall – an idea he later claimed was taken from Manchester meeting house of 1830. Later, when designing smaller meeting houses, he was aware that sound insulation in the main meeting room depended on good planning. This was achieved by planning the main room behind ancillary rooms; at Ealing Meeting House, designed in 1954, he ensured that the children's classrooms were not over the main room or adjoining to it, but in two separate wings. His designs also provide ample lobbies for social intercourse before and after meetings, as well as provision for cloakrooms, which he felt were particularly necessary if the meeting house was to be used as a social centre.

An issue that caused some consternation was fenestration and the problem of looking at individuals with a strong source of light behind them; also of whether the windows should be at a high level or take account of a fine view, and whether this added to or detracted from the spirit of communal worship. Lidbetter tended to place windows at an upper level; at Friends House, the large meeting house is lit by clerestory windows, screened from the road by an attic wall.

figure 4
Friends Meeting House, Bull Street,
Birmingham, 1931–33. View from the
burial ground, with Lewis's department
store behind. (photo Lidbetter
Collection, The Library, Friends House,
London)

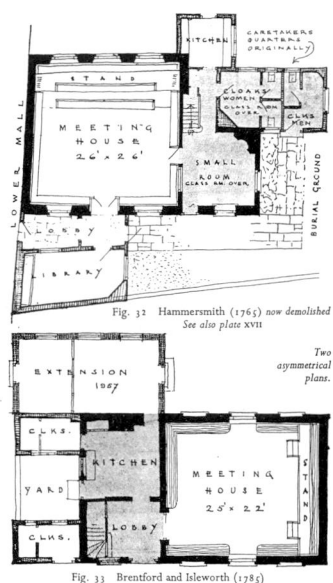

Fig. 32 Hammersmith (1765) *now demolished*
See also plate XVII

*Two
asymmetrical
plans.*

Fig. 33 Brentford and Isleworth (1785)

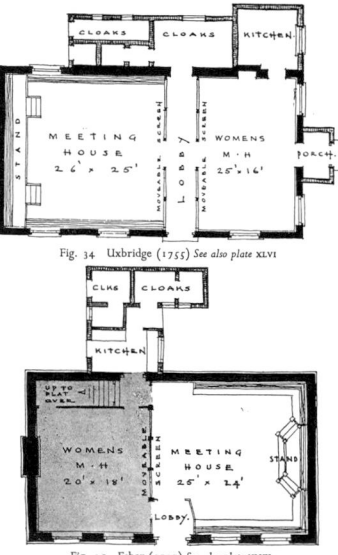

Fig. 34 Uxbridge (1755) *See also plate* XLVI

Fig. 35 Esher (1797) *See also plate* XLVII

figure 5
Plans of the old Meeting Houses at
Hammersmith, Brentford & Isleworth,
Uxbridge and Esher from Hubert
Lidbetter *The Friends Meeting House,* 1961
(William Sessions Ltd, The Ebor Press, York)

Following the success of Friends House, Lidbetter was commissioned by the Society of Friends to design two other large urban meeting houses at Birmingham (1931) and Liverpool (1941).[15] Both replaced earlier buildings. Birmingham Meeting House was financed by Lewis's department store, which required part of the site of the old building for expansion; Liverpool was financed by the Corporation who wanted the site for redevelopment and offered a new site and financed the new building. Their plans were based on Friends House, with corridors created around the outside of the meeting room. The meeting room itself was designed to be used for a variety of secular purposes, so the platform was used as a small stage or as a Minister's Gallery. Lidbetter argued that the need for greater economy in these buildings, compared to Friends House, dictated a more modern appearance.

Much of Lidbetter's involvement in the restoration, alteration and building of new meeting houses of the smaller 'domestic' type was due to his work as Surveyor to Six Weekly Meeting, which he served from 1935 to 1957. This group administers the property of the Society in the district known as London & Middlesex Quarterly Meeting – roughly the Greater London area. As their Surveyor, Lidbetter oversaw proposals by individual Meetings for alterations, extensions and new building work, such as at Hammersmith before the war; sometimes this led to a Meeting offering the work to Lidbetter. During the Second World War, he was responsible for organising the temporary repair of meeting houses which were damaged by enemy action and was consequently involved in rebuilding at least four of these: Hammersmith, Westminster, Croydon and Streatham.

Lidbetter's designs for these small meeting houses are on the whole plain and strictly functional, what Kenneth Lindley has called a 'serviceable and unobtrusive brick box'.[16] This was partly due to costs; money for new buildings had to come from the Meetings themselves, legacies, gifts and occasionally transactions in town-centre sites. Another reason for their plainness was the Quaker tradition of simplicity in their buildings and their deliberate rejection of their physical surroundings of worship: they preferred to spend little on their buildings in order to devote their resources to practical work.[17] This is evident from reports of the opening addresses at some meeting houses designed by Lidbetter when Friends adopted a strong moral stance that the building should never represent the Meeting. As David Butler writes 'The absence of features irrelevant to worship is easily taken to be mere emptiness or lack of initiative or of a sense of design, rather than the positive forbearance, which it represents in our tradition'.[18]

Lidbetter's designs for meeting houses around London include those at Watford (1953), Ealing (1954), Hammersmith (1955), Westminster (1956), Croydon (1956), Shenfield (1957), Stoke Newington (1957) and Streatham (1957). These are either single or two storey brick buildings, geometrically massed and use an Arts & Crafts approach to materials in the use of hand-made bricks, terracotta tiles and tile quoins. Neo-Georgian details, such as those used in Post Office building in the 1920s, are evident in the fenestration: circular, Palladian and sash windows. The plain interiors are occasionally relieved by textural features, such as brick pilasters which are used at Watford. Some of the buildings were based on earlier examples. Hammersmith, in its massing – the meeting room at the rear, and ancillary accommodation on either side – is reminiscent of the meeting house at Peckham of 1826. Lidbetter's other work involved restoring or extending existing meeting houses; that at Croydon was designed in 1956 to harmonise with an earlier Adult School hall by W. Curtis Green of 1908, its steep pitch roof and gable ends almost exact reproductions of the earlier building.

figure 6 · left
Friends Meeting House, Nigel Playfair Avenue, Hammersmith, 1955. View of the front entrance. (photo Author)

figure 7 · right
Friends Meeting House, Park Lane, Croydon, 1956. View of the Meeting House designed to harmonise with the large Adult School by W. Curtis Green of 1908, and linked to it by a colonnade. (photo Author)

APPENDIX

Friends meeting houses designed by Hubert Lidbetter are included in lists at the end of this journal. Of his other work to meeting houses:

Restoration work

1934   Blue Idol, Thakeham, Sussex (built 1691)

1952   Hertford, Hertfordshire (built 1670)

Alterations & additions

1938   Staines, Surrey (built 1844)

1955   Southend, Essex (built 1936)

1957   Amersham, Buckinghamshire (built 1689)

1958   Brentford, Hounslow, London (built 1785)

1962   Uxbridge, Hillingdon, London (built 1817)

Harrow, London (built 1935)

Ilfield, Sussex (built 1672)

Lidbetter also used details from his domestic work in his designs for meeting houses. For example, at The Forge, Totteridge Green, Hertfordshire, c.1932, he used overhanging pitched roofs with pantiles, decorative brickwork inside and out and plain white interiors with lightly stained oak joinery. Perhaps his most domestic meeting house is that at Streatham. Built on a council estate, it is a two storey pitched-roof building with a resident warden's flat on the first floor and a separate garage, looking every bit a quiet detached private house.

Hubert Lidbetter continued the Quaker tradition of building in which plainness and simplicity are used as a theological statement. His use of neo-Georgian details was not used to convey symbolically any meanings of authority, but rather to continue the tradition of making links with 18th and early 19th century meeting houses, which he so admired. His buildings do not easily fit into an architectural style, though the inherent functionalism of a meeting house tends to lend itself to a modern aesthetic. It is interesting to speculate what Lidbetter would have thought of the fact that many new Anglican churches of the post-war period imitate meeting houses in their accommodation, due to the move towards establishing the church as a social centre as well as worship space.

ACKNOWLEDGEMENTS

I would like to thank the following for their help and advice: H. Godwin Arnold; Adrian Betham; Dr Clyde Binfield; my colleagues at the RIBA British Architectural Library; Rachel Brown, National Monuments Record; David M. Butler for help compiling the list of Lidbetter's meeting houses; Sylvia Carlyle, Friends House Library; Norman Frith; Dr Roger Harper; Sherry S. Lee; Tom Manning; Jon North; Salvation Army Heritage Centre; Mr & Mrs William Sessions; Christopher Stell; Michael Sykes.

7 Merseyside Churches in a Modern Idiom: Francis Xavier Verlade & Bernard Miller

FIONA WARD

Merseyside Churches in a Modern Idiom:
Francis Xavier Verlade & Bernard Miller

FIONA WARD

Francis Xavier Velarde and Bernard Miller were contemporaries at the Liverpool School of Architecture under Charles Reilly and both went on to design churches, mainly in the North West of England. Miller designed mainly Anglican churches and Velarde mainly Roman Catholic ones although in 1931 they collaborated, in name at least, on the Anglican church of St Gabriel Blackburn. They tend to be discussed together, sometimes to the extent of making it appear as if they were in competition, but this is not the case. They are sufficiently distinctive to warrant consideration on their own merits. Yet they had enough in common to make comparison inevitable and such a comparison shows their work to be complementary.

Velarde was born in 1897 into a family of Spanish origin. After serving in the Navy and then the Army during the First World War, he joined the ex-servicemen's classes at the Liverpool School of Art for one year, after which he went to the Liverpool School of Architecture. He maintained his contacts with the school after graduation, as Professor Reilly instituted a series of half-time posts whereby practising architects were also engaged in teaching. Velarde was an instructor at the school on this basis. Before establishing his own practice, Velarde spent some time with Weightman and Bullen, where he eventually became a partner.

The work of both Miller and Velarde received wide and favourable coverage in the architectural periodicals during the inter-war years and much of this coverage was given to them by Professor Reilly, who was not above promoting his protégés through his writings or his position as an assessor in various competitions. Reilly himself had had a hand in church architecture with his St Barnabas, Dalston in North London. Features in this church occur in Velarde's work, particularly his first church of St Matthew, Clubmoor.

This part of Liverpool had been little more than a village up until the First World War. Queen's Drive, the 'ring road', was begun in 1904 and council houses were built there during the 1920s. The Catholic authorities first made mention of building a church there in 1922 in response to this building programme and the consequent increase in the area's population. The church which was to be built on the site was to be called St Matthew's after the Liverpool architect Captain Matthew Honan who died in the First World War and left 'a substantial sum of money'[1] for church building. Some of this went to Clubmoor and some to Coppull, in Lancashire. The Clubmoor money only covered part of the cost of building the church, the foundation stone of which was laid on 19th August 1928 and the church was opened on 16th March 1930.

St Matthew's is made a landmark by its high campanile, a feature which in one form or another was to appear throughout Velarde's church designs. The other main characteristic of his work is a preference for the rounded arch of early Christian architecture, rather than the pointed arch of the Gothic Revival. In this, he was following in the path set by J.F. Bentley with his Byzantine Westminster Cathedral. Reilly had said that this building '... showed that lofty plain wall surfaces, even of common stock brick, were more important in giving the idea of

figure 1
F.X. Velarde. St Matthew, Clubmoor, Liverpool, 1930 (photo from *The Book of the Liverpool School of Architecture*, 1932)

1. Transcript of commentary on slide talk presented as part of St Matthew's Golden Jubilee.

figure 2
F.X. Velarde. St Matthew, Clubmoor,
Liverpool, 1930 (photo E. Chambré
Hardman Trust)

2. Reilly, C.H. *'Some Architectural Problems of
Today'* University of Liverpool/Hodder &
Stoughton Liverpool, 1924, p.39.
3. *'St Monica's Church, Bootle'* in *The Builder*
vol.152, 15th January 1937, p.177.

remoteness and seclusion from the world than the richest clustered Gothic columns. The very simplicity of its round arches, its sheer unbroken walls and piers, its plain sedate domes, give it a solemnity which richer and more articulate structures like correct Gothic ones could not from their nature possess.'[2]

Plain brick walls were a consistent feature in Velarde's work, in both exteriors and interiors, compatible with the desire, increasingly expressed in the twentieth century, for Early Christian architectural forms and a move away from applied decoration in favour of basic geometric forms. For Roman Catholic churches this also had the appeal of a spiritual directness whilst having the practical advantage of economy.

It would be inaccurate and unfair to set Velarde's career out as a simple re-working of Early Christian, Byzantine and Romanesque ideas. Velarde did use history in an eclectic way in his churches, on occasion with confusing results (as on the exterior of the Church of the English Martyrs at Wallasey), but he was not entrenched in the past and his work at times has been radical to a degree that still startles today. An instance is Velarde's church of St Monica, Bootle.

This church was opened in 1937 and was commented upon widely and favourably in the architectural press on account of its appearance and plan. In St Monica's, Velarde has achieved visual impact through the inter-relationship of rectilinear forms something that is emphasised by the west tower, which serves to conceal the pitched roof of the nave and so to increase the rectilinear effect. This is a device which invites comparison with modernism, but Velarde's is not a stark and uncompromising modernism; rather a version which, with the number and size of window openings, seems to have been fused with Perpendicular Gothic. Within the church, the rounded arch is again introduced in various sizes and locations, although their use here is rather more sparing than at St Matthew's. Both the reredos (by Burden) and the exterior of the West Tower feature angels carved by Herbert Tyson Smith, a sculptor based at the Bluecoat Chambers in Liverpool. Tyson Smith's Portland stone angels and Pietas are as characteristic a feature of Velarde's churches, particularly the later ones, as are the campaniles; indeed, the figures are frequently placed on the campaniles and so make them a focal point at close range as well as from a distance.

St Monica's drew attention not only because of its cubo-rectilinear appearance, but also because of its plan and the disposition of elements within it, features which were '...not usually apparent in ecclesiastical design'.[3] The choir was

figures 3 and 4
F.X. Velarde. St Monica, Bootle,
Liverpool, 1936 (photos E. Chambré
Hardman Trust)

placed over the sacristies, which released space within the west end of the church, leaving the narthex to be divided from the nave by a high arch, a subtle and symbolic division, differentiating the different parts of the church rather than enforcing actual physical divisions, Velarde tended to use the same strategy with regard to communion rails. This, and the openness of the high arches, makes Velarde's designs compatible with the aims of the Liturgical Movement and its concern that the altar should be as visible as possible from all parts of the church and that the congregation should play as full as role in the proceedings as possible.

The names of Velarde and Miller tended to be mentioned in tandem in 1937. That year, apart from the Exhibition of British Architecture at the Royal Academy, there was an exhibition of the Liverpool School at the Royal Institute of British Architects in which the work of both men was included. The reviewer for the *RIBA* Journal stated '... one must remember the work of Mr. Bernard A. Miller in his Church of St Columba and his church of St Christopher, Withington, and that of Mr F.X. Velarde in his churches of St Matthew, St Gabriel and St Monica's. These two young architects seem to have established a kind of pre-eminence for Liverpool in the matter of churches, and I think the secret is that, charged with their somewhat emotional mission, they have ventured on the rough uncharted seas.'[4]

Miller's St Christopher's, Withington has recently been demolished, leaving the two surviving Liverpool churches of St Columba's, Anfield and St Christopher's, Norris Green, as the best known examples of his church architecture. Born in 1904, Miller had served with the 87th Field Ambulance in World War One and had trained under Reilly. He worked full-time at the Liverpool School for seven years and on a part-time basis for a further three, maintaining a connection there for around thirty years in all. He started in private practice as an assistant with Briggs and Thornley and then went to the firm Lockwood, Abercrombie and Saxon, setting up by himself in 1933.[5] Miller worked with Velarde on St Gabriel's, Blackburn, a competition for which Professor Reilly was Assessor and Advisor to the committee, though it was widely acknowledged that Miller's role was more of a consultative than a practical one.[6]

Reilly promoted the work of both men through his influence on committees

4. Towndrow, F.E. 'A Review of the Liverpool Exhibition' *Journal of the Royal Institute of British Architects* vol.44 8th May 1937, p.639.

5. Shennan, A.E. 'The Architects and Their Post War Work in Liverpool' *The Architects' Journal* 25th December 1995, p 775.

6. 'A New Church in Blackburn' *The Architectural Review* vol.73, June l933 p229.

figure 5 · above
Bernard Miller. St Christopher, Withington, Manchester, 1935, demolished (photo from *Fifty Modern Churches*, 1947)

figure 6 · right
Bernard Miller. St Columba, Anfield, Liverpool, 1932.
(photo of drawing by Bernard Miller, courtesy of Fr. Peter Cavanagh)

and through the architectural press, although he tended to favour Velarde as being more original of the two men. Writing in 1935 'Without being in any sense bizarre, like many of the new French and German churches, they seem to me both reverent and inspiring ... Velarde's is the more original and daring spirit, in that he will trust to the utmost simplicity, such as in the exterior of his church of St Gabriel's at Blackburn ... and out of nothing, as it were, produce a compelling and moving composition which is essentially religious. Miller is more like Maufe. Everything he does is graceful and full of feeling, and however novel his methods or materials, such as his Staybright steel and plywood stalls at St Columba's, his work is in essence based on the English tradition.'[7]

A comparison between St Columba's and St Monica's does reveal the latter church to be more simple in its massing. It is the complexity of St Columba's which makes it so distinctive and marks out within the neighbourhood in a way that Velarde's towers and campaniles do with his work.

St Columba's was built in 1932, in a new suburban development in Anfield; it can be regarded as an Anglican counterpart to St Matthew's, not far away. The church occupies a triangular site with entrances on two sides. The altar is at the point of the triangle, like an arrow head, pointing towards the city; Professor Reilly said of the church that it headed the housing massed behind it.[8] The building is silver-grey brickwork with Portland stone highlights such as lintels and fanlights. Like Velarde, Miller has used the round-headed arch in windows and again like Velarde's work there are large expanses of brickwork and comparatively little window; those windows are narrow and long, increasing in length at St Columba's from the west to the east end.

The church is made up of three blocks, rising in stages towards the altar, capped with pitched roofs of green pantiles. The stepping blocks are echoed on the outer walls of the sanctuary by a very tall Portland stone crucifix which rises in stepped formation from the foundation stone at the base and on the interior with the font by Bainbridge Copnall which also rises in steps. The Lady Chapel altar was painted by Mary Adshead and the interior of the church offers the viewer more decorative detail than is the case with Velarde's work. Together with the complexity in massing of the forms, so evident on the exterior, it illustrates Reilly's remark about the simplicity of Velarde's work in comparison with that of Miller. St Columba's was not completed as intended for lack of funds, as can be seen in the west facade, which shows a rather abrupt termination. In addition to the church itself, there was to have been a vicarage and church hall at either side of the west end, which would have further emphasised the arrow-head shape of the whole composition.

A scheme which was completed, including a church hall, children's court and cloister, was Miller's St Christopher, Norris Green of 1930–32. This church is known as the Children's Church because, when funds were being raised for it many activities and efforts were undertaken by Liverpool children. It was decided that rather than disperse the funds raised in this way across the programme, the children's money should all go towards one church: St Christopher's. Both St Columba's Anfield and St Christopher Norris Green received favourable mentions in Edward Maufe's talk on Modern Church Architecture at the RIBA in 1934.[9]

St Christopher's Norris is not composed of the rising blocks employed at St Columba's but has a central focus on the central, flat-roofed tower around which the surrounding blocks are massed. Generally the effect is more static than the arrowhead form at Anfield. St Christopher's also shares with St Columba's the characteristic feature of a large expanse of brickwork relieved by touches of Portland stone. Otherwise, from the point of view of the exterior, it is perhaps the least startling of Miller's churches. Nonetheless, it did provide a landmark and focus for the surrounding housing development and inside '... with its great vault

7. C.H. Reilly 'Some Recent Churches' The Architectural Review vol.77, April 1935, p.164.

8. ibid.

9. Maufe, E 'Modern Church Architecture' Journal of the Royal Institute of British Architects, 12th January 1935 pp.293–310.

figure 7 · right
Bernard Miller. St Christopher,
Withington, Manchester, 1935
demolished. Interior with reredos by
Mary Adshead. (photo from *Eyes on the
Wall*, Society of Mural Painters,
London, n.d.)

figure 8 · above
Bernard Miller. St Christopher,
Norris Green, Liverpool, 1930–32
(photo Alan Powers)

10. Reilly, C.H. op. cit. p.16.

rising from the ground without piers, it is solemn and impressive, with delightful silver gates to the chancel and a thin silver cross like a sword enshrined in baroque lines to complete the focus of the altar.'[10]

The interior at Norris Green, with its flamboyant arches and startling colour scheme in the sanctuary provoked much comment at the time that the congregation was never sure whether they were in a cinema or a church (while St Columba's had been likened by the locals to an ice-cream parlour). There is a menorah set in to the mosaics directly in front of the altar, while the windows feature the Star of David and the gates onto the road at the west end have the crescent moon of Islam described in the wrought iron-altogether, this is a striking examples of inter-faith eclecticism! There is no indication on the outside of the parabolic arches within and they make for a more open and lofty interior than might be guessed from the outside. Their effect is similar to the very high, though not parabolic, arches used by Velarde at St Matthew's and St Monica's. It is interesting to note that Velarde did use parabolic arches in Our Lady of Pity, Greasby, a much later church of 1951.

The effect produced by the arches in Our Lady of Pity is very different from that achieved by Miller at St Christopher's. It is a more rural site and the church is smaller, lower and altogether more earthbound and less lofty than the others. The low parabolic arches, placed close together in the interior make for a feeling of intimacy which is reinforced by the simple plan and the characteristic use of exposed brickwork.

Churches by both Miller and Verlade have, sadly, been demolished in the recent past. The most notable losses are Velarde's 1956 church of St Alexander, Bootle and Miller's St Christopher, Withington, Manchester of 1936. The reredos by Mary Adshead from Withington is, it is hoped, to be relocated at St Columba's Anfield if the funds can be raised. St Christopher's, again built of brick with Portland stone relief, was perhaps the most overtly Modern of all the churches by both architects. Despite a more or less traditional looking cruciform plan the building was flat roofed with tall narrow windows whose '... stepping-stone tops are typical of the Ostberg and Paris-1925 movement. The plan is not what one would expect. As you enter, the altar space is not facing you. The apse holds the baptistery instead, and the altar is at the left end, the nave filling the right part – a disturbing change of direction.'[11]

It had already been pointed out that the work of both Miller and Velarde was not Modern (or 'bizarre', as Professor Reilly would have it) in the extreme way of some of their French and German counterparts but that the Modernism in their work was more reminiscent of the Scandinavian approach. Neither architect rejected history; without slavish imitation, they acknowledged ecclesiastical tradition and reworked it, incorporating those aspects of Modernism which they felt to be useful or appropriate. They both took full advantage of modern materials and techniques when necessary without dispensing with the services of more traditional artists and craftspeople. It was a pragmatic approach and one which can be seen to have been vindicated by the enduring appeal of their work.

Both architects spent time on re-ordering churches as well as producing

11. Pevsner, N. *The Buildings of England: South-Lancashire*, Harmondsworth, 1969.

figure 9
F.X. Velarde. St Alexander, Bootle, 1956, demolished (photo from Bryan Little, *Catholic Churches since 1623*, 1966)

original schemes and the regard in which their contributions to church architecture was held is shown in the consultative posts held by each. In 1945 Miller was appointed by the Ecclesiastical Commissioners to the Church Building Advisory Panel, which reported in 1946 on the conditions relating to post-war church building. He was also architect to the fabric of Chester Cathedral. Velarde was one of an international committee of six (which also included Gio Ponti) set up in connection with the building of the basilica of St Pius at Lourdes. He was awarded the OBE in 1957.

Miller and Velarde died within four months of each other, Miller in August 1960 and Velarde in December of the same year. Velarde, who had moved to Formby, is buried at Southport and Miller at Woodchurch in Birkenhead. Their tombstones were both carved by Herbert Tyson Smith, the sculptor with whom they had worked so often during their respective careers.

figure 10
Bernard Miller. St Michael and All Angels, Tettenhall, Staffordshire, 1952–55 (photo from *Sixty Post-War Churches*, 1956)

8 Places of Christian Worship 1914–1990: A Selection

ELAIN HARWOOD & ANDREW FOSTER

Places of Christian Worship 1914–1990:
A Selection of Christian Places of Worship

ELAIN HARWOOD & ANDREW FOSTER

This list is arranged by architect, with cross-referencing where necessary. Some churches appear under more than one heading, if they occupy important places in the work of two practices, though this has been kept to a minimum. Works of restoration, rather than rebuilding, are not included. Neither are unbuilt schemes, though demolished churches are – suitably noted where known. Fixtures and fittings are not included. Though every attempt has been made to give an accurate address for each location, the recent reorganisation into unitary authorities may still cause some confusion and old 'counties' have been inserted where clarification may be thought helpful.

The order for each entry is as follows: denomination, dedication, address, date, date of other work (and of later work by other architects), listing status. Buildings not otherwise noted belong to the Church of England, Church in Wales or Church of Scotland in their respective countries. Dates are, where possible, those of construction rather than of design and may thus differ from those given in other works. Where the designer is not a qualified architect this has been noted.

The listing system is also different in different countries. In England and Wales grades I and II* denote buildings of international or major national significance in their type; grade II is the designation of special architectural interest into which some 90% of listings fall. Until 1974 churches had their own listing classification: A for major medieval or Georgian works; B for good examples of these and Victorian works; C for the rest. Since 1974 the conventional I, II* and II used for secular buildings in England and Wales has been adopted for churches also. Scotland has its own system of A, B and C (Statutory), where A is roughly equivalent to grades I and II*, B to grade II, and C is used for buildings listed primarily for group value. The Department of the Environment in Northern Ireland has a system of A, B+ and B which is otherwise similar to the English one.

The date 1914 has not been strictly adhered to. Where a church of 1914 belongs within the great tradition of Edwardian building it has not been included. But certain architects who straddle the boundary of the Great War are too important to miss out, so that all churches by Sir Giles Gilbert Scott and Sir Charles Nicholson are included – especially as so many of their early works had long building campaigns. With many other architects, including Temple Moore, W.D. Caröe and a number of Scottish architects, it has proved necessary to be more strict as most of their works fits into the earlier period. An effort has been made to include as many churches as possible from the years 1915–39, and to be more selective thereafter, particularly from 1970 onwards.

The C20 Society would like to thank English Heritage for its generous grant towards this project. The list was compiled by Andrew Foster and Elain Harwood, with help from Peter Arnold, Geoff Brandwood, Alan Brooks, Martin Cherry, Neville Doe, Eleanor Gawne, Pam Gray, Edward Holland, Roland Jeffery, Jill Kerry, Deborah Mays, Richard Morrice, Alan Powers, Martin Purdy and Peter Smith. Geoff Brandwood and Roland Jeffery edited the text. We would like to thank the many incumbents, churchwardens and enthusiasts who contacted the C20 Society about their churches following the 1997 exhibition *The Twentieth Century Church*.

T.G. Abercrombie
- Wallneuk Church, North Croft St, Paisley. 1913–15. B

Frank Abbey and Harrison
- St Francis Fixby, Huddersfield. 1954–5

Edward Adams
- Congregational church, Gatley, Cheshire. 1938

Stanley Adshead and Stanley C. Ramsey
- St Anselm, Kennington Cross, L B Lambeth. 1913–33. II

G.S. Agar
- German Evangelical. Dietrich Bonhoeffer Church, Dacres Rd, L B Lewisham

J.S. Ainsworth
- Baptist church, West Way, Ruislip Manor, L B Hillingdon. 1963–4

J.S. Alder
- St Mary the Virgin and All Saints, Potters Bar, Herts. 1914. Completed by Laurence King, 1967.
- St Catherine, Neasden, L B Brent. 1916. West front 1954 by E.B. Glanfield.

Aldington, Craig and Collinge
- Emmanuel, Broad St, Chesham, Bucks. 1989–90

John Alexander Ogg Allan, and Ross and Anderson
- Hall/Church, Garthdie, Grampian. 1955

W. Alison and R.F. Hutchinson
- R C St Gabriel, Prestonpans, Edinburgh. 1968
- R C St Andrew, Livingston, W. Lothian. 1968

W. Allan
- R C St Ninian, Culduthel Rd, Inverness, Highland. 1977

H.W. Allardyce
- St Augustine, Johnstone Rd, Thorpe Bay, Essex. 1934

Allcock and Grieves
- Methodist church, Loughborough, Leics. 1968

C.D. Allderidge
- R C Sacred Heart, Southcoates Lane, Hull. 1926–9

George P. Allen
- All Saints, Iddesleigh Rd, Bedford. 1914–22

Justin Henry Alleyn
- R C St Teresa, Weldon Way, Merstham, Surrey. 1959
- R C St Raphael, Ayles Rd, Yeading, L B Hillingdon. 1961
- R C St Clement, Kingston Rd, Ewell, Surrey. 1962
- R C St Augustine, Hoddesdon, Herts. 1962

W.H. Alleyn and Mansell
- Epiphany, Merstham, Surrey. 1955

H. Anderson
- St Mary, Little Chart, Kent. 1955

R. Rowand Anderson, William H. Kininmonth and A.F.B. Paul
- Drylaw Hall/Church, Edinburgh. 1957
- Brucefield Church, E. Main St, Whitburn, W. Lothian. 1962
- Craigsbank Church, Craigs Bank, Edinburgh. 1964–7
- See also William H. Kininmonth

W.E. Ellery Anderson
- Holy Trinity, Primrose Hill, Lydney, Glos. 1933
- St John, Little Thurrock, Essex. 1933
- St George, Nailsworth, Glos. Chancel 1937–8 to church of 1898–1900
- Holy Innocents, Sutton Park Rd, Kidderminster, Worcs. 1938
- St Oswald, Coney Hill, Gloucester. 1939
- Chapel, Llandovery College, Carmarthen
- Neyland Church, Pembrokeshire

Francis B. Andrews
- Baptist. City Rd Church, Edgbaston, Birmingham. 1922
- Baptist. Cannon St Memorial Church, Soho Rd, Handsworth, Birmingham. 1929–30

P.M. Andrews
- St Martin, Bexley, L B Bexley. 1937–8
- St Mary, Gravesend, Kent. 1939

Andrews and Winton-Lewis
- St Martin, Saltdean, Brighton. 1956–7

William Henry Ansell and Arthur Bailey
- Wesleyan Methodist Church, Westbury, Wilts. 1932 (W.H. Ansell)
- St Mary, Shortlands, Kent. 1953–5.
- Baptist. West Norwood Baptist Church, L B Lambeth. 1960
- Baptist. Westbourne Park Church, Porchester Rd, RB Kensington and Chelsea. 1961
- Holy Trinity, Twydall Green, Gillingham, Kent. 1963–4
- Cathedral Church of SS Peter and Paul, Sheffield. 1963– additions. I
- See also Arthur Bailey

F.S. Antliff and Sons
- Methodist church, King St, Alfreton (Watchorn), Derbys. 1929

APEC (Martin Purdy, Ken Fisher, Gary Dyhouse)
- St Bartholomew, Barking Rd, East Ham, L B Newham. 1977–83
- St Mark, Forest Gate, L B Newham. 1986–7
- St Matthias, Canning Town, L B Newham. 1983–8
- St Michael and All Angels, Romford Rd, Manor Park, L B Newham. 1990
- St Mark, Tollgate Rd, Beckton, L B Newham. 1986–9
- St Stephen, Copeland Rd, Walthamstow, L B Waltham Forest. 1988–94
- St Bede, Bryndale Ave, Brandwood End, Birmingham. 1992–4
- See also Peter Bridges and Martin Purdy; Martin Purdy

William G. Apps
- Lower Edmonth Church, Edinburgh. 1959

A.J. Hodsdon Archard and Partners
- R C SS Mary and Joseph, Hemel Hempstead, Herts. 1957
- R C Sacred Heart and St John, London Rd, Bushey, Herts. 1958–9
- R C St Joseph and St Walburga, Parkstone, Dorset. 1961–2
- R C St John, Egham, Surrey. 1962
- R C Our Lady of the Angels (Capuchin Fathers), Carlton Heath, Erith, L B Bexley. 1963
- St Michael and All Angels, Sycamore Rd, Amersham, Bucks. 1964–6. A. Hodson Archard.

George Arthur and Son
- Mure Memorial Parish Church, Maxwell Drive, Garrowhill, Glasgow. 1936–40

Ashby and Waring
- Congregational. Union Church, Queen Elizabeth St, Bermondsey, L B Southwark. 1957

H. Ascroft
- Congregational church, Gerrard's Cross, Bucks. 1920

Ashlin and Coleman
- R C Sacred Heart, Cloughoge, Newry, Co. Armagh. 1916. B
- R C Immaculate Conception, Artasooley, Co. Armagh. 1922. B
- R C St Malachy, Irish St, Armagh. 1935. B

Robert Atkinson
- St Catherine, Hammersmith. 1922–3. Demolished.
- All Hallows, Chertsey Rd, Twickenham, Richmond. 1939–40, incorporating Wren tower and fixtures from All Hallows, Lombard St, City of London. I

Austin and Paley
- Christ Church, Thornton, Lancashire. 1914 (chancel). Rest Leach, Rhodes and Walker 1963.
- St Mark, Basford, Staffs. 1914. West end 1969–71 by Charles Lewis.
- St Michael and All Angels, Ashton-on-Ribble, Preston. West end, 1915.
- All Saints, Station Rd, Becconsall, Lancs. 1925–6
- St Stephen-on-the-Cliffs, Blackpool, Lancs. 1925–6
- Chancel, Pennington-in-Furness, Cumbria. 1925–6
- St Hilda, Bilsborrow, Lancs. 1926–7
- St Luke, Orrell, Greater Manchester. 1927–38
- St Stephen, Whelley, Wigan. 1928–30, 1938.
- St Barbara, Rochester Rd, Earlsdon, Coventry. 1930–1. With H.T. Jackson.
- St Barnabas, Cromwell St, Coventry. 1932. With H.T. Jackson
- St Matthew, Haberham Eaves, Burnley, Lancs. Largely rebuilt 1928–31
- St Thomas, Blackpool, Lancs. 1930
- St Christopher, Bare, Morecambe, Lancs. 1932–4
- St John Evangelist, Abram, Greater Manchester. 1936–7
- St Mary Magdalene, Ribbleton, Preston, Lancs. New East end, 1938–42

Anthony Avenell
- Baptist church, West Howe, Bournemouth. 1956

Maxwell Ayrton
- Presbyterian. St Andrew, Northey Ave, Cheam, L B Sutton. 1931–3, addition 1956. Attached church hall Matley, Brotherton and Mills, 1924–7.

Lawrence M. Bader and Edward Miller
- Lutheran. St Andrew, Ruislip, L B Hillingdon. 1962

F.E.G. Badger
- R C St Teresa, Utting Ave East, Norris Green, Liverpool. 1937

Arthur Bailey
- Dutch Reformed Church, Austin Friars, City of London. 1950–4.
- St George in the East, Stepney, L B Tower Hamlets. 1958. Insertion within bombed Hawksmoor church, I
- See also Ansell and Bailey

Bailey and Piper
- St Columba, Highlands Rd, Fareham, Hants. 1961–3

George Baines and Son
- Methodist. Park Avenue Church, Northampton. 1924
- Baptist chapel, High Rd, Ilford, L B Redbridge. 1927
- Methodist church, Station Rd, Chingford, L B Waltham Forest. 1927
- Methodist church, Sevenoaks Rd, Orpington, L B Bromley. 1934–54

C.W. Baker and T.J. Denny

- RC Our Lady of the Annunciation, LB Croydon. 1946

Sir Herbert Baker

- St Andrew, The Drive, Ilford, LB Redbridge. 1923–4. II
- Christian Science. Ninth Church, Marsham St, Westminster. 1926–30. II*. With A. Scott.
- St Paul, Woldingham, Surrey. 1933. II
- Bearwood College Chapel, Bearwood Rd, Wokingham. 1934–5. II
- Haileybury College Chapel, Herts. Apse 1936. II*
- Presbytery Chapel, Church House, Dean's Yard, City of Westminster. 1935–9. II

F.R. Bales and C.F. Bales

- RC St Joseph, Cardiff. 1939

Balfour and Steward

- Congregational. Mosspark Church, Ladybank Drive, Glasgow. 1937–8

Joseph Lancaster Ball

- St Gregory the Great, Oldknow Rd, Small Heath, Birmingham. 1910–12, completed 1926–8, to revised plan with Holland W. Hobbiss. II
- Bluecoat School Chapel, Metchley Lane, Harborne, Birmingham. 1932–3 (with H.W. Simister)

Hugh C. Bankart

- RC Holy Redeemer, St Wulstan and St Eadburgha, Pershore, Worcs. 1958–9

Barber, Bundy and Greenfield

- Congregational church, Portsmouth Rd, Guildford, Surrey. 1965. By D. Bundy.

Raymond Turner Barker

- St Andrew, Southgate, LB Enfield. 1914

Leonard William Barnard

- School chapel, Oakleigh Hall, Cirencester, Glos. 1919
- Dean Close School Chapel, Cheltenham. 1932–3

J. Barrington-Baker and Partners

- St Giles, Bullsmoor Lane, LB Enfield. 1953–4
- St Michael, Golder's Green, LB Barnet. 1957. Now Greek Orthodox.

W.L. Barrow

- St Aidan, Princess Elizabeth Way, Plymouth. 1959

Arnold Montague Barrowcliff

- RC St Mary, Loughborough. Nave and aisles, 1924–5

Bartlett and Gray

- Friends' Meeting House, Clarendon St, Nottingham. 1960–2
- Congregational church, Worksop, Notts. 1968
- Friends' Meeting House, Goldwell Hill, Chesterfield, Derbys. 1971–2
- Friends' Meeting House, Rosemary St, Mansfield, Notts. 1972–3

Charles E. Bateman

- St Chad, Hollyfield Rd, Reddicap Heath, Sutton Coldfield, Birmingham. 1925–6

C.F. Bates

- RC St Joseph, New Zealand Rd, Cathays, Cardiff. 1936

F.R. Bates, Son and Price

- RC St Joseph, Port Talbot. 1930 (F.R. Bates and Son)
- RC St Francis of Assisi, Ely, Cardiff. 1960
- RC Blessed Sacrament, Wentloog Rd, Rumney, Cardiff. 1960
- RC St Benedict, Sketty, Swansea. 1961
- RC St Teilo, Old Church Rd, Whitchurch, Cardiff. 1964
- RC Our Lady of the Assumption, Briton Ferry, Neath Port Talbot. 1965
- RC St Theresa of Lisieux, Hirwaun, Rhondda Cynon Taff. 1966
- Methodist church, Sandfields, Port Talbot. 1966
- Holy Trinity, Fairway, Sandfields, Port Talbot. 1968
- RC Our Lady of Lourdes, Townhill, Swansea. 1968
- RC St Theresa of Lisieux, Southdown Rd, Sandfields, Port Talbot. 1969
- RC Our Lady Star of the Sea, Porthcawl, Bridgend. 1969
- RC St Mary, Merthyr Vale, Aberfan, Merthyr Tydfil. 1969–70

Geoffrey J. Beard

- Methodist. All Saints, Abingdon, Oxon. 1959

D.H. Beaty-Pownall

- St Andrew Mission Church, Molesey Rd, Horsham, Surrey. 1936

R.T. Beckett

- St Martin, Llay, Gresford, Denbighshire. 1923–5
- Holy Trinity, Llandudno Junction, Conwy. 1928

Gerald R. Beech

- Chapel at Abbey House, Glastonbury, Somerset. 1957
- St Alban, Northwood Rd, Prenton, Birkenhead. 1961
- Friends' Meeting House, Telegraph Rd, Heswall, Cheshire. 1961–2. With Dewi Prys Thomas.

Beney and Leech

- Baptist church, Osmaston Rd, Derby. 1972

T.P. Bennett and Son

- Mormon Temple, Newchapel, Lingfield, Surrey. 1957–9
- Mormon Kensington Temple, Exhibition Rd, RB Kensington and Chelsea. 1961
- RC St Mary Magdalene, Tilehurst, Reading. 1962
- Mormon Temple, Altrincham Rd, Northenden, Manchester. 1964
- Mormon. Jesus Christ and Latter Day Saints, Georgetown, Merthyr Tydfil. 1969

Ernest Bentley

- RC St Joseph, Seaholme Rd, Mablethorpe, Lincs. 1937

Osmund Bentley

- RC St Joseph, Kingston Rd, New Malden, RB Kingston. 1922–35

Arthur Gilbert Berry

- St George, Church Lane, Hindolveston, Norfolk. 1931–2. II

Harold Best

- St Mary and St Berin, Berinsfield, Oxon. 1962. Best was vicar of Dorchester.

Terry Bestwick

- Methodist. Bridgeway Hall Mission, Arkwright St, Nottingham. 1963–7
- Methodist. St John, Brook St, Strelley, Notts. 1966
- Methodist. St John, Sutton in Ashfield, Notts. 1972–3
- Methodist. St Andrew, Ilkeston, Derbys. 1973–5

R.J. Beswick and Son

- St Andrew, Raleigh Ave, Swindon. 1957–8
- Sindlesham House (Salvatorian Fathers), Sindlesham, Wokingham. Chapel 1963–4

J. Bevan

- RC Holy Cross, Bedminster, Bristol. 1930
- RC Corpus Christi, Weston-super-Mare. 1930

Beveridge and Dallachy

- United Free Church, Chalmers St, Dunfermline, Fife. 1936. By David Beveridge
- Church of Scotland. St Andrew, Main St, Cambuslang, Glasgow. 1961–6

William Henry Bidlake

- Emmanuel, Birmingham Rd, Wylde Green, Sutton Coldfield, Birmingham. Apse and chancel, 1925–7, completing a church of 1909. II
- Congregational. Sparkhill Church, Stratford Rd, Sparkhill, Birmingham. 1933. (now URC)

Bigland and Mouat

- Delting Parish Church, Voe, Shetland. 1953

Bingham Towner Associates

- RC St Mark, High St, West Wickham, LB Bromley. 1962–3

E.F.S. Biram and W.B. Fletcher

- St James, Eccleston Park, Prescot, Lancs. 1922

Biscoe and Stanton

- St Saviour, Warwick Ave, City of Westminster. 1973–6
- St Peter, Elgin Ave, City of Westminster. 1974–7

J.H. Black

- RC English Martyrs, Dalton, Huddersfield. 1971

W.H. Randoll Blacking

- Christ Church, Litton, Derbys. 1926–7
- Church of the Resurrection, Lampeter Ave, Drayton, Portsmouth. 1930
- St Augustine, Cooden Drive, Bexhill, E. Sussex. 1934. Completed 1960–3 by H. Hubbard Ford
- St Mary the Virgin, Littlehampton, W. Sussex. 1934 recasting of 1826 church by G. Draper.
- St John, West Bay, Bridport, Dorset. 1936. B
- St Alban, Broadmead Ave, Eastfield, Northampton. 1938
- St Edward the Confessor, Winchester Rd, Chandler's Ford, Hants. 1938.

J.P. Blake

- Congregational church, Perivale Park, LB Ealing. 1937–8

Trevor Blake

- Congregational church, Mount Rd, Chingford, LB Waltham Forest. 1952–3

Blackwood and Jury

- Church of Ireland. St Clement, Templemore Ave, Belfast. 1928–30. B
- Church of Ireland. St Polycarp, Finaghy, Belfast. 1932. B+

Michael Blee

- All Saints, Isleworth, LB Hounslow. 1967–70. Rebuilding incorporating C15 tower and C18 nave.
- Holy Innocents, Orpington, LB Bromley. 1980–1
- St Paul, St Paul's Rd, Brentford, LB Hounslow. 1990. Remodelling of F. & H. Francis church of 1868–9

Arthur C. Blomfield (junior)

- St Thomas, Bromyard Ave, Acton Vale, LB Ealing. 1915. Nave completed 1937–9 by Lester Richard. Demolished 1995.
- Chapel, Oundle School, Northants. 1922–3. B
- Epsom College Chapel, Epsom, Cheshire. 1925

Arthur Blomfield and A.J. Driver

- St Thomas, Haydon Rd, Becontree, LB Barking and Dagenham. 1926–7

D.M. Blouett

- RC St Anne Line, Grove Cres, S. Woodford, LB Redbridge. 1966

G.L.W. Blount and Williamson

- St George, Garrison Church, Bulford, Wilts. 1920–7

Detmar Blow and Frederic Billeray

- All Saints, Hundon, Suffolk. 1914–16

Edward Boardman and Son

- Trinity Presbyterian Church, Norwich. 1955–6

David Boddington

- St Luke, Halifax Drive, Leicester. 1960–6. With Colin Shewring (q.v.).

Body, Son and Fleury
- St Chad, Whitleigh Green, Plymouth. 1955–6

Lawrence Bond
- St Martin, Scartho Rd, Grimsby. 1938
- St Hugh, Ashby Rd, Old Brumby, Scunthorpe. 1939. II
- RAF College Memorial Chapel, Cranwell, Lincs. 1952. Rebuilt.
- Ascension, Harrowby, Grantham, Lincs. 1956
- All Saints, Capworth St, Leyton, LB Waltham Forest. 1973

Wilfrid Bond
- St Mary, Garthorpe, Lincs. 1913–24
- St Barnabas, Barnetby-le-Wold, Lincs. 1926–7
- St Martin, Grimsby, Lincs. 1938. With Lawrence Bond

Brian E. Bonskill
- All Saints, Hale Rd, Halebarns, Hale, Greater Manchester. 1966–7

P.L.B. Borthwick
- Church of Scotland. Cranhill Church, Bellrock St, Glasgow. 1963–5, replacing church of 1952–4 by Wylie, Shanks and Wylie which became parish hall.

Peter Bosanquet (Brett, Boyd and Bosanquet)
- St John, Hilltop, S. Hatfield, Herts. 1958–60
- St George, Norton Way North, Letchworth, Herts. 1961–4
- St Matthew, Drewery Drive, Wigmore, Gillingham, Kent. 1965
- Parish Centre, Newton Farm, Hereford. 1966–7
- Christ the King, Parish church and hall, Sonning Common, Reading. 1966–7

C.J. Bourne
- St Stephen, Brooks Rd, Cambridge. 1962–3

Bournville Village Trust Architects
- Prebyterian. Weoley Hill Church, Bryony Rd, Selly Oak, Birmingham. 1932 (now URC)
- St David, Shenley Green, Northfield, Birmingham. 1965

Stewart Powell Bowen (Bowen, Dann, Davies)
- RC Good Shepherd, Llanddoged Rd, Llanrwst, Clwyd. 1956. With Gwilyn Parry Davies
- RC Christ the King, Gors Rd, Towyn, Clwyd. 1973–4. By Bowen, Dann, Davies.
- RC St Illtud, Maes Onnan, Rhuddlan, Clwyd. 1975–6
- Calvinistic Methodist (Welsh Presbyterian). Capel-y-Groes Chapel, Wrexham. 1981–2. By Bowen, Dann, Davies.

John MacLintock Bowie
- Middlebie Parish Church, Dumfries and Galloway. 1928–9. B
- Mouswald Parish Church, Dumfries and Galloway. c.1929 remodelling and extension of church of 1816. C (S)

Denis Bowman
- St George, Chadderton, Oldham. 1957–8

Alan Brace
- Methodist Church, High St, Harpenden, Herts. 1929–30. II

Braddock and Martin-Smith
- See D.F. Martin-Smith

F.J. Bradford
- RC Corpus Christi, Grimsby Rd, Cleethorpes. 1930

Harold Brakspear
- St John, Swindon, Wilts. 1961

Peter Bridges and Martin Purdy
- Church at the Centre (Ecumenical Centre), Skelmersdale, Lancs. 1969–71
- Matchborough Church Centre, Redditch, Worcs. 1970–2
- United Reformed Church, Ormskirk St, St Helens, Merseyside. 1972–5
- See also APEC, and Martin Purdy

W.H. Brierley and J.H. Rutherford
- Durham School War Memorial Chapel, Durham. 1924–6
- St Chad, York. 1925–9
- Chapel, Liverpool College for Girls. 1926

Edward Percy Briggs
- Congregational church, Cleveleys, Lancs. 1920

Martin Shaw Briggs and A.W. Harwood
- Congregational church, Mill Hill, LB Barnet. 1920, 1937

Clive Broad
- RC Our Lady of Lourdes and St Vincent de Paul, Harrow Rd, City of Westminster. 1973–5

Francis George Broadbent and Partners
- RC Our Lady Queen of Peace, Sheen Rd, Richmond (Goodhart-Rendel, Broadbent and Curtis). 1953–4
- RC Chapel of the Tyburn Convent, Queensway, City of Westminster. 1958–62. Based on designs by H.S. Goodhart-Rendel.
- RC St Anne, Kingston Hill, RB Kingston. 1960
- RC St Thomas, Whyteleafe, Caterham, Surrey. 1960–1
- RC Holy Name, Arbrook Lane, Claygate, Surrey. 1961
- RC Our Lady of Lourdes, Hampton Court Way, Thames Ditton, Surrey. 1962. (By D.A. Reid).
- RC St John Fisher, Cannon Hill Lane, LB Merton. 1962
- RC Prinknash Abbey Church, Upton St Leonards, Glos. 1962–5
- RC St Thomas More, Knebworth, Herts. 1963
- RC St Andrew, Brook Rd, Thornton Heath, LB Croydon. 1970. (Broadbent, Hastings, Reid and Todd)

John S. Broadbent
- Congregational church, Upney Lane, LB Barking and Dagenham. 1929

Frank A. Broadhead and Eric V. Royle
- St John, Carlton, Notts. 1958
- Christ Church, Newark, Notts. 1958–9

Brocklebank and Co.
- Methodist church, Bebington, Birkenhead. 1927
- Methodist church, Platt Lane, Mosside, Manchester. 1932

Arthur Brocklehurst
- Methodist Central Hall, Woodhorn Rd, Ashington, Northumberland. 1923
- Methodist Central Hall, Dunscombe St, Grimsby. 1934

J.K. Brocklesby
- RC St Oswald and St Edmund, Liverpool Rd, Ashton-in-Makerfield, Wigan. 1930. II

John Sidney Brocklesby
- RC St Augustine of England, Woodborough Rd, Nottingham. 1921–3
- RC St Joseph, Hall St, Burslem, Stoke-on-Trent. 1925–7
- RC Sacred Heart, Queen's Ave, Tunstall, Stoke-on-Trent. 1925–30. II
- RC St Oswald, Ashton-in-Makerfield, Lancs. 1927

Margaret B. Brodie
- St Martin, Port Glasgow, Inverclyde. 1957–8

Bromilow, While and Smeeton
- St John the Baptist, Longbridge Lane, Longbridge, Birmingham. 1956–8. (George H. While)
- St Boniface, Quinton Rd West, Birmingham. 1958–9 (George H. While)
- Methodist. Sparkhill Church, Warwick Rd, Sparkhill, Birmingham. 1959
- St George, Bridge St West, Newtown, Birmingham. 1970 (Reginald Smeeton)

J. Brooke and C.E. Elcock
- St Peter, Hungerford Rd, Crewe, Cheshire. 1914–23. II

Cecil J. Brown
- St Stephen, Cambridge. 1962–3

Charles Brown
- Baptist Church, Green Lane, Walsall. 1972
- Church of England/URC. Balsall Heath Church Centre, Edward Rd, Birmingham. 1980

David Brown
- RC Immaculate Heart of Mary, Malvern Gardens, Lobley Hill, Gateshead. 1969
- RC St Augustine, Wealcroft, Lean Lane, Heworth, Gateshead. 1962
- RC St Joseph, Mill Lane, Gilesgate Moor, Durham. 1964–6
- RC SS Joseph, Patrick and Cuthbert, Church St, Coxhoe, Co. Durham. 1966
- RC Our Lady of the Rosary, Passfield Way, Peterlee, Co. Durham. 1966
- RC St Teresa, Heaton Rd, Heaton, Newcastle upon Tyne. 1972

George Talbot Brown
- Mormon Church, Newton Aycliffe, Co. Durham. 1961–2

Talbot Brown, Panter and Partners
- St Andrew, Wellingborough. 1930 (T. Brown and J.W. Fisher)
- St Barnabas, Wellingborough, Northants. 1951–3

Brown and Buttrick (Derek W. Brown)
- All Saints, East Common Lane, Scunthorpe. 1953
- Holy Spirit, Willoughby Rd, Scunthorpe. 1960 (Brown)
- RC St Bernadette, Ashby Rd, Scunthorpe. 1980 (E.S. Walton)

Brown and Sharp
- RC St Peter, Leicester Rd, Hinckley, Leics. 1958–60

John Bruce and Hay
- St Constantine, Govan, Glasgow. 1922

Arthur Bryan
- St Anne, Letchworth Rd, Leicester. 1933–4

Buckland and Haywood
- Royal Hospital School Chapel, Holbrook, Suffolk. 1925–33. II*

Building Design Partnership
- Methodist church, Lea, Preston, Lancs. 1961–2
- RC College Chapel, Kirkby Lonsdale, Cumbria. 1966
- Methodist church, Poulton-le-Fylde, Lancs. 1967–8. By Keith Ingham.

K.D. Bundy
- Methodist church, Woodbridge St, Guildford, Surrey. 1967

Burgess Partnership
- Tabernacle Chapel, Derwen Rd, Bridgend. 1988–9. Job architect Siarlys Evans.

Robert Burke
- RC Corpus Christi, Kelvin Grove, Gateshead. 1934
- RC Our Lady of the Annunciation, Gateshead. 1953
- RC Our Lady and St Wilfred, Gateshead. 1955

David R. Burles, Alexander John Newton and Partners

- RC St Augustine, Cranbrook Rd, Ilford, LB Redbridge. 1953–4
- RC St Basil, Barstable, Basildon, Essex. 1956
- RC St Michael, Tilbury Rd, East Ham, LB Newham. 1958–9
- RC St Stephen, Church Rd, East Ham, LB Newham. 1958–9
- RC St Augustine, Ilford, LB Redbridge. 1959
- RC St Aidan, Old Oak Common Lane, LB Hammersmith. 1958–61. By A.J. Newton.
- RC Immaculate Heart of Mary, Botwell Lane, Hayes, LB Hillingdon. 1961
- RC Our Lady Queen of the Apostles, The Green, Heston, LB Hounslow. 1964
- RC St Thomas, Harlow, Essex. 1965
- RC St Francis de Sales, Wellington Rd, Hampton Hill, LB Richmond. 1966
- RC St Anselm, South Rd, Southall, LB Ealing. 1967. By A.J. Newton.
- RC St Cedd, High Rd, Ilford, LB Redbridge. 1972
- RC Cathedral Church of St Mary and St Helen, Ingrave Rd, Brentwood, extensions and sanctuary 1972–3. See also Quinlan Terry
- RC St John the Baptist, Wanstead Park Rd, Ilford, LB Redbridge. 1967

Sir John Burnet and Partners (Sir John Burnet, Tait and Lorne)

- Second Church of Christ Scientist, Palace Gardens Terrace, RB Kensington and Chelsea. 1921–6 by Thomas Tait. II
- Glasgow University Memorial Chapel. 1929
- St Stephen, Edinburgh. Alterations and additions, 1947

John Burnet, Son and Dick

- RC Our Lady and St Columba, Newtonmore Rd, Kingussie, Highland. 1931–2. By Norman Dick. B

Cecil Burns and Guthrie

- Christian Science church, Tunbridge Wells, Kent. 1932–3
- St Andrew, Paddock Wood, Kent. 1953–5

Thomas H.B. Burrough and F.L. Hannam

- Holy Cross, Filwood Park, Bristol. 1949–50
- Prebyterian. Lockleaze Church, Bristol. 1952
- St Andrew, Brentry, Bristol. 1955–6
- St Mary Magdalene and St Francis, Lockleaze, Bristol. 1960–1

Eustace H. Burton

- Baptist church, Old King St, Bristol. 1956

David Bush

- St John, Meeting House Lane, Peckham, LB Southwark. 1965–6
- St Matthew, Chichester Rd, Croydon. 1965–72
- St Mark with St Margaret, Old Mill Rd, Plumstead Common, LB Greenwich. 1976

A.S.G. Butler

- RC Chapel for St David's Homes for ex-servicemen, Castlegar Hill, LB Ealing. 1919
- RC Chapel for St Vincent's Home, Eastcote, LB Hillingdon. 1921
- RC Sisters of Charity Chapel, Pinner, LB Harrow. 1924
- RC St Teresa, Warwick Rd, Beaconsfield, Bucks. 1926. Walsingham Chapel, west end and English Martyrs chapel, Adrian Scott 1934
- RC Sacred Heart, Vicarage Rd, Henley-on-Thames, Oxon. 1936, incorporating A.W.N. Pugin glass. II

Edward C. Butler

- Whitfield Memorial Church (American Church), Tottenham Court Rd, LB Camden. 1956

R.M. Butler

- RC Maguiresbridge Church, Co. Fermanagh, remodelling. 1922. B
- RC Chapel of Bon Sauveur Convent, Mill Bank, Holyhead. 1934–7. Now Ucheldre Centre. II

E. and J. Byrne

- RC Grange Church, Cranfield, Kilkeel, Co. Down. 1924. B

Peter A. Byrne

- RC St Anthony, Broadstone, Poole, Dorset. 1958–9
- RC St Bernadette, Galsworthy Square, Whipton, Exeter. 1960

Richard Byrom

- RC St Mary, Clayton-le-Moors, Lancs. 1958–9

Joseph Watson Cabré

- St Nicholas Blundellsands, Sefton, Merseyside. 1924–5. Restoration and additions. C

Nugent Francis Cachemaille-Day

- St Nicholas, Burnage, Manchester. 1931–2. II* (Welch, Cachemaille-Day and Lander).
- St Saviour, Middle Park Ave, Eltham, Greenwich. 1932–3. II* (Welch, Cachemaille-Day and Lander)
- St Alban, Burgess Rd, Swaythling, Southampton. 1933. II (Welch, Cachemaille-Day and Lander)
- St Catherine, Heald Green, Manchester. 1933
- St Nicholas, Middleton, Bognor Regis, W. Sussex. 1933
- St Barbara, Whale Island, Hants (Welch, Cachemaille-Day and Lander), 1933–4
- St Edmund, Larkswood Rd, Chingford, LB Waltham Forest. 1933–9. II

- St Mary, Grafton Rd, Dagenham, LB Barking and Dagenham. 1934–5. II (Welch, Cachemaille-Day and Lander)
- Baptist church, Cheam Rd, LB Sutton. 1934. II
- Bishops College Chapel, Cheshunt, Herts. 1934
- St Stephen, St Stephen's Rd, LB Hounslow. 1935 tower added to Ewan Christian church of 1875–6
- St Paul, Tiverton Rd, Ruislip Gardens, LB Hillingdon. 1936–52
- St Michael and All Angels, Orton Rd, Wythenshawe, Manchester. 1937. II*
- St Winifred, Salisbury Rd, Testwood, Southampton. 1937. II
- St Paul, Corbin's Lane, South Harrow, LB Harrow. 1937–8. II
- St George, Coventry. 1938
- St John the Divine, Heene, Worthing. 1938, 1964 (tower)
- St Thomas, Ipswich. 1938
- Good Shepherd Mission, Forest Hill Rd, Pallion, Sunderland. 1938
- Epiphany, Beech Lane, Gipton, Leeds. 1938. II*
- Holy Trinity, Hartshill, Nuneaton, Warks. 1938
- St Martin, Barton Hill Rd, Torquay, Torbay. 1938, 1961. II
- St Anselm, Belmont, Harrow. 1938–41. Incorporating remains of St Anselm, Davies St, Westminster. 1891 by Balfour and Turner.
- St Paul, Preston, Torbay. 1939
- Holy Cross, St Austell Rd, Caludon, Coventry. 1939
- St Paul, Dollis Hill Lane, LB Brent. 1939. Now Naharashta Mandal London
- St Luke, Rotherham Rd, Holbrooks, Coventry. 1939
- St Swithun, Purley, LB Croydon. 1939
- St Barnabas, Tuffley, Glos. 1939–40. II
- St Laurence, Hamilton Ave, Barkingside, LB Redbridge. 1939–40
- St Paul, Mill Hill, LB Barnet. 1946
- St Mary, Haggerston, LB Hackney. 1951
- All Saints, Uxbridge Rd, Hanworth, LB Hounslow. 1951–2, 1957. II
- St Peter, Westfield, Midsomer Norton, Bath. 1953
- St John the Evangelist, Gloucester Drive, Brownswood Park, LB Hackney. 1953
- St Richard of Chichester, Three Bridges, Crawley, W. Sussex. 1954. Demolished 1994.
- All Saints, Burton Rd, Clapton, LB Hackney. 1954
- All Souls, Oversbury St, Clapton, LB Hackney. 1954
- St Peter, Broadwater, Stevenage, Herts. 1954
- St Cuthbert, Kenton, LB Harrow. 1954
- Christ Church, Goldington Rd, Bedford. 1956–8
- St Mary Magdalene, Hatfield Hyde, Welwyn Garden City, Herts. 1955
- St Matthew, Upper Clapton, LB Hackney. 1955

- St Michael, Boreham Wood, Herts. 1955
- St Michael and All Angels, Hatfield, Herts. 1956
- St Michael, St Michael's Rd, N. Bemerton, Salisbury, Wilts. 1956–7
- St James, Clapham Park, LB Lambeth. 1957–8
- RC St Francis of Assisi, Links Rd, Radford, Coventry. 1957–9
- St Columba, Banners Gate Rd, Sutton Coldfield, Birmingham. 1957–60
- St Mary, Brentmead Gardens, Twyford, LB Ealing. 1958. II, because incorporates C17 and 1808 chapel.
- St Mary, Barton, Oxford. 1958
- St Paul, West Hackney, LB Hackney. 1958–60
- All Saints, Surrey Square, LB Southwark. 1959
- SS Faith and Matthias, Stoke Newington, LB Hackney. 1959
- Bishop Gorton Memorial Church (St Christopher), Winsford Ave, Allesey Park, Coventry. 1959–60
- St Thomas, Clapton, LB Hackney. 1960
- St Peter, Lee, LB Greenwich. 1960
- St Michael and All Angels, London Fields, LB Hackney. 1960
- St Stephen, Surrey Square, Walworth, LB Southwark. 1961
- St Edmund, Northwood Hills, LB Hillingdon. 1962
- St Philip, Avondale Square, Rotherhithe, LB Southwark. 1963

Cackett, Burns Dick and Mackellar

- Unitarian. Church of the Divine Unity, Ellison Place, Newcastle upon Tyne. 1939–40. II
- Methodist Church and hall, Cullercoats, N. Tyneside. 1961–2

Cairns and Ford

- Tron Moredun, Craigour Gardens, Edinburgh. 1951

A. Buchanan Campbell

- Church of Scotland. St George and St Peter, Boyndie St, Easterhouse, Glasgow. 1961–2
- Church of Scotland. St Christopher, Meikle Rd, Pollok, Glasgow. 1961–2
- Church of Scotland. Priesthill Parish Church, Freeland Drive, Pollok, Glasgow. 1971–3

D.A. Campbell and E.H. Honeybourne

- All Souls, Mather Ave, Allerton, Liverpool. 1927

G.C. Campbell

- Baptist church, College St, Buckhaven, Fife. 1914–15

A. Lorne Campbell

- Greenbank Church, Braidburn Terrace, Edinburgh. 1927
- Lochend Parish Church, Restalrig Rd South, Edinburgh. 1929

Alban D.R. Caröe and A.P. Robinson
▸ St Catherine, Aylsham Rd, Mile Cross, Norwich. 1935
▸ Ascension, Sherwood Park Rd, Mitcham, LB Merton. 1953 (Caröe and Partners, job architect Terence Can.)
▸ St John Evangelist, Causton St, City of Westminster. 1956–8
▸ Holy Trinity, Farrington Rd, Ettingshall Park, Wolverhampton. 1961

W.D. Caröe
▸ St Cadmarch, Llangammarch Wells, Powys. 1915–17, 1927 (tower)
▸ St Hilda, Hartlepool. 1921
▸ St Michael, Mill Hill, LB Barnet. 1921–39. West end by Alban Caröe.
▸ All Saints, Shaftesbury Rd, Luton, Beds. 1922–3
▸ St Helen, Church St, St Helen's. 1926. II
▸ Holy Trinity, Newcastle Emlyn, Ceredigion. 1926. (enlargement)
▸ St John, Romford, LB Havering. 1927, 1932 (with Hubert Passmore)
▸ St Francis, Woolbrook, Sidmouth, Devon. 1929
▸ Holy Trinity, Eccleshall, Staffs. Lady Chapel to C13 church. 1929–31. I
▸ RC Templewood Chapel, Browns Hill, Chalford, Glos. 1930
▸ St Matthew, Creighton Ave, Muswell Hill, LB Haringey. 1931–4. With Hubert Passmore.
▸ St Mary, Hawksworth Wood, Leeds. 1932–3
▸ St Oswald, Norbury, LB Croydon. 1933–4. With Hubert Passmore
▸ St Michael, Bishopswearmouth, Sunderland. 1933–5. (substantial remodelling)

Caröe and Martin
▸ Methodist Church, Laceby Rd, Grimsby. 1970

J. Cassells
▸ Episcopal. St Luke, Ninian Quadrant, Auchmuty, Glenrothes, Fife. 1960

Cassidy and Ashton
▸ Lancaster University Chaplaincy Centre, Lancaster. 1971–2

J. Coates Carter
▸ St Peter, Mill Rd, Dinas Powys, Vale of Glamorgan. Designed 1927, built 1929–30

H. Munro Cautley
▸ St Augustine, Felixstowe Rd, Ipswich. 1927

Peter MacGregor Chalmers
▸ Urr Parish Church, Haugh of Urr, Dumfries and Galloway. 1914–15
▸ Merrylee Parish Church, Merrylee Rd, Glasgow. 1915. B
▸ St Andrew, Bank St, Lochgelly, Fife. 1915. Recasting and extension of church of 1854–5
▸ Episcopal. Greyfriars, St Cuthbert St, Kirkcudbright, Dumfries and Galloway. 1919

Leslie Channing
▸ St Richard of Chichester, Forge Lane, Hansworth, LB Hounslow. 1964–5

A.J. Chaplin
▸ St Julian, St Julian's Alley, Norwich. 1953. Rebuilding of medieval church after bomb damage.
▸ RC St George, Sprowston Rd, Norwich. 1962

Charity, Thirtle and Duke
▸ Congregational church, Church St, Epsom, Surrey. 1963

C. Charlewood
▸ St Martin, Acklam Rd, Middlesbrough. 1940

George E. Charlewood
▸ St Aidan, Tintern Ave, Billingham, Teeside. 1954–60
▸ St Chad, E. Harrington, Co. Durham. 1962. With Ian Curry.

F.L. Charlton
▸ St Philip, Osmondthorpe, Leeds. 1933
▸ St Cross, Middleton, Leeds. 1936–7

Philip B. Chatwin and Anthony B Chatwin (as J.A. Chatwin and Son)
▸ RC Our Lady of Good Counsel and St Gregory, Three Shires Oak Rd, Bearwood, W. Mids. 1930
▸ St Faith and St Lawrence, Balden Rd, Harborne, Birmingham. 1935–7 (nave and tower); 1958–60 (chancel)
▸ Bishop Westcott Mission Church and Hall, Acocks Green, Birmingham. 1936 (now youth centre)

K.C. Cheeseman and S.E. Bragg
▸ Methodist church, Culver St, Colchester, Essex. 1971

Domenico Chiochetti
▸ RC Italian Chapel, Lamb Holm, Orkney. 1943–4. Prisoner of War chapel.

Chippindale and Needham
▸ Methodist church, Timperley, Greater Manchester. 1938

Philip Clarke
▸ RC All Saints, Golborne, Greater Manchester. 1927

Clarke Hall, Scorer and Bright
▸ St John, Ermine, Lincoln. 1961–3. II*

Clayton and Black
▸ Christian Science. First Church, Montpelier Rd, Brighton. 1921, recasting of c.1850 house

Clifford and Lunan
▸ Church of Scotland. Cathcart Old Parish Church, Carmunnock Rd, Glasgow. 1914, 1923–9. Completed by Watson, Salmond and Gray. B
▸ Titwood Church, Glasgow. 1923. (H.E. Clifford)

R.M. Close
▸ Church of Ireland. St Simon, Donegall Rd, Belfast. 1923–30. B

Cockrill and Eve
▸ St Cedd, Westcliff-on-Sea, Southend, Essex. 1954–5

A.E. Cogswell and Sons
▸ St Saviour, Jervis Rd, Tipner, Portsmouth. 1913–14
▸ Ascension, Stubbington Ave, Portsmouth. 1917
▸ St Nicholas, Battenburg Ave, Hilsea, Portsmouth. 1935

J.D. Coleridge
▸ St John, Simpson Rd, Rudmore, Portsmouth. 1915–16. II

Edward W. Collins
▸ Rutland Gospel Hall, Bedford. 1956

Herbert Collins
▸ Methodist church, Swaythling, Southampton. 1932. With cinema facilities (paid for by J. Arthur Rank). II

McCarthy Collings
▸ RC St Margaret Mary, Perry Common, Birmingham. 1936

John Ninian Comper
▸ St Cyprian, Clarence Gate (Glentworth St), Westminster. 1902–27. II*
▸ St Mary, Wellingborough, Northants. 1904–31. I
▸ St Giles, Wimborne St Giles, Dorset. 1910–42, rebuilding after fire. I
▸ St Martin's Chapel, Chailey Heritage, E. Sussex. 1913, 1927. II
▸ All Saints conventual church for the Community of All Saints, London Colney, Herts. 1927–38. II*
▸ St John the Baptist, Rothiemurcas, Highland. 1928–30. II
▸ County Hospital Chapel, Haywards Heath, W. Sussex. 1928–32
▸ Chapel of the House of Prayer, for the Community of the Servants of Christ, Burnham, Bucks. 1933–5.
▸ St Andrew's Cathedral, Aberdeen. Extension of chancel, 1934. A
▸ St Philip, Hawthorn Crescent, Cosham, Portsmouth. 1936–9. II*

J.B. Sebastian Comper
▸ St John, East Dulwich Rd, Southwark. 1951. Incorporating remains of Charles Bailey church, 1863–5
▸ RC St Gregory, Park Ave North, Northampton. 1952–4. Incomplete.
▸ St Helen, St Helen's Gardens, Kensington. 1954–5
▸ RC St Augustine, Amersham Hill, High Wycombe, Bucks. 1955–7
▸ Holy Trinity, Weston Lane, Weston, Southampton. 1960
▸ RC St Aidan, Manor Rd, Northampton. 1963

A.R. Conlon
▸ RC St Francis Friary Church, Tullideph Rd, Dundee. 1958. B

Connon and Chorley
▸ St Cuthbert and St Oswald, Winksley, Harrogate, N. Yorks. 1917. II

Alan D. Cooke
▸ Congregational church, High St, Stowmarket, Suffolk. 1953–5
▸ Congregational church, East Ham, LB Newham. 1957
▸ Congregational church, Wembley Park, LB Brent. 1957
▸ Congregational. Coverdale and Ebenezer Church, Stepney. LB Tower Hamlets. 1966–7

Samuel N. Cooke (S.N. Cooke and Partners after c.1950)
▸ St Hugh, Pineapple Grove, Stirchley, Birmingham. 1928 (mission church now incorporated into Church of the Ascension by Romilly B. Craze, q.v.)
▸ St Bartholomew, Allen's Farm Rd, Allen's Cross, Birmingham. 1936–8 (nave and tower); 1958 (chancel)
▸ Methodist. St George, Oakengates, Shrops. 1972

J. Coomans
▸ RC Sacred Heart, Middlesbrough. 1931–3. II

C.M. Cooper
▸ St Wilfrith, Moorends, W. Yorks. 1936

E. Priestley Cooper
▸ St Chad, Hutton-le-Hole, N. Yorks. 1957

Sir Edwin Cooper
▸ Chapel, Royal Star and Garter House, Richmond Hill, LB Richmond upon Thames, 1919–24. II
▸ Bryanston School Chapel, Dorset. 1930
▸ St Marylebone Cemetery Chapel, East End Rd, Finchley, LB Barnet. 1937. II

Donald M. Corder
▸ St Gabriel, Pitsea, Basildon, Essex. 1963

Thomas S. Cordiner
▸ RC St Brendan, Kelso St, Knightswood, Glasgow. 1947–9
▸ Church of Scotland. St Paul Provanmill, Greenrig St, Glasgow. 1948–51
▸ RC Immaculate Heart of Mary, Broomfield Rd, Springburn, Glasgow. 1950–2. B
▸ RC Our Lady of Fatima, Springfield Rd, Glasgow. 1953–6
▸ RC Our Lady of the Assumption, Bilsland Drive, Ruchill, Glasgow. 1953–6
▸ RC St Maria Gorletti, Bellrock St, Cranhill, Glasgow. 1954
▸ RC St Jude, Pendeen Rd, Barlanark, Glasgow. 1954–6
▸ RC St Thomas the Apostle, Smithycroft Rd, Glasgow. 1954–7. B
▸ RC St Gabriel, Marylee Rd, Cathcart, Glasgow. 1955
▸ RC Immaculate Conception, Maryhill Rd, Glasgow. 1955–6
▸ RC St Brigid, Prospecthill Rd, King's Park, Glasgow. 1955–7
▸ RC St Cadoc, Wellside Drive, Halfway, Glasgow. 1955–60
▸ RC St Margaret Mary, Dougrie Rd, Castlemilk, Glasgow. 1956–9. B
▸ RC Our Lady and St George, Sandwood Rd, Glasgow. 1957–9

▸ RC Christ the King, Carmunnock Rd, King's Park, Glasgow. 1957–9
▸ RC St Stephen, Dalmuin, Glasgow. 1958
▸ RC St Barnabas, Darleith St, Glasgow. 1960
▸ RC St Bernard, Wiltonburn Rd, Pollok, Glasgow. 1961–4
▸ Linn Crematorium, Lainshaw Drive, Glasgow. 1962. B
▸ RC St Gregory, Kelvindale Rd, Maryhill, Glasgow. 1965–71. Thomas Cordiner, Cunningham and Partners
▸ RC St Stephen, Fountainwell Drive, Sighthill, Glasgow. 1970–2

Cordingley and McIntyre
▸ All Saints, Lobley Hill, Gateshead. 1939
▸ St Clare, Central Ave, Newton Aycliffe, Co. Durham. 1951–5, 1966

Hector Corfiato
▸ RC Notre Dame de France, Leicester Place, Westminster. 1953–5
▸ RC Our Lady of Mount Carmel, Meins Rd, Blackburn. 1957–8
▸ RC Convent Chapel of the Adoration Reparatice, now Diocesan Training College, Beaufort St, RB Kensington and Chelsea. 1959
▸ RC St William of York, Du Cros Drive, Stanmore, LB Harrow. 1960

Hubert C. Corlette
▸ See also Sir Charles Nicholson
▸ St George, Frodingham Rd, Crosby, Scunthorpe. 1914–24
▸ St Paul, Ashby High St, Scunthorpe. 1925–7
▸ St Anselm, Station Rd, Hayes, LB Hillingdon. 1926–8

Frank Corr
▸ RC St Clement's Retreat Chapel, Antrim Rd, Belfast. 1966–7
▸ See also Liam McCormick

Covell, Matthews and Partners
▸ St Alban, Mottingham, LB Bromley. 1953
▸ St Francis, Sibthorpe Rd, Lee, LB Lewisham. 1953
▸ St Agnes, St Agnes Place, Kennington, LB Lambeth. 1956 (R. Covell)
▸ St George and St Andrew, Battersea, LB Wandsworth. 1956
▸ St Michael, Hatcham, LB Lewisham. 1957–8
▸ St Katherine, Eugenia Rd, Rotherhithe, LB Southwark. 1960
▸ St Mary, Charlton, LB Greenwich. 1961
▸ St Richard, Ham, LB Richmond. 1967
▸ St Laurence, Bromley Rd, Catford, LB Lewisham. 1967–8

Ronald Cowan
▸ Methodist church, Hartburn, Stockton-on-Tees. 1950

Cowper, Poole, Reynolds and Towns
▸ RC Pallotine Convent Chapel, Rochdale. 1966

George Bernard Cox
▸ RC Sacred Heart and St Margaret Mary, Aston, Birmingham. 1922. Tower by Cox, 1934
▸ RC Our Lady of Lourdes, Hednesford, Staffs. 1927–33
▸ RC Sacred Heart, Birmingham. 1935
▸ RC Sacred Heart and St Teresa, Coventry Rd, Coleshill, Warks. 1938–42. II
▸ RC St Augustine of Canterbury, Avenue Rd, Birmingham. 1939
▸ RC Sacred Heart, Warwick Rd, Acocks Green, Birmingham. 1940
▸ RC St Peter and Paul, Swadlincote, Derbys. 1957–8
▸ See also Harrison and Cox

Thomas A. Crawford
▸ St Francis, Acklam Rd, Middlesbrough. 1934–57
▸ RC St Thomas More, Easington Rd, W. Hartlepool. 1953
▸ RC St Cuthbert, Stockton Rd, W. Hartlepool. 1954
▸ RC St Anne, Welbeck Ave, Darlington, Co. Durham. 1956
▸ RC St Cuthbert, Yarm Rd, Stockton-on-Tees. 1958
▸ RC St John the Evangelist, Central Ave, Billingham, Teesside. 1959–60
▸ RC Our Lady of the Most Holy Rosary, Sidlow Rd, Billingham, Teesside. 1959–60
▸ RC St Mary, Central Ave, Newton Aycliffe, Co. Durham. 1960
▸ RC St John Vianney, King Oswy Drive, W. View Estate, Hartlepool. 1961
▸ RC English Martyrs, Hardwick Rd, Stockton-on-Tees. 1961. By Crawford and Spencer

Romilly B. Craze
▸ St Martin, Anlaby Rd, Hull. 1938–9
▸ St Paul, East Bank Rd, Arbourthorne, Sheffield. 1939
▸ RC St George Cathedral, Southwark. 1953–66, rebuilding and clerestory to Pugin's 1839–55 building. II
▸ St Peter, Irving Walk, Maybush, Southampton. 1956
▸ St Cuthbert, Wembley, LB Brent. 1958–9
▸ Ascension, Pineapple Grove, Stirchley, Birmingham. 1972–4

H.B. Creswell
▸ St Philip, Rugby, Warks. 1924
▸ St Alban, Mercer Ave, Coventry. 1929

Crickmay and Sons
▸ All Saints, Easton, Portland, Dorset. 1914–17
▸ St Edmund, Weymouth, Dorset. 1954

C.M. Crickmer
▸ RC St Ninian, Victory Ave, Gretna, Dumfries and Galloway. 1917. Government team led by Raymond Unwin. See C.E. Simmons. B
▸ All Saints Episcopal Church, Annan Rd, Gretna, Dumfries and Galloway. 1917. Govt. team led by Raymond Unwin. See Geoffrey Lucas. B
▸ St Andrew's Parish Church, Carnwath Rd, Gretna, Dumfries and Galloway. 1917. B
▸ Episcopal. St John the Evangelist, Ladysmith Rd, Eastriggs, Dumfries and Galloway. 1917.
▸ Farrington Girls' School chapel, Chislehurst, LB Bromley. 1934

W.H. Cripps
▸ Methodist church, Queen's Drive, Swindon, Wilts. 1959
▸ Methodist church (Mint), Fore St, Exeter. 1969–70 (Cripps and Stewart)

W.E. Cross
▸ Holy Trinity, High St, LB Hounslow. 1961

Crouch, Butler and Savage (partner responsible, W. Moss)
▸ Methodist. Hall Green Church, Reddings Lane, Hall Green, Birmingham. 1924
▸ Methodist. Beckminster Church, Birches Barn Rd, Penn Fields, Wolverhampton, W. Mids. 1926
▸ Methodist. New Rd Church, New Rd, Stourbridge, W. Mids. 1927–8
▸ Methodist. Warley Woods Church, Abbey Rd, Bearwood, W. Mids. 1928; demolished c.1993
▸ Methodist. Slade Rd Church, Erdington, Birmingham. 1931

J.J. Crowe
▸ St James, Clifton, Rotherham. 1934. With S. Careless
▸ St Michael, Gidea Park, LB Havering. 1937–8. With S. Careless
▸ St Peter, Harold Wood, LB Havering. 1939
▸ St Francis of Assisi, Fencepiece Rd, Ilford, LB Redbridge. 1956

Cruickshank and Seward
▸ St Luke, Roose Rd, Barrow-in-Furness. 1962–4
▸ Victoria Park Chapel, Manchester. 1968. By J.R.G. Seward.

C.W. Crush
▸ Chapel, Salford Training College, Salford. 1935

J. Arnold Crush
▸ RC Douai Abbey Church, Woolhampton, Berks. 1928. II*
▸ RC Our Lady of Lourdes, New Southgate, LB Enfield. 1935–6

T.J. Cullen
▸ RC Loretto Convent Chapel, Coleraine, Co. Londonderry. 1939. B

Edward Cullinan Associates
▸ St Mary, Church Rd, Barnes, LB Richmond-on-Thames. 1984–6; rebuilding after fire incorporating C16–17 tower. II*

Clifford Culpin and Partners
▸ RC St Joseph the Worker, Stanley Rd, Bracknell, Berks. 1961–2
▸ St Andrew, Cuffley, Herts. 1966–8

Cumbernauld Development Corporation
▸ Scottish Episcopal Church, Cumbernauld, North Lanarkshire. 1962

P.H. Currey and C.C. Thompson
▸ St Mary the Virgin, Dale Rd, Buxton, Derbys. 1914–15
▸ All Saints, Totley Hall Lane, Totley, Sheffield. 1924
▸ St Bartholomew, Nightingale Rd, Derby. 1927. adds. 1967 by Humphrey and Hurst (q.v.)
▸ Theological College for Society of the Sacred Mission, Kelham Hall, Newark, Notts. 1927–8. II
▸ St Stephen, Sinfin Lane, Normanton, Derby. 1935. P.H. Currey.

W.T. Curtis and D. Robertson (Middlesex CC)
▸ Shenley Hospital Chapel, Shenley, London Colney, Herts. 1938

W.J. Dacombe
▸ Christian Science. First Church, Christchurch Rd, Bournemouth. 1926

John L. Seaton Dahl
▸ Norwegian Lutheran. St Olav, Albion St, Bermondsey, LB Southwark. 1927. II

Lawrence Dale
▸ St Alban the Martyr, Oxford. 1933
▸ St Michael, Marston Rd, New Marston, Oxford. 1954–6
▸ St Swithun, Kennington, Oxford. 1956–8

Thomas L. Dale
▸ St Alban the Martyr, Oxford. 1935
▸ St Michael and All Angels, Marston Rd, Oxford. 1956–7

Thomas Llewelyn Daniels
▸ Welsh Presbyterian Church, Green Man, Leytonstone, LB Waltham Forest. 1957

Clifford H. Dann
▸ Methodist church, Heartsease Lane, Norwich. 1955–6

Trevor Dannatt
▸ Congregational church, Lawn Terrace, Blackheath, LB Lewisham. 1957 incorporating Brandon and Richie church, 1853
▸ Society of Friends Meeting House, Lawn Terrace, Blackheath, LB Lewisham. 1973–4

Darnton, Elgee and Wrightson
▸ Swedish Lutheran, Linthorpe Rd, Middlesbrough. 1963
▸ St Hilda, Redcar, Cleveland. 1971–2. With Jackson and O'Connor.

Peter J. Darvall
▸ Christ Church, Kennington, LB Lambeth. 1959–60

Norman Davey
▸ St Aldhelm, Regent St, Swindon. 1967

T.E. Davidson and J.R. Sherwood
▸ Christian Science. First Church, Kingston-on-Thames. 1933
▸ Christian Science. First Church, Leytonstone, LB Waltham Forest. 1933. By J.R. Sherwood

William Davidson
▸ St Barbara, Stilbottle, Northumberland. 1929

G. Parry Davies and Associates
▸ RC St Joseph, Bryn Stanley, Denbighshire. 1968

R.K. Davies
▸ Methodist church, Greens Lane, Hartburn, Stockton-on-Tees. 1975–6

N. Davis
▸ St Francis, Laurel Rd, Priory Estate, Dudley, W. Mids. 1932

Geoffrey Davy
▸ St Andrew Methodist Church, Old Lane, Beeston, Leeds. 1956

Ivor Day and O'Brien
▸ RC Holy Family, Marlowe Rd, Park North, Swindon, Wilts. 1967–9
▸ RC St John Fisher, Thanet Rd, LB Bexley. 1974

Wilfred T. Deacon and Laing
▸ RC St David, Childwall, Liverpool. 1945
▸ RC Holy Spirit, Liverpool. 1945
▸ RC St Mary Magdalene, Stony Stratford, Milton Keynes. 1957–8

G.B. Deas and Henry Hubbard
▸ Templehall Church, Beauly Place, Kirkaldy, Fife. 1955–6

George D. Denbigh
▸ Methodist church, Mereside Estate, Blackpool, Lancs. 1958

C.F.W. Dening
▸ St Christopher, Hampstead Rd, Arnos Vale, Bristol. 1931
▸ St Barnabas, Daventry Rd, Knowle, Bristol. 1938

John L. Denman
▸ Chapel at Royal Masonic School for Girls, Rickmansworth, Herts. 1928–33. II
▸ St George, Shirley, LB Croydon. 1953

E.D. Dennis
▸ St Mark, Layton, Blackpool, Lancs. 1923

Denny and Brian
▸ RC Our Lady of the Annunciation, Wellesley Rd, LB Croydon. 1964

Donald C. Denton-Smith
▸ Methodist church, Tuddenham, Suffolk. 1952

Louis de Soissons
▸ St Francis of Assisi, Church Road, Welwyn Garden City, Herts. 1934–5
▸ St Francis of Assisi, St Albans, Herts. 1940
▸ Baptist. Old George St Chapel, Catherine St, Plymouth. 1958
▸ Unitarian Chapel, Notte St, Plymouth. 1958
▸ RC St Teresa, Blandford, Efford, Plymouth. 1958

W.J. Devlin
▸ RC Convent of the Good Shepherd, Colinton, Edinburgh. 1928. B

Arthur Stansfeld Dixon
▸ Bishop's Chapel, Bishop's Croft, Harborne, Birmingham. 1923
▸ St Giles, Rowley Village, Rowley Regis, W. Mids. 1923–6 (incorporating east end of a church of 1904; with H.W. Hobbiss, q.v.)

J.E. Dixon-Spain
▸ Evangelical Church (St Alphage), Burnt Oak, LB Barnet. 1928. Reconstructed 1952 after war damage.

Archibald M. Doak and Alexander R. Whitelaw
▸ St Nicholas, Calder Rd, Sighthill, Edinburgh. 1955

Eduardo Dodds
▸ RC St Thomas of Canterbury, Gillingham, Kent. 1958. With Kenneth C. White.
▸ RC English Martyrs, Frindsbury Rd, Strood, Kent. 1963–4

L. Dodsley
▸ St Mowden, Sutton-in-Ashfield, Notts. 1936

Dodson, Gillatt and Partners
▸ St Peter and St Andrew, Beanfield Ave, Corby, Northants. 1966–7

W.J. Doherty
▸ RC St Columbkille, Straw, Draperstown, Co. Derry. 1926, remodelling of 1853 church.

J.L. Donnelly
▸ RC St Joseph, Cooneen, Co. Fermanagh. 1939–42

J.A. Douglas (MPBW)
▸ RC Our Lady Queen of Peace, Home Rd, Bulford, Wilts. 1961–9

George Downie
▸ Presbyterian. Rankin Memorial Church, Lorenzo Drive, Norris Green, Liverpool. 1930–1

H.P. Burke Downing
▸ St Barnabas, Gorringe Park Ave, Mitcham, LB Merton. 1914
▸ Chapel, Brighton Training College, Brighton, E. Sussex. 1921
▸ St John, Walthamstow, LB Waltham Forest. 1921–2
▸ St Margaret, Putney, LB Wandsworth. 1924
▸ All Saints, London Rd, Hackbridge, LB Sutton. 1931
▸ St Augustine, Broadwater Rd, Tooting, LB Wandsworth. 1931

J.F. Doyle and S.J. Doyle
▸ St Barnabas, Liverpool. 1925

E.P. Drongle
▸ RC St Joseph, Nympsfield, Glos. 1923, perhaps from a design by Charles Hansom.

Henry M.R. Drury
▸ St Paul, Burnthouse Lane, Exeter, Devon. 1951–2

George Drysdale
▸ RC Holy Family, Coventry Rd, Small Heath, Birmingham. 1928
▸ RC Memorial Chapel, Catterick Camp, N. Yorks. 1930
▸ RC Immaculate Heart of Mary, Hayes, LB Hillingdon. 1931
▸ RC St Chad, Whitworth Rd, South Norwood, LB Croydon. 1932
▸ RC Our Lady of the Rosary and St Teresa of Lisieux, Parkfield Rd, Saltley, Birmingham. 1933
▸ RC St Joseph, Westham Rd, Weymouth, Dorset. 1934
▸ RC Our Lady and St Hubert, Bleakhouse Rd, Warley, W. Midlands. 1934–5
▸ RC Sacred Heart, Pembroke Rd, Ruislip Manor, LB Hillingdon. 1939

Edward Ford Duncannon
▸ Congregational church, Gerrard's Cross, Bucks. 1922

John Walter Dudding and Partners
▸ RC St John, Stapleford, Notts. 1952
▸ Methodist church, Carlton, Notts. 1958

P. Dunham, Widdup and Harrison
▸ St Francis, Carteret Rd, Luton, Beds. 1959–60

Edwin T. Dunn
▸ St Margaret of Antioch, Perth Rd, Ilford, LB Redbridge. 1913–14
▸ St Luke, Baxter Rd, Ilford, LB Redbridge. 1914–15
▸ St Mary the Virgin, High Road, Ilford, LB Redbridge. Chancel. 1919–20

Austin Durst
▸ St Paul, Bushey, Herts. 1923–31

S.E. Dykes Bower
▸ All Saints, Hockerill, Bishops Stortford, Herts. 1936
▸ St Vedast-alias-Foster, City of London. 1953–62 rebuilding within Wren walls firebombed 1940. I
▸ Holy Spirit (St Matthew), Fawcett Rd, Southsea, Portsmouth. Restoration of Micklethwaite and Nicholson (q.v) church, 1956–8
▸ St John, Newbury, Berks. 1955–7. Hall 1982–3 by Roderick Gradidge. II
▸ St Nicholas, Great Yarmouth, Norfolk. 1957–60. Rebuilding within medieval walls after firebomb 1942. A
▸ St Nicholas Ferrar (Church of the Good Shepherd), Arbury Rd, Cambridge. 1957–8, 1963–4
▸ St Edmundsbury Cathedral (St James), Bury St Edmunds, Suffolk. 1960–; transepts, crossing, sanctuary and cloister to 1503– parish church. I

▸ Lancing College Chapel. West end, 1962, to chapel of 1868–1911. I

William Parker Dyson and B.A. Hebeler
▸ St Cuthbert, Hermingthorpe, Rotherham. 1935

Robert G. Easdale
▸ St Helen, Carlton, Barnsley. 1954–5

John Easton
▸ Jesus Christ and Latter Day Saints, Kinfauns Drive, Drumchapel, Glasgow. 1961–4. Now Kinfauns Centre. B

Arthur Eaton and Son
▸ St Edmund, Sinfin Ave, Allenton, Derby. 1939
▸ Christian Science Church, Derby. 1939–40

A. Eden and Associates
▸ St Michael and All Angels, Bradford. 1968

F.C. Eden
▸ All Saints, All Saints Rd, Weston-super-Mare. S. aisle and Lady chapel, to G.F. Bodley 1898–1902 church. II*
▸ All Saints, Pembridge Rd, Clifton, Bristol. 1928. Alterations and sacristy. See also R. Potter.
▸ St George, Wash Common, Newbury. 1933
▸ King Charles the Martyr, Dugdale Hill Lane, Potter's Bar, Herts. 1939

Wilfrid B. Edwards
▸ Venerable Bede, Benwell Grove, Newcastle upon Tyne. 1936–7
▸ St Peter, Cowgate, Newcastle upon Tyne. 1952–3. With Roy M. Manby.
▸ St Francis, Heaton, Newcastle upon Tyne. 1957–8

Charles Ernest Elcock and John Brooke
▸ St Peter, Earle St, Crewe, Chester. 1914–23

Frank H. Elder
▸ St Augustine, Bromley Common, LB Bromley. 1957–8

Elder and Cannon
▸ RC Holy Name, Pentland Rd, Glasgow. 1983–4

E.W.T. Elford
▸ RC Holy Family, Beacon Park Rd, Pennycross, Plymouth. 1955. Completed 1961 by Louis de Soissons and Partners.

Anthony Ellis
▸ RC St Anthony of Padua, Queen's Drive, Mossley Hill, Liverpool. 1931–2

William Ellis
▸ RC Holy Rosary, Fitton Hill, Oldham. 1954–5

Arnold England
▸ St Anne, Blackpool, Lancs. 1928

R.E. Enthoven
▸ Chapel Royal, Foundation of St Katharine, Butcher's Row, LB Tower Hamlets. 1951–2

Raymond Erith

▸ St Andrew, St Andrew's Rd, Felixstowe, Suffolk. 1929–31. With Hilda Mason. II*
▸ St Mary, Paddington Green, City of Westminster. 1972–3. With Quinlan Terry. Internal remodelling. II*

Frederick Etchells

▸ St Andrew, West Dean, W. Sussex. 1934 remodelling of C13 and C18 church after fire. II*
▸ St James, Abinger, Surrey. 1950 rebuilding of bombed medieval church, 1964 rebuilt after fire. II*

Cecil W.T. Evans

▸ St Luke, Battery Hill, Winchester, Hampshire. 1960

Evans and Powell

▸ RC St Thomas, Bampfylde Way, Southway, Plymouth. 1964
▸ RC Our Lady Star of the Sea, Brixham, Torbay. 1967
▸ RC St Peter, Tavistock Rd, Crownhill, Plymouth. 1967–70. By John Evans

Conor P. Fahy

▸ RC St Joseph, Merton High St, LB Merton. 1966

Arthur Fairbrother and Partner

▸ RC St Catherine of Siena, School Lane, Didsbury, Manchester. 1928–9
▸ RC Sacred Heart, Rochdale. 1957–8
▸ RC Our Lady at Lourdes, Leasowe, Wallasey, Wirral. 1959
▸ St Michael, Oldham. 1959–60
▸ RC St Anthony, Farnham Rd, Farnham Royal, Bucks. 1960. Completed 1964 by Desmond Williams and Associates.
▸ St Andrew, Orford, Warrington, Cheshire. 1965

Fairbrother, Hall and Hodges

▸ Presbyterian. St George, Blackpool, Lancs. 1956

Harry S. Fairhurst

▸ St Martin, Hall Rd, Wythenshawe, Manchester. 1958

Reginald Fairlie (Reginald Fairlie and Partners from c.1950)

▸ Crichton Stuart Memorial Chapel, Falkland, Fife. 1912–14. Unfinished.
▸ House of Falkland Memorial Chapel, Edinburgh. 1912–16. B
▸ RC St Benedict's Abbey Church, Fort Augustus, Highland. 1914–80. (Completed by A.R. Conlon, later by C.W. Gray)
▸ RC Our Lady and St Bride, Stenhouse St, Cowdenbeath, Fife. 1921–3
▸ RC Chapel, St Joseph's Convent of Mercy, Dundee. 1921. B
▸ RC St Serf, Highvalleyfield, Culross, Fife. 1922
▸ RC St Joseph, Kelty, Fife. 1922
▸ RC St Agatha, Methil, Fife. 1923
▸ RC St Andrew, Rothesay, Isle of Bute, Argyll and Bute. 1923. A
▸ RC Church, Tarbrax, Midlothian. 1923
▸ RC St Thomas, Addiewell, Midlothian. 1923–4

▸ RC Convent Chapel, St Mary of Egypt Home, Barrhead, East Renfrewshire. 1924
▸ Parish Church, Methil, Fife. 1924–5
▸ Episcopal Church of Scotland. St Aidan, Gullane, East Lothian. 1926. B
▸ RC Holy Cross, Edinburgh. 1927
▸ RC St Patrick, Cowgate, Edinburgh. 1928–9. Facade.
▸ RC St Margaret, Roy Bridge, Lochaber, Highland. 1929
▸ RC St Peter and St Paul, Byron St, Dundee. 1929. B
▸ RC St Columba, Birnam, Dunkeld, Perth and Kinross. 1932
▸ RC St Ninian, Derran Drive, Bowhill, Fife. 1932
▸ RC St Francis Friary, Tullideph Rd, Dundee. 1933. B
▸ RC Chapel, Sacred Heart Convent, Craiglockhart, Edinburgh. 1933. B
▸ Chapel (The Temple), Belladrum, Kitarlity, Highland. 1935
▸ RC Notre Dame Convent Chapel, Clerkhill, West Dumbarton. 1935
▸ RC Holy Family, Dunblane, Perth and Kinross. 1935. C (S)
▸ RC St Patrick, Mallaig, Lochaber, Highland. 1935. C (S)
▸ Cloister at RC St Matthew, Carruthers St, Rosewell. 1935. B
▸ See also Archibald Macpherson.
▸ RC St Mary and Immaculate Conception, Belford Rd, Fort William, Highland. 1936–8. A
▸ RC Sacred Heart and St Anthony, Armadale, West Lothian. 1937
▸ RC Sacred Heart, Cowie, Stirling. 1937
▸ RC St Mary, Jedburgh, Scottish Borders. 1937. B
▸ RC Our Lady and St Bean, Marydale, Cannich, Highland. 1938
▸ RC Our Lady Star of the Sea, Queen St, Tayport, Fife. 1938–9. B
▸ RC St Margaret Mary, Boswall Parkway, Edinburgh. 1939
▸ RC St John Vianney, Fernieside Gardens, Edinburgh. 1952
▸ RC St Anne, Corpach, Highland. 1952
▸ RC St Catharine Labourne, Lamont Rd, North Balornock, Glasgow. 1952–3
▸ RC St Augustine, Ashgill Rd, Milton, Glasgow. 1954–6. B
▸ RC St Laurence, Kinfauns Drive, Drumchapel, Glasgow. 1954–7. B
▸ RC St Paul, Dumbarton Rd, Whiteinch, Glasgow. 1957–60

Peter Falconer

▸ St Barnabas, Box, Minchinhampton, Glos. 1953
▸ RC Chapel of Our Lady of Victories, Brown's Hill, Chalford, Glos. 1960
▸ Presbyterian. St Andrew, Dartford, Kent. 1962
▸ RC Church, Stonehouse, Glos. 1966 (with Anthony Thompson)
▸ RC St Thomas More, Cheltenham, Glos. 1967–8

Thomas Falconer

▸ St Alban, Parliament St, Stroud, Glos. 1915–16
▸ St George, Nailsworth, Glos. 1957–8 (successor practice)

H.E. Falmer

▸ St Anne, Coventry. 1930–1

Cyril Farey

▸ St Michael, Tokyngton, LB Brent. 1932. East end rebuilt 1966
▸ St Mark, Ferry Rd, Teddington, LB Richmond. 1938–9
▸ St Peter, Vera Ave, Grange Park, LB Enfield. 1941
▸ All Hallows, Horsenden Lane, N. Greenford, LB Brent. 1942

Michael A. Farey

▸ St Andrew Roxbourne, Malvern Ave, Pinner, LB Harrow. 1956. With John J. Adams.
▸ St Luke's Church centre, Kilburn, LB Brent. 1960
▸ Good Shepherd, LB Hounslow. 1960
▸ RC Christ the Redeemer, Allenby Rd, Southall, LB Ealing. 1964

Farquharson, McMorran and Whitby

▸ Free Church, Woodside Rd, Amersham, Bucks. 1960–2

B.H. Fawcett

▸ St Luke, Scalby Rd, Scarborough, N. Yorks. 1932, enlarged 1956

Sidney Colwyn Ffoulkes

▸ Baptist chapel, Park Rd, Ruthin, Denbighshire. 1934

Sir Bernard Fielden

▸ Presbyterian Church, Unthank Rd, Norwich. 1954–5

T. Phillips Figgis

▸ United Reformed Church. St Columba, Alfred St, Oxford. 1916

Cecil E.M. Fillmore

▸ Congregational (URC). Broadway Church, Broadway, Walsall, W. Mids. 1959

John Finlayson and I. Langlands

▸ URC. St John, Somerset Rd, LB Barnet. 1967–8

Kenneth Finlayson

▸ Methodist Church, Huntly St, Inverness, Highland. 1964–5

John J. Fisher, Harold J. Hollingsworth and Partners

▸ Baptist church, Coronation Rd, Hull. 1957
▸ Methodist. St Mark, Ashby Rd, Scunthorpe. 1960

Gilbert Flavel

▸ RC Holy Rood, Abingdon Rd, Oxford. 1959–61
▸ RC St Peter, Eynsham, Oxford. 1967, incorporating work begun 1939

J.B. Fletcher

▸ St Alban, Llangyfelach Rd, Treboeth, Swansea. 1927–8

Hugh H. Ford

▸ St Richard hall/church, Langney Village, Eastbourne, E. Sussex. 1956–8

Thomas F. Ford

▸ St Michael, Upper Wickham Lane, East Wickham, LB Bromley. 1932
▸ St Barnabas, Eltham, LB Greenwich. 1933
▸ St John, Waterloo Rd, LB Lambeth. 1951 restoration of 1822–4 church by Francis Bedford as the Festival of Britain church. II*
▸ St Mary the Virgin, Wickham St, Welling, LB Bexley. 1954–5
▸ St Michael and All Angels, Paulsgrove, Portsmouth. 1955
▸ St Faith, Charles St, Landport, Portsmouth. 1956
▸ All Saints, Ripon Rd, Woolwich, LB Greenwich. 1956
▸ All Hallows, Pepper St, LB Southwark. 1957
▸ St Peter, Bexleyheath, LB Bexley. 1957–8
▸ St Michael and All Angels, Bishop Ken Rd, Harrow Weald, LB Harrow. 1958
▸ St Crispin, Southwark Park Rd, LB Southwark. 1958–9
▸ Christ Church, Battersea Park Rd, LB Wandsworth. 1959
▸ Holy Trinity, Rotherhithe St, LB Southwark. 1960
▸ St Alban, Gossops Green, Crawley, W. Sussex. 1961–2

W.A. Forsyth

▸ St Andrew, Church Lane, Kingsbury, LB Brent. 1934. Rebuilding of St Andrew, Wells St, City of Westminster.
▸ Cathedral Church of St Mary, Blackburn. 1820–6, extended 1926. Laurence King corona, 1961. II*

Reginald C. Foster

▸ St Erkenwald, Lovett Rd, LB Barking and Dagenham. 1954–5
▸ St Edmund, Loughton, Essex. 1957–8

Foster and Barber

▸ Methodist church, Ramsgate, Kent. 1957

Fosbrooke and Bedingfield

▸ RC Sacred Heart, Leicester. 1924

C.H. Fowler

▸ St George, East Boldon, Sunderland. 1920–3. Extended by Edmund Oakley, 1933
▸ Ascension, Seaside Lane, Easington Colliery, Co. Durham. 1925–8. Interior by J.N. Comper 1951.

Eric C. Francis

▸ RC St Teresa of Lisieux, Taunton, Somerset. 1958

Freeman and Ogilvy

▸ All Saints, Gobowen, Shrops. 1928, 1934. Tower 1945

Peter French

▸ RC St Michael, Ashtead, Surrey. 1966–7

W.W. Friskin

▸ RC St Teresa (formerly St Michael), Graham St, Dundee. 1938. B

E.M. Galloway and Partners
- RC Christ the King, Bitterne Rd, Bitterne, Southampton. 1960

A. Gardiner (of Gardiner and McLean)
- Church of Scotland. St David, Boreland Drive, Knightswood, Glasgow. 1938–9. B

Alfred H. Gardner and Baldwin
- Christchurch, Cheylesmore, Coventry. 1954–8
- Friends Meeting House, Queens Rd, Leicester. 1955

Bradshaw Gass and Hope
- Holy Angels, Claremont, 1926. II. Demolished 1996
- Congregational church, Ross-on-Sea, Denbighshire. 1932
- Congregational church, Caernarvon, Gwynedd. 1932

William Gauldie (of Gauldie and Wright)
- St Ninian's Episcopal Church, Longston Rd, Dundee. 1938. B

Alick Gavin
- Methodist. St Andrew, The Grove, Slough, Berks. 1965–7

A.E. Geens, M.G. Cross, R.H. Sims
- St Joseph College Chapel, Ipswich. 1967

Sir Alfred Gelder (Gelder and Kitchen)
- Methodist church, South Rd, Southall, LB Ealing. 1916. II
- Methodist church, Cottingham Rd, Hull (Newland). 1927–8 (Gelder and Kitchen)
- Methodist church, Derringham Bank, Willerby Rd, Hull. 1934 (Gelder and Kitchen). Chapel on adjoining site by B.W. Blanchard, 1957–8
- St Cuthbert, Marlborough Ave, Hull. 1956 by Douglas Potter of Gelder and Kitchen.

Sir Frederick Gibberd
- RC Liverpool Metropolitan Cathedral of Christ the King. 1960–7. II*
- RC Hopwood Hall, former chapel, now library, De la Salle College, Hopwood, Greater Manchester. 1963–5. II
- RC Douai Abbey Church, Woolhampton, Berks. extended 1964. II*
- Ecumenical. St George's Chapel, Heathrow Airport, LB Hillingdon. 1968. With Jack Forrest.
- Baptist. Thomas Cooper Memorial Church, High St, Lincoln. 1973–4

J. Harold Gibbons
- St Michael, St Michael's Ave, Bramhall, Cheshire. 1910–38. Tower by G.G. Pace.
- St Francis, Charminster Rd, Bournemouth. 1929–30
- St Francis, Gladstone Park, LB Brent. 1933. II
- St Jerome, Dawley Rd, Harlington, LB Hillingdon. 1933–40
- St Mary, St Leonard's Ave, Kenton, LB Harrow. 1935–6. II*
- St Barnabas, Raglan Way, Northolt, LB Ealing. 1939. II
- Transfiguration, Kempston, Bedford. 1939
- SS Peter and Paul, LB Bromley. 1948–57, rebuilding after bombing, retaining medieval tower. II
- St Cyprian, Frecheville, Derbys. 1953
- St Barnabas, Raggan Way, Northolt Park, LB Ealing. 1954
- St Philip and St James, Whitwell Rd, LB Newham. 1954–5
- Ascension, Preston, LB Brent. 1957

Gibson and Taylor
- Church of Ireland. St John Evangelist, Castlereagh Rd, Belfast. 1955–7. B

Fr. Gilbert
- RC Our Lady of Lourdes and St Joseph, Leigh Rd, Southend-on-Sea. 1926

Gilbert and Hobson
- RC Sacred Heart, Shanklin, Isle of Wight. 1956–7

P.S. Gilby
- RC St Philip Neri, Catharine St, Liverpool. 1914–20
- RC Holy Name, Longmoor Lane, Fazakerley, Liverpool. 1964–5. (P.S. Gilby and Associates)

Robert Gibson and Ernest D. Taylor
- Church of Ireland. St Christopher, Mersey St, Belfast. 1931. With Henry Seaver.
- St John the Evangelist, Orangefield, Belfast. 1957

N.N. Gilkinson
- Church of the Nazarene, Broomhill Drive, Glasgow. 1969–72

Eric Gill
- RC St Peter the Apostle, Gorleston-on-Sea, Norfolk. 1938–9. II*

Macdonald Gill
- Findon Valley Mission Church and hall, near Chichester, W. Sussex. 1935

Gillespie, Kidd and Coia (Isi Metzstein and Andy McMillan designers from 1956–)
- RC St Anne, Whitevale St, Dennistoun, Glasgow. 1931–5. A
- RC St Patrick, Orangefield Place, Greenock, Inverclyde. 1935. A
- RC St Columba of Iona, Hophill Rd, Maryhill, Glasgow. 1937. A
- RC St Peter-in-Chains, S. Crescent Rd, Ardrossan, North Ayrshire. 1938. A
- RC Pavilion, British Empire Exhibition, Bellahouston Park, Glasgow. 1938. Demolished.
- RC St Columbkille, Main St, Rutherglen, Glasgow. 1939–40. A
- RC Holy Family, Port Glasgow, Inverclyde. 1946–59. A
- RC St Eunan, E. Thomson St, Clydebank, W. Dunbartonshire. 1950
- RC St David, Meadowhead Rd, Plains, Airdrie, N. Lanarks. 1950
- RC St Kevin, Rosebank Terrace, Bargeddie, Coatbridge, N. Lanarks. 1950
- RC St Matthew, Kinkintilloch Rd, Bishopsbriggs, E. Dunbartonshire. 1950. C
- RC St Lawrence, Kilmacolm Rd, Greenock, Inverclyde. 1951–4 A
- St Michael, Cardross Rd, Dunbarton, W. Dunbartonshire. 1952–4. B
- St Andrew, Whinhall Rd, Airdrie, N. Lanarks. 1953
- RC SS Peter and Paul, Arrochar, W. Dunbartonshire. 1953
- RC St Joachim, Inzievar Terrace, Carmyle, Glasgow. 1954–5. C
- RC St Paul, Warnut Rd, Auchmuty, Glenrothes, Fife. 1956–7. B
- RC St Paul, Shettleston Rd, Sandyhills, Glasgow. 1957–9. B
- RC St Kessog, Balloch Rd, Balloch, W. Dunbartonshire. 1957
- RC St Charles, Kelvinside Gardens, Glasgow. 1958–60. B
- RC St Peter's College, Cardross, W. Dunbartonshire. 1959–66. A
- RC St Vincent de Paul, Main St, Thornliebank, E. Renfrewshire. 1959
- RC St Martin, Ardencraig Rd, Castlemilk, Glasgow. 1959–61. B
- RC St Mary of the Angels, Camelon, Falkirk. 1960–1. A
- RC St Mary, Dean Rd and Linlithgow Rd, Bo'ness, Falkirk. 1962
- RC St Joseph, Faifley Rd, Duntocher, W. Dunbartonshire. 1961–4. Destroyed by fire 1993.
- RC St Patrick, Low Craigends, Kilsyth, N. Lanarks. 1961–4. B
- RC St Bride, East Kilbride, S. Lanarks. 1963–4. A. Campanile destroyed 1983.
- RC St Benedict, Westerhouse Rd, Easterhouse, Glasgow. 1962–5. B
- RC Sacred Heart, Kyle Rd, Kildrum, Cumbernauld, N. Lanarks. 1964. A
- RC Our Lady of Good Counsel, Craigpark, Dennistoun, Glasgow. 1964–6. A
- RC College Chapel and Convent, Sisters of Notre-Dame-de-Namur, Bearsden, S. Lanarks. 1966

- RC St Benedict, Drumchapel Rd, Glasgow. 1964–70. Demolished 1991.
- RC St Margaret, Sinclair St, Clydebank, W. Dunbartonshire. 1970–2. B
- Robinson College Chapel, Cambridge. 1974–80

Gillespie and Scott
- Martyr's Church, St Andrew's, Fife. 1926–8, incorporating earlier work by John Milne. B
- Baptist church, Church St, Glenrothes, Fife. 1961–2. Formerly St Luke's Episcopal.

E.B. Glanfield
- Methodist church, Neasden, LB Brent. 1937–8

Gerard Goalen
- RC Our Lady of Fatima, Harlow, Essex. 1958–60
- RC Good Shepherd, Woodthorpe, Notts. 1962–4.
- RC St Gregory the Great, Victoria Rd, S. Ruislip, LB Hillingdon. 1966–7
- RC St Gabriel, St John's Villas, Upper Holloway, LB Islington. 1966–8
- RC St James, Harlow, Essex. 1969
- RC St Christopher, Cranford, LB Hounslow. 1969–71.
- RC University Chaplaincy Centre, Cambridge. 1976.

W. Emil Godfrey
- Christ Church, Northcourt Rd, Abingdon, Oxon. 1961. Converted C13 barn. B

Henry Goddard and Partners
- St Elizabeth, Nether Hall Rd, Leicester. 1959

E. Goldie
- RC Our Lady and St Peter, Garlands Rd, Leatherhead, Surrey. 1922–3

Joseph Goldie
- RC St Dunstan, Woking, Surrey. 1927. With G.R.G. Topham.
- RC St Thomas More, Lordship Lane, Camberwell, LB Southwark. 1929
- RC St Patrick, Pentrebane St, Cardiff. 1929–30
- RC Assumption of Our Lady, Englefield Green, Surrey. 1930–1

Felix Goldsmith
- Presbyterian. John Knox Church, Stepney, LB Tower Hamlets. 1956

H.S. Goodhart-Rendel
- St Mary the Virgin, Graham Terrace (Bourne St), City of Westminster. 1922–36. Clergy house, porch and south aisle. II
- St Wilfrid, Elm Grove, Brighton. 1932–4. II. Converted to flats.
- Holy Spirit, Ewloe, Flintshire. 1937–8
- Chapel of the Royal School for Daughters of the Officers of the Army, Bath. 1937–41, 1960s. Not completed to Goodhart-Rendel's design.
- St Mary the Virgin, Worton Rd, LB Hounslow. 1937–55
- Convent of the Poor Clares Collettines, Hawarden, Flintshire. 1944

St John the Evangelist, St Leonard's on Sea. 1951–8. II. Rebuilding of Arthur Blomfield church, incorporating original tower and baptistry.
▸ RC Our Lady of the Seven Sorrows, Stoppage Lane, Liverpool. 1951
▸ RC St Thomas More, Maresfield Gardens, Hampstead, LB Camden. 1951–4. Extension to church converted from artist's studio by Sir R. Blomfield.
▸ RC Chapel to John Fisher School, Peaks Hill, Purley, LB Croydon. 1951–9.
▸ Household Brigade Memorial Cloister, Royal Military Chapel, Birdcage Walk, City of Westminster. 1954–5. II. See also Trew and Dunn.
▸ RC St Cecilia, Stonecot Hill, North Cheam, Surrey. 1954–9
▸ RC Sacred Heart, Cobham, Surrey. 1955–9
▸ RC SS Francis and Anthony, Crawley, W. Sussex. 1955–62 (completed by H. Lewis Curtis)
▸ RC SS Ninian, Martin and John, Whithorn, Dumfries and Galloway, 1955–60.
▸ RC Holy Trinity, Dockhead, LB Southwark. 1951–60 (completed by H. Lewis Curtis).
▸ RC Our Lady of the Rosary, Old Marylebone Rd, City of Westminster. 1959–63 (completed by H. Lewis Curtis)

Alexander F. Gordon and William G. Day
▸ Old Kirk, Pennywell Rd, Edinburgh. 1952. By Stanley Ross-Smith.
▸ St David, Broomhouse, Edinburgh. 1965

Esmé Gordon, William Day and Stanley Ross-Smith
▸ Innerleven East Church, Methilhaven Row, Buckhaven, Fife. 1939–41. By Esmé Gordon
▸ Dual-purpose church and hall, Pennywell Rd, W. Pilton, Northants. 1952

Henry Gordon
▸ Convent of St Clare, Freeland, Oxon. Chapel 1960

C.L. Gotch and Partners (Gotch, Saunders and Surridge)
▸ Church of Scotland. St Ninian, Beanfield Ave, Corby, Northants. 1967–8

Laurence M. Gotch and Partners
▸ Church of the Resurrection, S. Woodingdean, Brighton. 1958–9

A.R. Gough
▸ St Gregory, Filton Rd, Horfield, Bristol. 1934

C.A.B. Gowers
▸ RC St Mary the Virgin, St Albans Rd, Adeyfield, Hemel Hempstead, Herts. 1958

George Graham
▸ Holy Trinity, LB Hounslow. 1959

John Graham
▸ Mormon Church of Jesus Christ of Latter Day Saints, Thirlestaine Rd, Cheltenham, Glos. 1964

Gratton and McLeen
▸ Castlemilk West Parish Church, Glasgow. 1962–4

Charles W. Gray
▸ RC St John the Baptist, Parkgrove Avenue, Edinburgh. 1926
▸ RC St Philip, Drumlochy Rd, Ruchazie, Glasgow. 1954–8
▸ RC Church of the Holy Name, Station Rd, Oakley, Fife. 1958
▸ RC Our Lady of Perpetual Succour, Mitre Rd, Broomhill, Glasgow. 1962–5
▸ RC St Teresa, Niddrie Mains Rd, Edinburgh. 1963
▸ RC Our Lady of Lourdes, Bathgate Rd, Blackburn, W. Lothian. 1965
▸ RC St John, St John's Rd, Caol, Lochaber, Highland. 1970

Arthur B. Grayson
▸ St Mary and All Saints, Yeovil, Somerset. 1959–60

William Curtis Green
▸ St George, Barrow Rd, Waddon, LB Croydon. 1932. II
▸ St Christopher, Cove, Farnborough, Hants. 1934
▸ St Francis, Rough Close, Stoke-on-Trent. 1940
▸ Diocesan Training College Chapel, Salisbury, Wilts. 1948
▸ All Saints, Shirley, LB Croydon. 1952–6

Greenaway and Newberry
▸ St John Baptist, Avenue Rd, Belmont, LB Sutton. 1915
▸ St Mary, Sanderstead Hill, LB Croydon. 1920–6
▸ See also Newberry and Fowler

Harold Greenhalgh (Greenhalgh and Williams)
▸ RC St Patrick, Livesey St, Manchester. 1936. II (Greenhalgh, Hadfield and Cawkwell)
▸ RC St Columba, Bolton. 1957. With Geoffrey S. Williams.
▸ RC St Anne, Crescent Rd, Crumpsall, Manchester. 1957 (Greenhalgh and Williams)
▸ RC St Bernadette, Princess Rd, Withington, Manchester. 1960–3. By A. Walmsley of Greenhalgh and Williams.

Padraic Gregory
▸ RC Dominican Convent Chapel, Falls Rd, Belfast. 1926. B+
▸ RC St Columcille, Upper Newtownards Rd, Belfast. 1927–9. Apse and chancel fittings added to older building.
▸ RC St Theresa, Somerton Park, Belfast. 1934. B
▸ RC chapel, Dominican Convent of St Mary, Portstewart, Co. Derry. 1935
▸ RC Church of Christ the King, Drumaness, Co. Down. 1936. B
▸ RC St Malachy, Coleraine, Co. Derry. 1937. B+
▸ RC St Anthony, Cregagh Rd, Belfast. 1938. B
▸ RC St Patrick, Agahagallon, Co. Antrim. 1941. B
▸ RC Our Lady of the Assumption, Tullyallan, Killeshill, Co. Tyrone. 1951. B
▸ RC St Macnissis College Chapel, Carnlough, Co. Antrim. 1956. B
▸ RC Ederney Church, Co. Fermanagh. 1957. B
▸ RC St Bernadette, Rosetta Rd, Belfast. 1966. With B. Gregory

Gribbon, Foggitt and Brown
▸ RC St Augustine, Leeds. 1937
▸ RC Venerable Bede, Stanningley, Wyther, Leeds. 1938

Edward A. Gunning
▸ RC St Matthew, York Ave, Monkton, Co. Durham. 1958
▸ RC St Peter, Kells Lane, Low Fell, Gateshead. 1962

Gunton and Gunton
▸ Methodist church, Boscombe, Bournemouth. 1930–1

Gutteridge and Gutteridge
▸ St Barnabas, Lodge Rd, Southampton. 1956
▸ St Jude, Warren Ave, Shirley Warren, Southampton. 1956

T. Harley Haddow
▸ RC St Kentigern, Parkgrove Ave, Edinburgh. 1966

Charles M.E. Hadfield and R. Cawkwell
▸ All Saints, Glossop, Derbys. 1914–23
▸ RC Sacred Heart, Hillsborough, Sheffield. 1936

H. Norman Haines
▸ St John the Baptist, Hillingdon. Refurbishment after war damage. 1953
▸ Christ Church, Kingston Rd, Staines, Surrey. 1961–2
▸ Christ Church, Lake Rd North, Llanishen, Cardiff. 1963–4
▸ St Michael and All Angels, Field Lane, Bartley Green, Birmingham. 1965–6

E. Stanley Hall
▸ St Cuthbert, Hayling Ave, Copnor, Portsmouth. 1914–15. With E.T. Hall.
▸ Chapel, Bronllys TB Sanatorium, Pont-y-Wall, Powys. 1920. With E.T. Hall. II

Franklyn Halliday and C.G. Agate
▸ Unitarian church, Cross St, Manchester. 1959
▸ Methodist church, North Rd, Longsight, Manchester. 1959–60
▸ Methodist church, Sale, Cheshire. 1963
▸ See also below.

F.L. Halliday, P.H. Meecham and Partners
▸ Methodist. Hazel Grove Church, Stockport. 1972

Ian B.M. Hamilton
▸ St Peter, Aylesham, Kent. 1927

Denis O'D. Hanna
▸ Church in Ireland. St Comgall, Rathcoole, Newtownabbey, Co. Antrim. 1955–6. B
▸ Church in Ireland. St Molua, Stormont, Belfast. 1961–2. B+
▸ Cregagh Presbyterian Church and Hall, Belfast. 1961–3. B
▸ Church in Ireland. Church of the Pentecost, Mount Merrion Ave, Cregagh, Belfast. 1961–3

Cecil Handisyde and Douglas Rogers Stark
▸ Congregational, now Methodist: Trinity Church, Lansbury, LB Tower Hamlets. 1950–1

Ronald Hardy
▸ RC St Oswald, Barnes, LB Richmond-upon-Thames, 1956

C.G. Hare
▸ St Benet, Lupton St, LB Camden. 1908, 1927.
▸ All Saints, Southsea, Portsmouth. 1922. With A.V. Heal.
▸ St Nicholas, Dilham, Norfolk. 1931. Rebuilding, medieval stump of tower remains.
▸ St Mildred, Addiscombe, LB Croydon. 1931–2

J. Morgan Harries
▸ Bethany Baptist Chapel, Heol Llanishen Fach, Rhiwbina, Cardiff. 1963–4

E. Vincent Harris
▸ Church and Sunday School, Stewartby, Beds. 1930
▸ Mary Harris Memorial Chapel, Exeter University, Devon. 1943–58. II

Geoffrey Stanley Harrison
▸ Congregational church, Romford Road, Stratford, LB Newham. 1957

Harrison and Cox
▸ RC St Catherine of Siena, Bristol St, Birmingham. 1964–5.
▸ RC Our Lady of Lourdes, Yardley, Birmingham. 1965
▸ RC St Patrick, Green Lane, Walsall. 1965–6. By B.V. James.
▸ See also George Bernard Cox

Rev. D.E. Hart-Davies
▸ Episcopal. St Thomas, Glasgow Rd, Edinburgh. 1937–8

W. Alexander Harvey and Herbert Graham Wicks

▸ St Francis of Assisi, Linden Rd, Bournville. 1922–5, extended 1933, 1938. II
▸ Robin Hood Cemetery Chapel, Streetsbrook Rd, Solihull, Birmingham. 1930
▸ Bembridge School Chapel, Isle of Wight. 1931–4
▸ St Francis of Assisi, Friar Park, West Bromwich, W. Mids. Designed 1935–7, built 1938–41. II
▸ Immanuel, Highters Heath Lane, Birmingham. 1939 nave and aisles; 1960, east end to reduced plan.
▸ St Anne, West Heath, Birmingham. 1966 (H.N. Wright)

Hately, Winterbottom and Thorne

▸ St Aidan, Kersal, Salford. 1971–2

Michael Hattrell (W.S. Hattrell and Associates)

▸ Anglican and RC shared. St Andrew, Elmshott Lane, Cippenham, Slough. 1968–70

Patrick J. Haughey

▸ RC St Theresa, Sion Mills, Co. Tyrone. 1962. B
▸ RC St Patrick, Dunnamanagh, Co. Tyrone. 1969–72
▸ RC St Mary Mellmount, Strabane, Co. Tyrone. 1970

Neville Hawkes

▸ St Mary, Bearley, Warks. 1961–2

Louis Hayes (S.N. Cooke and Partners)

▸ RC St Vincent de Paul, Francis St, Duddeston, Birmingham. 1968

William Hayne

▸ Baptist. Central Mission, Barking Rd, W. Ham, LB Newham. 1921

A.R. Haynes

▸ St Barnabas, Gunness, Scunthorpe, N. Lincs. 1952
▸ St Hugh, Langworth, Lincs. 1960–2. By Haynes and Johnson, with fabric from Walmsgate Hall chapel, 1901.

E.H. Heazell

▸ St Margaret, Apsley Lane, Aspley, Nottingham. 1934–6
▸ St Martin, Trevose Gardens, Sherwood, Nottingham. 1937. II

Evelyn Hellicar

▸ St John, Roseacre Rd, Welling, LB Bexley. 1925

Hellmuth, Obata and Kassabaum

▸ St Barnabas, Calton Ave, Dulwich, LB Southwark. 1994–6. By Lawrence Malcic.

Hemel Hempstead Development Corporation

▸ St Alban, Hemel Hempstead, Herts. 196–8

E.M. Hemsall

▸ Hall Green Ecumenical Church, Birmingham. 1971

A.G. Henderson

▸ MacNicol Memorial Church, Croftfoot, Glasgow. 1950

P.D. Hepworth

▸ RC St David, Park Cres, Newport. 1938

Clarence L. Heslop

▸ RC St Joseph, Durham. 1955

L. Keir Hett

▸ St Andrew, Moulscombe, Brighton. 1932–4
▸ Ascension, Peacehaven, Brighton. 1954–5
▸ Christ the King, S. Patcham, Brighton. 1958

H.L. Hicks and G.E. Charlewood

▸ St Mary Magdalene, Wilson St, Millfield, Sunderland. 1929 (Hicks, Charlewood and Steel)
▸ St Augustine, Derby Rd, Birdholme, Chesterfield, Derbys. 1931
▸ Holy Cross, Ovington Grove, Fenham, Newcastle upon Tyne. 1935–6

Graeme I.C. Highet

▸ Presbyterian. St Andrew, Woking, Surrey. 1951–2

Hickton, Madeley and Stanley Thomas Salt

▸ Annunciation, Yew Tree Estate, West Bromwich, W. Mids. 1956–7

Higgins Group

▸ Baptist church, Cann Hall Rd, LB Waltham Forest. 1992

C.H. Hignett

▸ Elim Pentecostal Church, Norton Way North, Letchworth, Herts. 1925

R.S. Hill

▸ Church of Ireland. St Columbanus, Ballyholme, Bangor, Co. Down. 1939. B

Hill, Sandy and Norris

▸ RC St John Baptist, Dowling St, Rochdale. 1924
▸ RC St Alphonso, Agnes Rd, Stretford, Greater Manchester. 1936
▸ RC St Bernadette, Liverpool. 1936
▸ See also E. Bower Norris

Denys Hinton

▸ St George, Hillmorton, Rugby, Warks. 1962–3
▸ St Chad, Pheasey, W. Mids. 1964
▸ St Michael, Rowlands Rd, S. Yardley, Birmingham. 1964–5
▸ St Richard, Ridpool Rd, Lea Hall, Birmingham. 1965–9
▸ St Paul, St Paul's Rd, W. Smethwick, Sandwell, W. Mids. 1967
▸ Methodist church, Station Rd, Cheadle Hulme, Cheshire. 1967–8
▸ URC. Carrs Lane Church Centre, Birmingham. 1968

Alfred William Hoare

▸ Zion Baptist Chapel, Hawkesbury, Coventry. 1922

Hobart and Heron

▸ Gardenmore Presbyterian Church, Larne, Co. Antrim. 1915. B
▸ McCracken Memorial Presbyterian Church, Malone Rd, Belfast. 1933. B

Holland W. Hobbiss (in partnership with Maurice A.H. Hobbiss and Noel Hastilow after c.1950

▸ St Cadoc Mission Church, Gwynfa Dale, Highfield Rd, Hall Green, Birmingham. 1923. Demolished. New church (St Peter) 1964 by Norman T. Rider (q.v.)
▸ St Giles, Rowley Village, Rowley Regis, W. Mids. 1923–6, incorporating east end of 1904 church with A.S. Dixon q.v.; 1926 porch; 1933, lychgate.
▸ Christ Church, Burney Lane, Ward End, Birmingham. 1933–5
▸ St Mary and St John, Alum Rock Rd, Shaw Hill, Birmingham. 1934–5, nave and aisles; 1957–8, east end and hall.
▸ Holy Cross, Brigfield Rd, Billesley Common, Birmingham. 1935–7 nave and aisles; 1965 sanctuary and vestries; 1971 Lady chapel.
▸ St Mary Magdalen, Vicarage Rd, Hazelwell, Birmingham. 1936, recasting of church of 1915 by Gerald McMichael and H.C. Weston (q.v.); with new tower, chancel, vestries and extended nave.
▸ St Edmund, Reddings Lane, Tyseley, Birmingham. 1938–40, nave, aisles, tower; 1961, sanctuary and apse.
▸ Chapel, Queen's College, Somerset Rd, Edgbaston, Birmingham. 1939–40, 1947
▸ King Edward VI Grammar School, Edgbaston Park, Birmingham. 1952 incorporating old fabric. II*
▸ St Barnabas, Over Green Drive, Kingshurst, Solihull, W. Mids. 1954–7

W.H. Hobday and F.J. Maynard

▸ St Michael and All Angels, Ravenscroft Rd, Beckenham, LB Bromley. 1955–6

Charles Holden

▸ Sutton Valence School Chapel, Sutton Valence, Kent. 1928–30 (Adams, Holden and Pearson)
▸ Torbay Hospital Chapel, Newton Rd, Torquay. 1930. II

Ernest F. Hooper

▸ St Mark, Pinhoe Rd, Exeter, Devon. 1934–7

E.B. Hoare and M. Wheeler

▸ St Cuthbert, Grimscar, Yorks. 1926
▸ St Paul, Goodmayes, LB Redbridge. 1931

Horsley and Currall

▸ RC Holy Trinity, Boundary Rd, Newark, Notts. 1975–80

Honeyman, Jack and Robertson

▸ Church of Scotland. St Matthew, Beil Drive, Knightswood, Glasgow. 1950–2
▸ Church of Scotland. St Mark, Kinfauns Drive, Drumchapel, Glasgow. 1955–6
▸ Scottish Presbyterian. Anderston Kelvingrove Church and Community Centre, Argyle St, Glasgow. 1970–2
▸ Presbyterian Church of Broom, Newton Mearns, E. Renfrewshire. 1959

R.C. Hosford

▸ RC St Thomas More, High St, Blindley Heath, Surrey. 1959

H.R. Houchin

▸ Methodist church, New Malden, RB Kingston-upon-Thames. 1932
▸ Methodist church, Banstead, Surrey. 1934–5
▸ Congregational church, Sanderstead, LB Croydon. 1934–5
▸ Free Church, Wembley Park, LB Brent. 1935–7
▸ See also Smee and Houchin

James Houston and Partners

▸ Penilee St Andrew, Bowfield Crescent, Glasgow. 1951–2
▸ St Andrew, Muirhead Rd, Bailleston, Glasgow. 1973–6

Thomas T. Houston

▸ Stormont Presbyterian Church, Upper Newtownards Rd, Belfast. 1950–5
▸ Strabane First Presbyterian Church, Co. Tyrone. 1955–7. B

Peter Howe

▸ RC St Theresa, Canon St, Clock Face, St Helens. 1930. Howe was a stonemason who worked as his own architect here.

T. Cecil Howitt

▸ St Cyprian, Carlton Hill, Sneinton, Nottingham. 1934–5
▸ St Mary, Wollaton Park, Nottingham. 1937–9. II
▸ St Barnabas, Lenton Abbey, Nottingham. 1939
▸ St Christopher and St Philip, Colwick Rd, Nottingham. 1952. Rebuilding of 1910 church after bomb damage.

E. Douglas Hoyland

▸ St Luke, Buckhall Rd, LB Waltham Forest. 1914

J. O'Hanlon Hughes

▸ RC St Edmund, Beckenham, LB Bromley. 1938

T. Harold Hughes

▸ Scottish Episcopal. St Matthew, Balmore Rd, Glasgow. 1935–7

Hughes and Bicknell

▸ Methodist. Meadowlands Church, Newmarket Rd, Cambridge. 1960

Hulme, Upright and Partners

▸ Methodist church, Bradwell Lane, Wolstanton, Staffs. 1966
▸ Methodist. St John, Victoria Ave, Bloxwich, Walsall. 1966
▸ Methodist Central Mission, Swan Square, Burslem, Stoke-on-Trent. 1969–71

Derek Humphrys and Hurst

▸ St Paul, Stratford, LB Newham. 1953
▸ St Paul, Playhouse Square, Harlow, Essex. 1959–61
▸ St Peter, Eastbourne Grove, Westcliff-on-Sea, Essex. 1963
▸ St Mark, St Mark's Place, Worple Rd, Wimbledon, LB Merton. 1968–9

Percival J. Hunt

▸ St Chad mission church and hall, Waterloo Rd, Hay Mill, Yardley, Birmingham. 1936 (now URC)
▸ St Luke, Caversham Rd, Kingstanding, Birmingham. 1937
▸ St Andrew Mission Church, Audley Rd, Stechford, Birmingham. 1938

Hutchison, Locke and Monk

▸ Emmanuel, Clive Rd, LB Lambeth. 1967–8
▸ St Luke, Uxbridge Rd, Hammersmith. 1976–8. By A.J. Monk

Hutton and Taylor

▸ King's Park Parish Church, Castlemilk Rd, Glasgow. 1931–2
▸ Calton Parkhead Church, Helenvale St, Parkhead, Glasgow. 1934–5. B

Geddes Hyslop

▸ Bishop Andrewes Church, Wigmore Rd, St Helier, Morden, LB Merton. 1933
▸ All Saints, Orpington, LB Bromley. 1957–8. Incorporating medieval church as side chapel. B

Herbert G. Ibberson

▸ Congregational church, Elmers End, LB Bromley. 1931
▸ Christian Science Church, Recorder Rd, Norwich. 1934–5. II

William Illingworth

▸ Methodist church, Frinzinghall, Bradford. 1954–5

Keith Ingham (Building Design Partnership)

▸ Methodist church, Chester Ave, Poulton-le-Fylde, Lancs. 1965–6

Gordon W. Jackson and Partners

▸ St James, Exeter. 1959
▸ Congregational. Boulevard Church, Weston-super-Mare. 1959

Herbert Jackson and Reginald Edmonds

▸ Congregational church, Digbeth-in-the-Fields, Birmingham. 1960

Ralph E. James

▸ Baptist church, Chalk Farm, LB Camden. 1960

Rev. David Jenkins

▸ St John, Pentre, Rhondda Cynon Taff. 1985–7, incorporating fragments from church previously on site and other local demolished churches.

Peter Jenkins

▸ St Paul, Haringey, LB Haringey. 1990–3

Jennings, Homer and Lynch

▸ RC St Peter, High St, Bloxwich, Walsall, west end 1952–4
▸ RC St Thomas of Canterbury, Dartmouth Ave, Coalpool, Walsall. 1959–60
▸ RC St Anthony of Padua, Headley Way, Oxford, 1960
▸ St Andrew, Westlands, Newcastle-under-Lyme, Staffs. 1961–2
▸ RC St Catherine Labouré, Edison Rd, Beechdale, Walsall. 1961–3

Holgar Jensen (with Armstrong and MacManus)

▸ Danish Lutheran. Seamen's Mission in Foreign Parts, Commercial Rd, Stepney, LB Tower Hamlets. 1958–9. Now (Methodist) London City Mission.

H.N. Jepson

▸ All Saints, Chilvers Coton, Warks. 1946–51.

Johns, Slater and Haward

▸ Congregational. Castle Hill Church, Ipswich, Suffolk. 1956–7.

Francis Johnson

▸ Ascension, Calvert Rd, Hull. 1957–8, extension of mission church by Wellstead, Dossor and Wellstead, 1935
▸ Holy Nativity, Eastfield, Scarborough, N. Yorks. 1954–5
▸ St Michael and All Angels, Orchard Park Rd, Hull. 1957–8

D.T. Johnston and R. Wright

▸ St Elisabeth, Harraby, Carlisle. 1967

Ivan A. Johnston and Associates

▸ (Mormon). Jesus Christ and the Latter Day Saints, Bramhill Lane, Stockport. 1962–4

James Johnstone

▸ Wilson Memorial Church (Portobello United Free), Moira Terrace, Edinburgh. 1933. B

Marcus Johnston

▸ St John, Meldrum Rd, Kirkaldy, Fife. 1976–7
▸ Dalgety Parish Church, Dalgety Bay, Fife. 1980–1

G. Raymond Jones and Associates

▸ Congregational. Ebenezer Chapel, Chester Rd, Wrexham. 1974–5

John L. Jones (Barnard and Partners)

▸ St John Evangelist, Herbert Jennings Ave, Rhosnesni, Wrexham. 1973–4

Maurice Jones

▸ St Mary, Sherrards Green, Worcs. 1957

Ronald Potter Jones

▸ Unitarian church, Cambridge. 1922
▸ Unitarian church, W. Kirby, Wirral. 1929. With E. Thornely.

William A. Jones and J.E. Stocks

▸ St Richard, Seacroft, Leeds. 1955

Jopling and Wright

▸ RC St Vincent de Paul, Queen's Rd, Hull. 1932–3. II

E.J. Kay

▸ RC St Edward, Park Parade, Whitley Bay, N. Tyneside. 1928

B.D. Kaye

▸ RC St John Fisher, Langdale Gardens, Perivale, LB Ealing. 1970–3
▸ RC English Martyrs, Wembley, LB Brent. 1971

W. Keay

▸ St Christopher, Marriott Rd, Leicester. 1928. See Roger Keene

Arthur Keen

▸ Mission church, Waterloo Rd, Uxbridge, LB Hillingdon. 1932

Roger Keene Partnership

▸ St Gabriel the Archangel, Kerrysdale Ave, Leicester. 1963–4
▸ St Christopher, Marriott Rd, Leicester. 1967–8. Attached to church of 1928 by W. Keay.

Percy Kelly (Hastie Winch and Kelly)

▸ RC St Joseph, Austenwood Lane, Chalfont St Peter, Bucks. 1962–3 adds to 1913 church by Percy Lamb, now north transept.

G.R.M. Kennedy

▸ St Martin of Tours, Tranent, E. Lothian. 1967

J.S. Kennedy

▸ First Dunboe Presbyterian Church, Articlave, Co. Derry. 1936. B

Arthur W. Kenyon

▸ St Alban, Church Drive, LB Harrow. 1936–7. II
▸ St Barnabas, Three Bridges, Crawley, W. Sussex. 1955

Keppie and Henderson

▸ St Enoch Hogganfield, Cumbernauld Rd, Glasgow. 1927–30
▸ Croftpark Parish Church, Croftpark Ave, Glasgow. 1934–5. B

Francis A. Kerr

▸ St Christopher, Lees Rd, Hurst, Ashton-under-Lyne, Greater Manchester. 1956

L.F. Kimber

▸ Congregational church, Bury Rd, Gosport, Hants. 1957

J. Thompson King and Partners

▸ Blawarthill Church, Millbrix Ave, Garscadden, Glasgow. 1960–4

Laurence King

▸ St George, Brentwood. 1934–5. With J.J. Crowe and S. Careless
▸ St Mary, Fairway, South Ruislip, LB Hillingdon. 1958–9
▸ St Peter, Hinckley, Leics. 1960
▸ Cathedral Church of St Mary, Blackburn. Corona and flèche, 1961
▸ St Mary, Little Walsingham, Norfolk. 1962–4. Rebuilding of medieval church gutted by fire 1961.
▸ St Mary with St Nicholas, Federal Rd, Perivale, LB Ealing. 1963
▸ St Michael, Town Square, Letchworth, Herts. 1966–8
▸ St Mary with SS Mary and Edward, Albert Rd, LB Newham. 1968
▸ St John, Woolwich, LB Greenwich. 1969

William Kininmonth

▸ Drylaw Parish Church, Groathill Rd North, Edinburgh. 1956. See also R. Rowand Anderson etc.

Edmund Kirby and Sons

▸ RC St Catherine and St Martina, Birkenhead Rd, Hoylake, Wirral. 1926–8
▸ RC St Edmund, Ivy St, Runcorn, Cheshire. 1956

Kitson, Parish, Ledgard and Pyman

▸ St Stephen, Moortown, Leeds. 1954
▸ St Andrew, Old Lane, Beeston, Leeds. 1957
▸ St Cyprian with St James, Harehill, Leeds. 1960
▸ St David, Beeston, Leeds. 1961–2

W.H. Kitching and Co.

▸ Methodist church, Perth St, Hull. 1930–1

A.B. Knapp-Fisher

▸ Chapel at Gunnersbury Burial Ground, near Acton, LB Hounslow. 1928–30
▸ St Leonard, Langley Green, Crawley, W. Sussex. 1955
▸ St Stephen, Chatham, Kent. 1956–7
▸ St Paul, Crofton, Orpington, LB Bromley. 1958

Walter John Knight

▸ St Leonard, Elmdon Rd, Marston Green, Solihull, W. Mids. 1938 (incomplete)

Felix J. Lander and James C. Stevens

▸ St Mary, Goldington, Bedford. 1957
▸ See also N.F. Cachemaille-Day.
▸ See also Welch and Lander.

J.A. Lane, D.S. Bremner and D.J.S. Garnett

▸ RC St Joseph, Cumbernauld, N. Lanarkshire. 1971–2

J.H. Langtry Langton

▸ RC First Martyrs, Heights Lane, Chellow Grange, Bradford. 1935. II
▸ RC Our Lady of Perpetual Succour and St Clare, Fagley, Bradley, W. Yorks. 1957

Lavender and Twentyman (post-war, Lavender, Twentyman and Percy)
- See under Richard Twentyman; Twentyman Percy and Partners

Graham C. Law and James D. Dunbar-Nasmith
- Blackburn Church, Edinburgh, 1963
- St Columba Ecumenical Church, Livingston, W. Lothian. 1966. By Graham Law.

Geoffrey Lawson
- St Lawrence, Towcester, Northants. 1962

Frederic W. Lawrence
- Congregational. Immanuel Church, Southbourne Rd, Southbourne, Southampton. 1930
- St Saviour, Holdenhurst Ave, Iford, Bournemouth. 1934–5
- Congregational Church of the Peace of God, Oxted, Surrey. 1935

Cecil Lay
- Baptist church, Aldringham, Suffolk. 1915

Alexander Leach, Herbert Rhodes and Albert Walker
- St Peter, White Moss, Blackley, Lancs. 1958
- All Saints, Wood St, Middleton, Greater Manchester. 1963–4

T. Greenshields Leadbetter
- Bedrule Parish Church, Bedrule, 1914. B

Egbert Leah
- RC St Augustine, Matson, Glos. 1962

J. Leask
- RC St Bernadette, Bristol. 1968

Leathart, Grainger and Webber
- Chapel, Liverpool College, Mossley Hill, Liverpool. 1934

Cecil Leckenby
- St Hilda, Tang Hall Lane, York. 1933–4

R.W. Leggatt
- Baptist. Immanuel Church, Victoria Rd North, Southsea, Portsmouth. 1953–7

John Anthony Lewis
- St Barnabas, Bethnal Green, LB Tower Hamlets. 1958

Hubert Lidbetter
- (Society of) Friends Meeting House, Euston Rd, LB Camden. 1925–7. II
- Friends Meeting House, Bristol Rd, Selly Oak, Birmingham. 1928
- Friends Meeting House, Bull St, Birmingham. 1931–3
- Friends Meeting House, Hunter St, Liverpool, Merseyside. 1941
- Methodist Church, Teddington, LB Richmond. 1946
- Friends Meeting House, Church Rd, Watford, Herts. 1953
- Friends Meeting House, Woodville Rd, LB Ealing. 1954
- Friends Meeting House, Nigel Playfair Ave, LB Hammersmith. 1954–5
- Friends Meeting House, St Martin's Lane, City of Westminster. 1956
- Friends Meeting House, Park Lane, LB Croydon. 1956–9. School hall by Curtis Green, 1908
- Friends Meeting House, Hutton Rd, Shenfield, Essex. 1957
- Friends Meeting House, Yoakley Rd, Stoke Newington, LB Hackney. 1957
- Friends Meeting House, Redlands Way, Ropell Park, LB Lambeth. 1957
- Baptist. Bow Church, Old Ford Road, LB Tower Hamlets. 1959 (with Hubert Martin Lidbetter)
- Friends Meeting House, Hartshead, Sheffield. 1962–4 (with Hubert Martin Lidbetter)

Ian G. Lindsay
- RC St Finnan, Invergarry, Highland. c.1935–8. B
- Livingston Kirk, Livingston, W. Lothian. 1949
- Episcopal. St John the Evangelist, Burnside, Moffat, Dumfries and Galloway. 1951–3
- Colinton Mains Kirk, Edinburgh. 1954

Lingard and Williams (Brian Hallwood)
- RC church, Menai Bridge, Isle of Anglesey. 1951

Liverpool City Architect's Department (Ronald Bradbury, City Architect)
- West Derby Cemetery Chapel, Liverpool. 1965

T. and H. Llewelyn
- Welsh Presbyterian church, High Rd, Leytonstone, LB Waltham Forest. 1958

Thomas Alwyn Lloyd
- St Margaret, Chester Rd, Wrexham. 1927–8. Completed 1976–8
- Lutheran church, Fairwater, Cardiff. By Alexander J. Gordon. 1962

C.M. Lock and Partners
- Baptist church, Stotfold, Beds. 1968
- Baptist church, Biggleswade, Beds. 1969
- Baptist church, Arnold, Gedling, Notts. 1968–9
- Methodist. Trinity Church, Huntingdon, Beds. 1969

E.E. Lofting
- St James and St Basil, Fenham Hall Drive, Newcastle upon Tyne. 1927–31. II

E.E. Lofting and E. Priestley Cooper
- St Columba, Laburnum Ave, Hull. 1926–9

Charles A. Lomas and Derek H. Pooley
- Christ Church, Pound Hill, Crawley, W. Sussex. 1957–8

Sir Robert Lorimer
- RC St Peter, Falcon Ave, Edinburgh. 1906–29
- St Andrew, Queen's Ave, Aldershot, Hampshire. 1927
- Stowe School Chapel, Stowe, Bucks. 1927–8. II
- St Peter Edinburgh. Additions 1929, with J.F. Matthew.
- Church of Scotland, St Margaret, Great Western Rd, Knightswood Cross, Glasgow. 1929–32. Completed by J.F. Matthew after Lorimer's death in 1929

Thomas Lovatt
- Congregational church, Drubbery Lane, Longton, Stoke-on-Trent. 1969.

H.W.W. Lovegrove
- Presbyterian (URC). Holly Lane Chapel, Erdington, Birmingham. 1934

Ralph Lovegrove
- RC St Anselm, West Hill, Dartford, Kent. 1973–5

George C. Lowe
- St Barnabas, Purley, LB Croydon. 1961–2

William L. Lowe and Partners, with E.S. Gray, F. Evans and F.H. Crossley
- Christian Science. First Church, Bury. 1948

Lowther and Rigby
- RC St Joseph, Plymouth Grove, Chorlton-on-Medlock, Manchester. 1914–15

Geoffrey Lucas
- Episcopal. All Saints, Annan Rd, Gretna, Dumfries and Galloway. 1917. B

Lucas, Roberts and Brown
- St Sidwell, Sidwell St, Exeter. 1950 from a Nissen hut. 1957–8

Anthony F. Lucy
- Church in Ireland. Church of the Holy Name, Greenisland, Co. Antrim. 1954. B
- Glengormley Presbyterian Church, Belfast. 1956
- St Dorothea, Belfast. 1956
- St Katharine, Belfast. 1956

David F. Lumley
- Methodist church, Ilford, LB Redbridge. 1961–2

Sir Edwin Lutyens
- St Jude, Central Square, Hampstead Garden Suburb, LB Barnet. 1909–35. I
- Free Church, Central Square, Hampstead Garden Suburb, LB Barnet. 1910–23. I
- St Martin, London Rd, Knebworth, Herts. 1914. Completed by Sir Albert Richardson 1963–4. II*
- Temple of Music, Tyringham Hall, Stoke Goldington, Bucks. 1926. II*
- RC Chapel, Campion Hall, Oxford. 1933–6. II

T.H. Lyon
- Corpus Christi College Chapel, Cambridge. 1921

P.J. Mabley
- RC Holy Family, Vale Lane, Acton, LB Ealing. 1967

John McAlery
- Presbyterian. Abbots Cross Church, Belfast. 1956–7

Alexander McAnally
- RC St Conval, Hapland Rd, Pollok, Glasgow. 1953–6
- RC St Pius X, Bayfield Terrace, Drumchapel, Glasgow. 1954–7. B
- RC St Teresa of Lisieux, Saracen St, Glasgow. 1956–60
- RC St Mark, Fernhill Rd, Burnside, Glasgow. 1957–61
- RC St Michael, Gallowgate, Glasgow. 1965–8
- RC St James Crookston, Crosstobs Rd, Pollok, Glasgow. 1965–8
- RC St Monica, Castlebay St, Glasgow. 1970–4

Francis MacArdle
- RC Our Lady's Convent Chapel, Beechmount, Falls Rd, Belfast. 1934–5. B+
- RC Our Lady of Perpetual Succour, Old Park Rd, Belfast. 1959

Richard MacCormac
- Chapel, Fitzwilliam College, Cambridge. 1992–3

Lawrence McConville
- RC Chapel of the Annunciation, St Brigid's Convent, Cookstown, Co. Tyrone. 1963–5

Liam McCormick
- RC St Mary, Fanad Drive, Creggan, Londonderry, Co. Derry. 1959 (Corr and McCormick)
- RC Holy Family, Redbridge Mill, Millbrook, Southampton. 1965–6
- RC Our Lady of Lourdes, Steelstown, Londonderry, Co. Derry. 1975. See also J.J. Tracey.
- RC church, Maghera, Co. Derry. 1975
- RC St Patrick's Cathedral, Armagh. 1977–82 remodelling of 1840 building. A
- RC St Mary, Altimire, Park, Co. Derry. Remodelling, 1978

Alister MacDonald and Partners
- Methodist church, Harlesden, LB Brent. 1956
- St John, Amersham, Bucks. 1961. By D.K. Compton

Frank F. Macdonald
- Congregational. Knightswood Church, Dunterlie Ave, Glasgow. 1933. B

J.J. MacDonell
- RC Our Lady of Lourdes, Moneyglass, Co. Antrim. 1925. B+

Leslie Grahame MacDougall
- See Leslie Grahame Thomson

John MacGeagh
- Presbyterian. Smyth Halls, Lisburn Rd, Belfast. 1930–3
- Presbyterian. Gospel Hall, Albertbridge Rd, Belfast. 1935–6
- Duneane Presbyterian Church, Co. Antrim. 1936. B+
- St Barnabas, Duncairn Gardens, Belfast. 1956–7
- St Silas, Cliftonville Rd, Belfast. 1957–8
- Church of Ireland. St Anne's Cathedral, Donegall St, Belfast. Transepts, 1968–81. A. See also Sir Charles Nicholson

S. McIlveen
- Downpatrick Presbyterian Church, Co. Down. 1954. B

A. Marshall Mackenzie
- Cults West Church, Peterculter. 1915–16. B
- All Saints, Hilton, Aberdeen. 1936–7
- St Nicholas, South St, Kincorth. 1954–5 (A. Marshall Mackenzie and Sons)

Arthur M. McKewan and McKewan
- Lyndon Methodist Church, Birmingham. 1958–9
- Elmwood Congregational Church, Handsworth Wood, Birmingham. 1969

Gordon K. McKnight
- Orangefield Presbyterian Church, Castlereagh Rd, Belfast. 1955–7. B.
- Knockbreda Presbyterian Church, Belfast. 1970–1
- High Kirk, Ballymena, Co. Antrim. 1976
- Corrymeela Worship Centre, Co. Antrim. 1978

James McLachlan
- Morningside United Church, Bruntsfield Place, Edinburgh. 1926–9. B
- St Christopher, Craigentinny Rd, Restalrig, Edinburgh. 1934–8

T. McLean
- RC Stella Maris Church, Strangford, Co. Down. 1932. B
- RC Church of the Angels, Clonvaraghan, Co. Down. 1937. B

McLean & Forte
- RC Chapel, Convent of Sacred Heart, Castle St, Lisburn, Co. Down. 1967
- RC Our Lady Mother of the Church, Larne Rd, Ballymena, Co. Antrim. 1968

Gerald McMichael and Howard C. Weston
- St Mary Magdalen mission church, Vicarage Rd, Hazelwell, Birmingham. 1915–16. Altered 1936 by H. Hobbiss (q.v.)

Archibald Macpherson
- RC St Matthew, Carruthers St, Rosewell, W. Lothian. 1925. B. See also Reginald Fairlie.
- RC Our Lady and St Ninian, Quakerfield Rd, Bannockburn, Stirling. 1927. C(S)
- RC Sacred Heart, Grangemouth, Stirling. 1928

John H.D. Madin
- Good Shepherd with St John, Lyttleton St, W. Bromwich, W. Mids. 1967–8

Robert Maguire and Keith Murray
- St Paul, Bow Common, LB Tower Hamlets. 1958–60. II*
- St Matthew, Perry Beeches, Birmingham. 1962–4. II
- All Saints, Crewe, Cheshire. 1964–5.
- Abbey Church of St Mary, West Malling, Kent. 1964–6
- St Joseph the Worker, Yeading Lane, LB Ealing. 1967–9
- Ascension, Hulme, Manchester. 1968–70
- RC St Augustine, Crescent Rd, Tunbridge Wells, Kent. 1975

T.K. Makins
- St Francis, Riders Lane, Leigh Park, Havant, Hants. 1962

H.J. Manchip
- Baptist church, Harehills Lane, Leeds. 1931

Wilfrid C. Mangan
- RC St Saviour, Totland, Isle of Wight. 1923
- RC St Joseph and the Sacred Heart, Newbury, Berks. 1923–8
- RC English Martyrs, Tilehurst Rd, Reading. 1926
- RC Our Lady, New Milton, Hants. 1926–7
- RC St Boniface, Shirley Rd, Shirley, Southampton, 1927
- RC St Teresa, Bishopsford Rd, St Helier, LB Merton. 1930
- RC St Paul, Hazelgrove Rd, Hastings, E. Sussex. 1930
- RC Our Lady of Willesden, Acton Lane, Harlesden, LB Brent. 1930–1. II
- RC St Barnabas, Vine Rd, W. Molesey, Surrey. 1931
- RC St Paul, Hayward's Heath, W. Sussex. 1931
- RC Holy Cross, North St, Carshalton. LB Sutton. 1933
- RC St Edward the Confessor, Home Park Ave, Peverell, Plymouth. 1934 nave, sanctuary, s aisle and baptistry to 1911 church by Scoles and Raymond (q.v.)

- RC Holy Family, Oxlow Lane, Becontree, LB Barking and Dagenham. 1934
- RC St Gregory, Blackpool Rd, Preston, Lancs. 1935–6
- RC St Patrick, Portsmouth Rd, Woolston, Southampton. 1938
- RC St Bede, Carlisle. 1959
- RC Corpus Christi, Hood Walk, Collier Row, LB Havering. 1964–5

Michael Manser
- Baptist church, Waterlooville, Hants. 1966–7
- Baptist church, Battersea, Wandsworth. 1972

E.M. Marriner
- St John Baptist, High St, Harborne, Birmingham. 1959–60
- St James, Hartlebury Rd, Lion Farm (Rounds Green), Oldbury, W. Mids. 1963–4

Alexander Marshall
- Holy Trinity, Dromore, Co. Tyrone. 1957
- Church of Ireland. St Peter, Culmore Rd, Londonderry, Co. Derry. 1963–7

C.T. Marshall and W. Tweedy
- Congregational church, Potters Bar, Herts. 1939

Donald Plaskett Marshall
- RC Our Lady of Grace and St Edward, Chiswick, LB Hounslow. 1953. Remodelling after war damage.
- RC Sacred Heart, Camberwell New Rd, LB Southwark. 1953
- St Augustine's Convent Chapel, Brighton. 1958–9
- RC St Joseph, St Mary Cray, LB Bromley. 1958–9
- RC Our Lady Help of Christians, W. Byfleet, Surrey. 1958–9
- RC St Boniface, Stepney, LB Tower Hamlets. 1960

W.H.H. Marten with G.A. Burnett
- Holy Rosary, Leeds. 1940

A.C. Martin
- St Luke, Farnborough Way, Camberwell, LB Southwark. 1953–4. Completed by Milner and Craze.

Arthur C. Martin
- St Olave, Church Walk, Mitcham, LB Merton. 1931
- St Luke, Milber, Newton Abbot, Devon. 1936 from concept by J. Keble Martin, incumbent and architect's brother.
- St Luke, Farnborough Way, Camberwell, LB Southwark. 1953–4. Completed by Milner and Craze.

R. Martin
- St Margaret, Hapton, Lancs. 1926–7
- St James, Woolford, Bury. 1931

Donald F. Martin-Smith
- John Keble Church, Dean's Lane, Mill Hill, LB Barnet. 1934–7. II
- St Mary, Southgate, Crawley, W. Sussex. 1956–8. With Henry Braddock.
- Holy Cross, Doncaster. 1957. With Henry Braddock.
- Little St Peter, Claremont Rd, Cricklewood, LB Brent. 1958
- St Paul, LB Barking. 1959
- St James, Hardwick Rd, Stockton-on-Tees. 1961, 1966. With Henry Braddock.
- Epiphany, Elizabeth St, Corby. 1961–2. With Henry Braddock.
- St Andrew, Maylands Drive, Sidcup, LB Bexley. 1964. By Braddock, Martin-Smith and Lipley.

George W. Martyn
- RC Our Lady of Grace and St Teresa of Avila, Kings Rd, Chingford, LB Waltham Forest. 1931

Hilda Mason and Raymond Erith
- St Andrew, St Andrew's Rd, Felixstowe, Suffolk. 1929–31. II*

Massey and Massey
- RC St Raphael, Millbrook, Greater Manchester. 1963
- St Aidan and St Oswald, Royton, Greater Manchester. 1964–5 (E. Massey)

Andrew Mather
- Methodist church, Ruskin Rd, Carshalton, LB Sutton. 1926

Mather and Nutter
- St Boniface, Great Cheetham St, Salford. 1960–1

George A.J. Mathers, Thomas and Associates
- RC St Bartholomew, Vesta Ave, St Albans, Herts. 1962–4
- RC St Mary, Old Hatfield, Herts. 1970

Matheson and Mackenzie
- Free Presbyterian Church, Dingwall, Highland. 1959

Matkin and Hawkins
- RC St Anne, Hylton Rd, Pennywell, Sunderland. 1957

John F. Matthew
- Granton Parish Church, Boswall Parkway, Edinburgh. 1934
- Robin Chapel, Thistle Foundation, Niddrie Mains Rd, Edinburgh. 1950–3

Robert Matthew, Johnson-Marshall and Partners
- Loretto School Chapel, Edinburgh. 1965–7

Mauchlen and Weightman
- Methodist church, Seahouses, Northumberland. 1925

Sir Edward Maufe

- St Bede, Clapham Rd, LB Lambeth. 1923
- St Saviour (Centre for Deaf People), Old Oak Rd, Acton, LB Ealing. 1924–7
- Religious Broadcasting Studio, BBC Broadcasting House, Portland Place, City of Westminster. 1931. Destroyed.
- St Thomas the Apostle, Boston Rd, Hanwell, LB Ealing. 1933–4. II*
- Cathedral Church of the Holy Spirit, Stag Hill, Guildford. 1936–61. II*
- St John the Evangelist, Hook, Hampshire. 1938
- Bishop Hannington Memorial Church, Hove. 1938. II
- St George, Goodrington, Torbay. 1939–65
- All Saints, Weston Green, Surrey. 1939
- Scottish Presbyterian. St Columba, Pont St, RB Kensington and Chelsea. 1950–4. II
- Cathedral Church of St Peter, Bradford. Additions 1951–65. I
- St Mary, Hampden Park, Eastbourne, E. Sussex. 1952–4
- Gray's Inn Chapel, Gray's Inn, Holborn, LB Camden. 1954. II. Rebuilt after war damage.
- County Grammar School Chapel, Lewes, E. Sussex. 1958–60
- St Alphege, Edmonton, LB Enfield. 1959
- St Nicholas, Saltdean Vale, E. Sussex. 1962

Paul Mauger and Partners

- Methodist church, Bow Road, LB Tower Hamlets. 1951
- Methodist church, Welwyn Garden City, Herts. 1951, 1957. With A.J. May.
- Methodist church, S. Ruislip, LB Hillingdon. 1951–2
- Christian Science church, Welwyn Garden City, Herts. 1954
- Methodist church, Borehamwoood, Herts. 1956
- Methodist church, Denbigh Rd, RB Kensington. 1957–8. With Alexander G. Gavin.
- Methodist church, Clapton, LB Hackney. 1958. With George A.J. Matthews and John Mitchell
- Methodist. St Andrew, The Stow, Harlow, Essex. 1959–61
- Methodist church, Holmwood Road, LB Bromley. 1967 (with Alexander G. Gavin)

Maxwell, Stewart and Maxwell

- RC St Philomena, Royston Rd, Provanmill, Glasgow. 1939–40

Arthur J. May

- Methodist church, Westpole Ave, Oakwood, LB Enfield. 1958
- Methodist church, Putmore, Beds. 1956–7
- See also Paul Mauger

N.D. Melhuish, Wright and Evans

- RC Christ our Hope, Beare Green, Surrey. 1971

Tom Mellor

- Housing Scheme incorporating circular private chapel, Lytham St Annes, Lancs. 1951
- All Saints, New Longton, Lancs. 1963–5
- St Wilfrid, Mereside Estate, Blackpool, Lancs. 1965–6

John B. Mendham

- St Michael, Glassonbury Drive, Bexhill, E. Sussex. 1929
- St Ethelburga, Filsham Rd, Hastings, E. Sussex. 1929
- RC St Anselm, Tooting Bec, LB Wandsworth. 1931–3

Alan Mercer

- Baptist church, Rosyth, Fife. 1970

Percy W. Meredith

- Congregational church, Stanley Park Rd, Wallington, LB Sutton. 1928
- Congregational church, Southall, LB Ealing. 1933
- Congregational church, Leatherhead, Surrey. 1936
- Congregational church, Eltham, LB Greenwich. 1937

Mewès and Davis

- Armenian. St Sarkis, Iverna Court, RB Kensington and Chelsea. 1922–3. II

Middleton, Fletcher and Partners

- St Mark, Bishopton Rd, Fairfield, Stockton-on-Tees. 1963

C.W. Milburn

- St Matthew, Brinkburn Rd, Darlington. 1936

Stanley W. Milburn and Partners

- St Francis, Prince Charles Ave, Mackworth, Derby. 1953–4
- St Philip, Chaddesden, Derby. 1955
- Presbyterian. St Columba, Marsh House Ave, Billingham, Teesside. 1956–7
- Methodist church, Seaburn Dene, Fulwell, Sunderland. 1960

W. and T.R. Milburn

- Lutheran church, Queen Alexandra Road, Sunderland. 1962

Bernard Miller

- St Christopher, Lorenzo Drive, Norris Green, Liverpool. 1930–2. II*
- St Columba, Pinehurst Rd, Anfield, Liverpool. 1932. II
- St Christopher, Minehead, Withington, Manchester. 1935. II*. Demolished 1995
- St Thomas, Heaton Moor, Stockport. 1938
- St Saviour, Langshaw Estate, Blackburn, Lancs. 1947
- St Michael and All Angels, Tettenhall, Wolverhampton. 1951–5. II. Rebuilt after fire, incorporating medieval tower.

- St Chad, Stowlawn, Bilston, Staffs. 1953–5
- St Aidan, Speke, Liverpool. 1953–5
- Christ the King, Pendeford Ave, Aldersley, Wolverhampton. 1956
- St Aidan, Wheatley Hills, Doncaster, S. Yorks. 1956
- St Hugh, New Cantley, Doncaster, S. Yorks. 1956

J.C. Miller

- Lochside Parish Church, Lochside Rd, Dumfries. 1961–2, 1964–5

Robert Miller and O.D. Black

- Baptist. Harper Memorial Church, Glasgow. 1922
- Baptist. Partick Church, Crow Rd, Partick, Glasgow. 1927
- Gospel Hall, Fulton St, Glasgow. 1932
- Church of Scotland. St Nicholas, Hartlaw Crescent, Cardonald, Glasgow. 1935–6
- Church of Scotland. South Carntyne Church, Cartyne Rd, Glasgow. 1935–6

Edward Mills

- Methodist Mission, Colliers Wood, LB Merton. 1937. Now a nursery.
- Methodist church, High St, LB Greenwich. 1954
- Congregational church, Stevenage, Herts. 1955
- Methodist church, Stoke Mandeville, Bucks. 1958
- Methodist church, Cricket Green, Mitcham, LB Merton. 1958–60
- Methodist church, Cutthome Rd, Loundsley Green, Chesterfield, Derbys. 1962–4
- Methodist church, Chelsfield, Kent. 1964
- Methodist church, Upper Norwood, LB Croydon. 1965
- Methodist church (Trinity), Brewery Rd, Woking, Surrey. 1966
- Methodist. Trinity and Woodsmoor Church, Stockport. 1967
- Methodist. St Paul, Bedford. 1968–9
- Congregational and Methodist church, Cheadle, Cheshire. 1970
- Methodist church, Daventry, Northants. 1972
- Methodist church, Trinity at Bowes, Bowes Park, LB Enfield. 1973

Oswald P. Milne

- Christian Science. Eleventh Church, Seymour Place, City of Westminster. 1926–7

W. Milner and R.B. Craze

- See also Romilly B. Craze
- Shrine of Our Lady of Walsingham, Holt Rd, Little Walsingham, Norfolk. 1931–7
- St Alban, Becontree, LB Barking and Dagenham. 1933–4
- St Matthew, Owthorne, Hull Rd, Withernsea, E. Yorks. 1934–5
- St Aidan, Southcotes Ave, Hull. 1935
- St George, Becontree, LB Barking and Dagenham. 1938

- St Alban, Hall Rd, Hull. 1938. Part reconstructed 1955–6
- St Thomas, Prince George Ave, Oakwood, LB Enfield. 1939
- All Saints, Queensbury, LB Harrow. 1954
- St Columba, Laburnum Ave, Hull. 1958–60

Milton Keynes Development Corporation (Derek Walker and Peter Barker)

- RC Our Lady of Lourdes, Coffee Hall, Milton Keynes. 1974–6

Milton Keynes Planning Design Development Ltd

- Ecumenical Church of Christ the Cornerstone (City Church), Saxon Gate, Milton Keynes.

Thomas Mitchell and Associates

- Royal Air Force College Chapel, Cranwell, Lincs. 1962

Mitchell and Bridgwater

- Ascension mission church and hall, Preston, Wembley, LB Brent. 1937
- Golders Green Crematorium Chapel, LB Barnet. 1938

Hedley A. Mobbs

- Methodist church, Sandy Bank, Lincoln. 1954

Montague Associates

- RC Christ the King, Prince Charles Ave, Derby. 1971–2

Francis G. Montgomery

- RC Church of the Blessed Sacrament, Walton Vale, Liverpool. 1956–7
- RC St Winefride, Bootle, Sefton. 1957
- RC Our Lady of the Assumption, Belle Vale, Liverpool. 1958–9

Leslie T. Moore

- St John the Evangelist, Rosmead Ave, Hull. 1924–5. Restored 1952
- St George and St Michael, Castleton, N. Yorks. 1924–6. II
- St Wilfrid, Duchy Rd, Harrogate, N. Yorks. 1924–8, tower, transepts; 1935 Lady chapel; to Temple Moore church 1905–14. A
- St Hilda, Windmill Lane, Shiregreen, Sheffield. 1924, 1937
- All Saints, Basingstoke, Hants. Additions 1930. II
- All Saints, Dormanstown, Redcar, N. Yorks. 1932
- St Oswald, Grove Hill, Middlesbrough. 1934.
- St Luke, Luton. 1936
- St Oswald Mission Church and Hall, Croxley Green, Watford. 1937
- St Francis, Cornyx Lane, Elmdon Heath, Solihull, W. Mids. 1939, 1946–50
- St Leonard, Norwood, Sheffield. 1951
- St Mary, Hobs Moat, Solihull, W. Mids. 1955

Louis Moore

- Christian Science. Sixth Church, Putney, LB Wandsworth. 1940

Temple Lushington Moore

- St Cuthbert, Lytham Rd, Preston, Lancs. Designed 1912–13, built 1914–16
- St Thomas, London Rd, Boston, Lincs. 1912, chancel 1933.
- St Aidan, Manchester Rd, Rochdale. 1913–15. II
- St Augustine, Gillingham, Kent. Designed 1913, built 1915–16
- St Mary, Nunthorpe, Middlesbrough. Designed 1914, built 1924–26. II Built by L.T. Moore.
- St Cyprian, Longsight, Manchester. 1914–17. Demolished.
- St Mary, Sculcoates, Hull. Designed 1914–15, built 1915–16. West extention 1925–6 by L.T. Moore. II
- All Saints, Victoria St, Basingstoke, Hants. Designed 1915, built 1915–17. II.
- St Columba, Dean Rd, Scarborough, N. Yorks. Designed 1911–14, built 1922–6. Built by L.T. Moore.

W.J. Moore

- RC Cushendall Church, Co. Antrim. 1914. B
- RC Our Lady Start of the Sea, Portstewart, Co Derry. 1916. B
- RC Milltown Church, Glenariff, Co. Antrim. B

Guy Morgan and Partners

- RC Holy Mary, Bepton Rd, Midhurst, W. Sussex. 1957

Morgan and Branch

- Unitarian church, Palace Gardens Terrace, RB Kensington and Chelsea, 1976–7

Morley and Bolden

- St Michael, Hamworthy, Poole, Dorset. 1958–9

Morris, Smith and Partners

- RC St John, St John St, Tamworth, Staffs. 1954–6. Adds to 1829 church.

J. Inch Morrison

- St Aidan, Stenhouse Grove, Edinburgh. 1933

S.P. Morter and W.G. Dobie

- St Andrew, Clubmoor, Liverpool. 1930
- Presbyterian. Rankin Memorial Church, Norris Green, Liverpool. 1931
- Presbyterian church, Allerton, Liverpool. 1932
- United Reformed Church. St Columba, Weelsby Rd, Grimsby. 1932

W.J. Moscrop

- St Paul, Bishopton Rd, Stockton-on-Tees. 1925–6. West end completed 1964–6

A.H. Mottram

- RC St John and St Columba, Crossroads Place, Rosyth, Fife. 1926
- Parish Church, Queensferry Rd, Rosyth, Fife. 1929–31

John Mottram

- RC Polish Church of Divine Mercy, Farnham Rd, Slough. 1983–4

Glendinning Moxham

- St Hilary, Killay, Swansea. 1925–6.

Geoffrey Mullins

- St Francis, Willett Way, Petts Wood, LB Bromley. 1934–5

James F. Munce and Kennedy

- Imakee Presbyterian Church, Dunmurry, Belfast. 1960–1

J.M. Munro and Son

- Church of Scotland. Calton New Parish Church, Bain Square, Glasgow. 1925–6 rebuilding of 1836–7 church gutted by fire.

Padraig Murray

- RC Our Lady of Bethlehem Abbey, Portglenone, Co. Antrim. 1962–71. B

Murray, Ward and Partners

- Gordonstown School Chapel, Scotland. 1966

Narracott, Tanner and André

- Central Church, Torquay, Torbay. 1970

Naylor, Sale and Widdows

- St Paulinus, Ollerton, Notts. 1933
- St Luke, Loscoe, Derbys. 1938
- St Alkmund, Kedleston Rd, Derby. 1967–72

Kenneth Nealon

- Methodist church, Redcliffe Crescent, Bristol. 1956

Hamilton Neil

- United Free. Sherwood Church, Paisley. 1925

J.K. Nelson

- St Leonard, Bootle, Sefton. 1950

J.E. Newberry and C.W. Fowler

- All Saints, E. Sheen Ave, E. Sheen, LB Richmond. 1929
- St Martin, Goresbrook Rd, Becontree, LB Barking and Dagenham. 1931–2
- St Patrick, Park Hill Rd, Wallington, LB Sutton. 1932
- St James, Bodley Rd, New Malden, LB Kingston. 1934
- Good Shepherd, Collier Row Lane, Romford, LB Havering. 1934–5
- St Andrew, Electric Ave, Westcliff-on-Sea, Essex. 1935
- St John, Selsdon, LB Croydon. 1935–6
- St Francis of Assisi, West Wickham, LB Bromley. 1935–6
- SS George and Ethelbert, Burford Rd, East Ham, LB Newham. 1936–7
- Ascension, Chelmsford, Essex. 1939
- See also Greenaway and Newberry

Newcombe and Newcombe

- Holy Spirit, Denton, Manchester. 1962

A.J. Newton. See Burles, Newton and Partners

W.G. Newton and Partners

- Chapel for the Sisters of Bethany, Boscombe, Bournemouth. 1928–30

C. Nicholas and J.E. Dixon Spain

- St Alphage, Hendon, LB Barnet. 1937
- RC St Joan of Arc, Elstead Rd, Farnham, Surrey. 1929–31. With H. Faulkner and M. Aylwin.
- RC St Hugh, Letchworth, Herts. Designed 1938, built 1960

Sir Charles Nicholson

- Holy Spirit (formerly St Matthew), Fawcett Rd, Southsea, Portsmouth. 1904–26. Completion of J.T. Micklethwaite church; restored after bombing by S.E. Dykes Bower, 1956–8
- St George, Minworth, Sutton Coldfield, Birmingham. 1909, later alterations
- St Paul, Yelverton, Devon. 1910–14
- St Paul, Queen's Rd, Halifax. 1912. C
- St Lawrence, Oswald Rd, Frodingham, Scunthorpe. 1913
- St Alban, Copnor Rd, Copnor, Portsmouth. 1914. West end rebuilt 1956. C
- St Michael, Holderness Rd, Sutton Ings, Hull. 1915 (Nicholas and Corlette)
- Cathedral Church of SS Peter and Paul, Sheffield. 1919–48, adds to C15 raised to Cathedral status in 1914. I. See also Ansell and Bailey
- St John, College St, Long Eaton, Derbys. 1922 (designed 1916)
- Memorial Chapel, Rugby School, Dunchurch Rd, Rugby, Warks. 1922. II*
- Cathedral Church of St Mary, Chelmsford, Essex. East end chapter house and vestries. 1923–6. B
- Ascension, Cobden Ave, Bitterne Park, Southampton. 1924–6
- St Dunstan, Bellingham Green, LB Lewisham. 1925–6. Unfinished.
- Church of Ireland. St Anne's Cathedral, Donegall St, Belfast. W front 1925–7, baptistry 1928, chapel 1930–2, apse and ambulatory 1947–59. A. See also J. MacGeagh.
- St Mary, Springbourne, Bournemouth. 1926–34. II
- St Michael and All Angels, Leigh-on-Sea, Southend, Essex. 1926–57
- St Michael, Smawthorne Lane, Castleford, W. Yorks. 1927–9
- St John, Bromley Rd, Southend, LB Lewisham. 1925–8, unfinished. C
- St John the Evangelist, Dudley Wood Rd, Netherton, W. Mids. 1928
- St John, Weston Rd, Stafford. 1928
- St Barnabas, Downham Way, LB Lewisham. 1928–9
- St Laurence, Upminster, LB Havering. Additions 1928–9, 1937
- St Mary Magdalene, Old Rd, Frinton, Essex. 1928–9
- St Andrew, Burnt Ash Lane, LB Bromley. 1929
- St George, Woodford Ave, Barkingside, LB Redbridge. 1931–2
- St Margaret, Lime Ave, Leigh-on-Sea, Southend, Essex. 1931. II
- All Saints, Long Lane, LB Hillingdon. 1932
- St Peter, Bishopsford Rd, St Helier, Morden, LB Merton. 1932
- Holy Cross, Airedale, Wakefield. 1932. With T.J. Rushton

- St Elizabeth, Wood Lane, Becontree, LB Barking and Dagenham. 1932
- St Lawrence, Bridle Rd, Eastcote, LB Hillingdon. 1932–3
- St Luke, Northover, Downham, LB Lewisham. 1934
- St Thomas, Camelford, Cornwall. 1938. With T.J. Rushton
- Cathedral Church of St Thomas, Portsmouth. 1938–9. Westward extensions and alterations to church founded 1180, parish church 1320, cathedral status 1927. I
- St Hugh, Northampton Rd, Market Harborough, Leics. 1938–40
- College Chapel, Ellesmere, Cheshire. 1957. By T.J. Rushton
- St David, Eastwood, Essex. 1965–7. By H.T. Rushton.
- Methodist. St Andrew, St Peter's Ave, Cleethorpes. 1978. By Sir Charles Nicholson, Rushton and Smith.

Nicholson and Jacobsen

- RC St Joseph, Fullarton Ave, Glasgow. 1978–80

Richard S. Nickson

- St Chad, Tonge Fold, Bolton. 1937

William Nimmo and Partners

- Church of Scotland. Carnwadric Church, Boydestone Rd, Glasgow. 1952

Richard M. Noad and A.F. Wallace

- Scottish Episcopal. Good Shepherd, Hillington Rd, Glasgow. 1939–40
- United Free Church, Croftfoot, Croftpark Ave, Glasgow. 1949
- St Mark's Episcopal Church, E. Kilbride, S. Lanarks. 1957

E. Bower Norris and F.M. Reynolds

- RC Convent of St Paul, Selly Park Rd, Birmingham. Chapel 1914. E.B. Norris
- RC Our Lady's Convent, Southam, Warks. Chapel 1925
- RC St Paul, Birmingham. 1928
- RC St Joseph, Leyton, LB Waltham Forest. 1928
- RC St Gerard, Coleshill, Warks. 1928
- RC Our Lady of Lourdes, Cambridge Park, Wanstead, LB Waltham Forest. 1928. By E.B. Norris.
- RC St Cecilia, Liverpool. 1931
- RC St Anne, Blackburn, Lancs. 1931–3
- RC SS Peter and Paul, Atherton St, Wallasey, Wirral. 1932–5
- RC English Martyrs, Sparkhill, Birmingham. 1933
- RC Sacred Heart, N. Walsham, Norfolk. 1934–5
- RC St John Fisher and St Thomas More, Benchill, Wythenshawe, Manchester. 1935
- RC Our Lady and St Brigid, Frankley Beeches Rd, Northfield, Birmingham. 1936
- RC St Bernadette, Allerton, Liverpool. 1936–7
- RC St Alphonsius, Manchester. 1936–7
- RC St Dunstan, Moston Lane, Manchester. 1937. II

- RC St Joseph, Waterloo Rd, Burslem, Stoke-on-Trent. 1937. E. Bower Norris.
- RC Sacred Heart, Preston New Rd, Blackburn. 1937–8
- RC Sacred Heart, Bilton, Warks. 1959. E. Bower Norris
- See also Hill, Sandy and Norris
- See also Reynolds and Scott
- See also Sandy and Norris

Herbert Luck North and P.M. Padmore
- St Winifred's Chapel, Woodard School, Llanfairfechan, Caernarvon. Demolished
- Church Hostel chapel, Bangor, Wales. 1933. Now the University Anglican Chaplaincy Centre. Extended by P.M. Padmore 1953–4, and altered by Bowen, Dann, Davies in 1978. II
- Holy Spirit, Harlescott, Shrewsbury. 1936 (now community centre)
- St Catherine, Blackwell, Worcs. 1939–40

Northampton Development Corporation
- Emmanuel Shared Church, Weston Favell Centre, Northampton. 1973

Peter B. Nuttall
- RC St Joseph, Macleod St, Nelson, Lancs. 1962–4

David Evelyn Nye
- St Mark, Westmoreland Rd, LB Bromley. 1953 incorporating tower and arcades by Evelyn Hellicar of 1897–8. With T.W.G. Grant
- St Swithun, Purley, LB Croydon. 1954
- St Faith, Sunray Ave, Herne Hill, LB Southwark. 1958–9
- Christ the King, Salfords, Surrey. 1958–67
- St Andrew with St Thomas, Short St, LB Lambeth. 1960
- Good Shepherd, Pyrford, Surrey. 1963–4
- St Alban, W. Leigh, Havant, Hants. 1966

Edmund Oakley
- St George, E. Boldon, Sunderland. 1933

Sir George Oatley
- St Edyth, Avonleaze, Sea Mills, Bristol. 1928. Altered 1993
- Lancing Chapel transept, W. Sussex. 1929, with G.C. Lawrence. I

C.S. Oldfield
- Elim Pentecostal Church, Halifax. 1972

John S. O'Doherty
- RC St John, Moneymore, Co. Derry. 1956
- RC St Joseph and St Malachy, Drumullan, Coagh, Co. Tyrone. 1958

Oldreave, Bell and Patterson
- Bristol Baptist Church, Queensferry Rd, Edinburgh. 1932–5. By William Patterson

Paul Oliver
- Mormon. Jesus Christ and Latter Day Saints, Edinburgh Rd, Dumfries. 1963–6

Richard O'Mahoney and Partners
- RC St Michael and All Angels, New Hey Rd, Woodchurch, Birkenhead. 1963–5. Scheme inherited from F.X. Velarde and Partners
- RC Our Lady of the Rosary, Donnington, Liverpool. 1970
- RC St John Stone, Woodvale, Lancs. 1972

Gordon O'Neill
- St Cedd, Beckton Rd, Canning Town, LB Newham. 1938–9
- RC St Francis of Assisi, Halstead, Suffolk. 1958. With George R. Fordham.

J.P. Osborne and Son
- St Matthew, Aldridge Rd, Perry Beeches, Birmingham. 1939 (now hall to 1962–4 church by Maguire and Murray, q.v.)
- All Saints, Coneyford Rd, Shard End, Birmingham. 1955–7 (F.J. Osborne)
- Methodist church, Bristol Rd South, Northfield, Birmingham. 1956
- St Stephen, Rednal, Birmingham. 1957
- St Paul, Belchers Lane, Bordesley Green, Birmingham. 1968 (John Osborne)
- St Peter, Tile Cross, Birmingham. 1968
- St Cuthbert, Castle Vale, Birmingham. 1973

Charles D. Ostick
- Methodist church, Bloomfield, Belfast. 1955

Oxley and Bussey
- St Peter, Greenhill, Sheffield. 1964–5

George G. Pace
- Llandaff Cathedral, Cardiff. 1949–64. Reconstruction after war damage. A
- All Saints, Intake, Doncaster. 1951–6
- St James, Acomb Moor, York. 1955.
- Holy Trinity, Christchurch, Newport, Wales. 1955–8. Rebuilding after fire. II
- St Martin-le-Grand, York. 1956–68. Rebuilding after war damage. II
- St Michael's College Chapel, Llandaff, Cardiff. 1957–9
- St Leonard and St Jude, Doncaster. 1957–60
- Scargill Chapel, Kettlewell, N. Yorks. 1958–61.
- St Mark, Broomfield Rd, Broomhill, Sheffield. 1958–63. New church to 1871 tower.
- St Luke, Penarth, Vale of Glamorgan. 1959–60
- Holy Redeemer, Acomb, York. 1959–63.
- St Mark, Chadderton, Oldham. 1960–3.
- St Michael, St Michael's Ave, Bramhall, Cheshire. 1960–3 tower only.
- St Teilo, Cockett, Caer Eithin, Swansea. 1961–3

- All Saints, Branston, Lincs. Chancel, 1964. II*
- Ecumenical. Keele University Chapel, Newcastle-under-Lyme, Staffs. 1964–5
- William Temple Memorial Church, Wythenshawe, Manchester. 1964–5
- St John's College Chapel, York. 1965–6, 1969
- St Saviour, Fairweather Green, Bradford. 1966
- St Mark, Rawcliffe, York. 1967–9
- St Mark, Thornaby-on-Tees, Cleveland. 1968–70
- St John, Wawne Rd, Bramsholme, Hull. 1968–73
- St Thomas and St Paul, Scarborough, N. Yorks. 1969
- Church of the Ascension, Woolston, Warrington. 1970
- St James the Deacon, Acomb, York. 1970–1

D.J. Pamplin
- St Francis of Assisi, Galahad Ave, Strood, Kent. 1960
- St Philip and St James, King George's Rd, Walderslade, Kent. 1961–2

Paul J.J. Panter
- St Barnabas, St Barnabas St, Wellingborough. 1950–4

Barry Parker
- The Free Church, Norton Way South, Letchworth, Herts. 1923. II

Frank W. Parkinson
- Congregational church, Four Lane Ends, Shear Brow, Blackburn. 1925

J.F. Parkinson
- United Reformed. St Ninian, Chanterlands Ave, Hull. 1931

Pascall and Watson
- Baptist church, Days Lane, Sidcup, LB Bexley. 1966

Kenneth W. Patterson and John S. Macaulay
- Congregational church, Hoole, Chester. 1958
- St Martin, Suez Rd, Cambridge. 1960–2
- St John, Macclesfield, Cheshire. 1962
- St Columba, Liverpool. 1964–5
- Methodist church, Church Rd, Tranmere, Birkenhead. 1966 (Patterson, Macaulay and Owens).

F. Barry Peacock
- RC Sacred Heart and St Catherine of Alexandria, Worcester Rd, Droitwich, Worcs. 1919–32

Paul Pearn
- RC St Margaret Mary, Quarry Park Rd, Plymstock, Devon. 1956–61
- RC St Paul, Torridge Rd, Efford, Plymouth, Devon. 1963. Pearn and Proctor.
- RC Buckfast Abbey, Buckfastleigh, Devon. Blessed Sacrament Chapel. 1965. See also Walters and Kerr Bate. II*

Lionel Pearson
- Sandham Memorial Chapel, Burghclere, Hants. 1927. I

Pearson and Burrell
- Congregational church, Shirley, Southampton. 1926

Dick Peddie and Walker Todd
- Episcopal. St Ninian, Comely Bank, Edinburgh. 1921. Now church hall to church of 1952 by R.H. Taylor.
- Episcopal. St Catherine, Cadzow Crescent, Bo'ness, W. Lothian. 1925
- Episcopal. St Peter, High St, Linlithgow, W. Lothian. 1928. B
- Episcopal. St Andrew and St Aidan, Hay Drive, Edinburgh. 1935

P.N. Perkins
- St Stephen, Upper Basildon, Berks. 1964–5

Perry, Shaw, Hepburn, Kehoe and Dean
- American Military Cemetery, Madingley, Cambridge. 1952–4

Ronald A. Phillips and Partners
- Holy Epiphany, Bournemouth. 1953

P. Phipps
- Christian Science. Seventh Church, Wright's Lane, RB Kensington. 1927
- Christian Science. First Church, Sevenoaks, Kent. 1937–8
- Christian Science. First Church, LB Croydon. 1937–8

Pick, Everard and Keay
- Holy Apostles, Fosse Rd South, Leicester. 1923–4

Z. Jan Piet (with Brian and Norman Westwood)
- RC Most Holy Name, Military Rd, Shorncliffe Camp, Sandgate, Kent. 1967–9

Michael Pigott
- Baptist Church, W. Green, Crawley, W. Sussex. 1953

J.A. Pinckheard and Partners
- Magdalen College School Chapel, Oxford. 1967–8

Pinckney and Gott
- St Michael, Weyhill Rd, Andover, Hants. 1962–4. By R.A.P. Pinckney.
- All Saints, Redbridge, Southampton. 1964–5
- All Hallows, Witts Hill, Midanbury, Southampton. 1965–6

A. Beresford Pite
- Monkton Down School Chapel, Monkton Combe, Somerset. 1925. With J.S. Hodges

William A. Pite
- St Peter, Southfield Rd, Acton Green, LB Ealing. 1914–15. Church hall by Morley Horder
- St Jude, Thornton Heath, LB Croydon. 1927–8 (Pite, Son and Fairweather)
- St John the Baptist, Beckenham, LB Bromley. 1932 (Pite, Son and Fairweather)
- Holy Cross, Hornchurch, LB Havering. 1932–3 (Pite, Son and Fairweather)
- Christ Church, Orpington, LB Bromley. 1940 (Pite, Son and Fairweather)

Donald Plaskett, Marshall and Partners
▸ RC St Boniface, German Mission, Adler St, LB Tower Hamlets. 1959–60

Edward Playne and John S. Lacey
▸ Chapel to Queen Mary College, Mile End Rd, LB Tower Hamlets. 1962–3

Rev. C.P. Plummer
▸ RC Our Lady and St Philip Neri, Uckfield, E. Sussex. 1957–61

Francis Pollen
▸ RC Assumption of Our Lady and St Thérèse, Presteigne, Powys. 1952–4
▸ RC Convent of Jesus and Mary, Willesden, LB Brent. 1955
▸ RC Our Lady Help of Christians, Hurst Green, E. Sussex. 1959
▸ RC Church of Our Lady, Help of Christians, Worth Abbey, Kent. 1965–75
▸ RC St John Bosco, Woodley, Reading. 1966
▸ RC St Peter, Marlow, Bucks. 1973 extension to church by A.W.N. Pugin of 1845. 1973. II*

Bernard Arthur Porter
▸ Baptist. Grey Memorial Church, Twickenham, LB Richmond. 1914

Robert Potter (Potter and Hare)
▸ St Leonard, Bristol. 1936–7
▸ St Francis, Castle Rd, Salisbury, Wilts. 1936–9. II
▸ St Francis, Ashton Gate, Bristol. 1952–3. With Richard Hare
▸ Bridgemary Church/Hall, Rowner, Gosport, Hants. 1953–5
▸ Ascension, Crownhill, Plymouth. 1956. With Richard Hare
▸ All Saints, Wavell Rd, Swanage, Dorset. 1956–7
▸ St George, Oakdale, Poole, Dorset. 1959–60. With Richard Hare
▸ St Mary, St Mary's Rd, Peckham, LB Southwark. 1961–2
▸ All Saints, Pembroke Rd, Clifton, Bristol. 1963–6. II. Reconstruction after war damage, incorporating Street tower. See also F.C. Eden.
▸ St Aldate, Gloucester. 1964. With Richard Hare
▸ St Anthony's College Chapel, Leweston, Dorset. 1968–70. Brandt Potter Hare Partnership.
▸ St Paul, Covingham, Swindon, Wilts, with library. 1971. Brandt Potter Hare Partnership.

Harry R. Poulter and B.A. Poulter
▸ RC St Joseph, Aldershot, Hants. 1923

Charles B. Powell
▸ RC St Mary, North Rd, Lowe House, St Helens. 1924–30

G. Sworler Powell
▸ St James, St James's Ave, Elmers End, LB Bromley. 1934, major extension to A.R. Stenning church of 1879–88.

Frederick R. Pratten
▸ RC St Pius X, Bristol. 1961–2

Ernest Prestwich
▸ Methodist. Peter Lee Memorial Church, Bede Way, Peterlee, Co. Durham. 1957–8

J.C. Prestwich and Sons
▸ Methodist. Butler St Church, Manchester. 1964

L.A.G. Prichard, Son and Partners
▸ RC English Martyrs, School Lane, Litherland, Merseyside. 1935 (Prichard)
▸ St Jude, St Paul's Ave, Worsley Mesnes, Wigan. 1963–4
▸ St Agnes, St Mary's Rd, Huyton, Merseyside. 1964–5
▸ RC St Columba, Plas Newton Lane, Newton, Chester. 1966
▸ RC Christ the King, Queen's Drive, Wavertree, Liverpool. 1966–7
▸ RC St Swithun, Gill Moss, W. Derby, Liverpool. 1966–7 (Francis Leo Prichard)

B. Prichard
▸ RC St Joan of Arc, Bootle, Liverpool. 1962–3

J.P. Prichett and Son
▸ St Mary, Cockerton Green, Darlington, Durham. 1926

G.H. Fellowes Prynne
▸ St Michael, New Town, Beaconsfield, Bucks. 1914–16. East end 1954–5. Lady chapel 1963

Pugin and Pugin
▸ RC St Robert Ballarmine, Peat Rd, Glasgow. 1955–9

Pullan and Ronchetti
▸ RC St Joseph, High St, Aylesbury, Bucks. 1934–5

C.H. Purcell
▸ RC St Ninian, Knightswood Rd, Glasgow. 1956–9. Completed by S. Stevenson-Jones. B

Donovan C. Purcell and Frederick K. Johnson
▸ RC Our Lady and St Thomas of Canterbury, Wymondham, Norfolk. 1955–6
▸ RC Sacred Heart and St Margaret Mary, E. Dereham, Norfolk. 1956

Martin T. Purdy
▸ St Philip and St James, Hodge Hill, Birmingham. 1965–8
▸ See also APEC, Peter Bridges and Martin Purdy

C.H.B. Quennell
▸ St John, Edmonton, LB Enfield. 1926–7

Quiggan and Gee
▸ Christ Church, Sedgmoor Rd, Norris Green, Liverpool. 1931–2
▸ St Anne, Wigan. 1953
▸ St Oswald, St Oswald's Lane, Netherton, Liverpool. 1960–1

David M. Rae
▸ Mormon. Church of Jesus Christ and Latter Day Saints, Nightingale Lane, LB Wandsworth. 1966

H. Rainger
▸ Emmanuel, Ewlyn Rd, Cheltenham, Glos. 1936

Walter N.W. Ramsay
▸ Church of Scotland. Castlemilk East Church, Barlia Terrace, Glasgow. 1956–9

R.B. Rankin and Associates
▸ Baptist. Springburn Church, Springburn Rd, Glasgow. 1980

E. Ravenscroft
▸ St Agnes, Northumberland Ave, Reading. 1938

Geoffrey Raymond (Scoles and Raymond)
▸ Chapel to St Ann's Convent, Southampton. 1922–3
▸ RC Assumption of Our Lady, Maldon, Essex. 1924

Reavell and Cahill (Thomas J. Cahill and Mary J. Cahill)
▸ RC Immaculate Heart of Mary, Durham Rd, Springwell, Sunderland. 1954
▸ RC Holy Family, Park Rd, Gateshead. 1959
▸ RC Holy Rosary, Gateshead. 1962

Claude Redgrave and Partners
▸ Methodist Central Hall, Warwick Lane, Coventry. 1932
▸ Methodist church, Lockhurst Lane, Coventry. 1957

W. Beddoe Rees
▸ Baptist. Ararat English Baptist Church, Merthyr Rd, Whitchurch, Cardiff. 1914–15

Dalby Reeve
▸ RC St Anne, Eastern Esplanade, Margate. 1926. E. end H. Curtis, 1964

Alan Reiach
▸ Parish church, Bogwood Rd, Easthouses, Dalkeith, Midlothian. 1954–5
▸ St John's Parish Church, Oxgangs, Edinburgh. 1956

Douglas Reid
▸ RC Christ the King, Gower St, Brora, Sutherland. 1973

J.T. Reid (Reid Partnership)
▸ RC St Mary Queen of Martyrs, Bransholme, Hull. 1976

Reid and Forbes
▸ Richmond Craigmillar Church, Niddrie Mains Rd, Edinburgh, 1934

Edwin F. Reynolds (as Wood Kendrick and Edwin F. Reynolds from 1926)
▸ All Saints, Belwell Lane, Four Oaks, Sutton Coldfield, W. Mids. 1908 (nave and aisles – see also Wood Kendrick and Williams). II*

▸ St Germain, City Rd, Edgbaston, Birmingham. 1915–17
▸ St Mary, Padstow Rd, Pype Hayes, Birmingham. 1929–30. II
▸ St John Evangelist, Essington, Staffs. 1932.
▸ St Gabriel, Shenley Lane, Weoley Castle, Birmingham. 1934 (incomplete)
▸ St Mark, Thimblemill Rd, Londonderry, Sandwell, W. Mids. 1935
▸ St Alban, Stanhope St, Highgate, Birmingham. Tower 1938 (added to church of 1879–81 by J.L. Pearson). II*
▸ St Hilda, Pottery Rd, Warley Woods, Sandwell, W. Mids. 1938–40

Peter Reynolds
▸ Baptist. John Bunyan Church, Crowell Rd, Cowley, Oxford. 1959
▸ RC St Dominic Barberi, Littlemore, Oxon. 1969

Reynolds and Scott
▸ RC St Willibrand, North Rd, Openshaw, Manchester. 1938. II
▸ RC St Thomas More, Knighton, Leicester. 1952
▸ RC St Joseph, High Rd, Wembley, LB Brent. 1956–7
▸ RC Sacred Heart, Moreton, Wallasey, Wirral. 1957
▸ RC Mother of God, New Parks Boulevard, Leicester. 1957
▸ RC St Patrick, Beaumont Leys Lane, Leicester. 1958
▸ RC St Ambrose, Princess Rd, Chorlton-cum-Hardy, Manchester. 1958
▸ RC St Teresa, Blacon Ave, Chester. 1957–9
▸ RC Holy Cross, Watnall Rd, Hucknall, Notts. 1959
▸ RC Sacred Heart, Levenshulme Rd, Longsight, Manchester. 1962
▸ RC St Mary, Barnard Ave, Brigg, Lincs. 1963–4
▸ RC Our Lady of Lincoln, Lincoln. 1963–4
▸ RC Our Lady of Lourdes, Chapel Lane, Partington, Cheshire. 1964
▸ RC St Peter and Paul, Skellingthorpe Rd, Boultham, Lincoln. 1968
▸ RC Our Lady of Good Counsel, Peebles Way, Leicester. 1975

Sir Albert Richardson
▸ St Mary, Eaton Socon, Cambs. 1930 rebuilding of medieval church gutted by fire.
▸ Bricket Wood Mission Church and hall, Herts. 1936
▸ St Christopher, Round Green, Luton, Beds. 1936–7
▸ Holy Cross, Ferrymead Gardens, Greenford, LB Ealing. 1939–41. II*
▸ Ridley Hall Chapel, Cambs. 1950. Rebuilding after war damage.
▸ St Cuthbert, Colburn, N. Yorks. 1957 (Richardson and Houfe)
▸ Strawberry Hill Chapel, Twickenham, LB Richmond-on-Thames, 1960–4

T.W.T. Richardson
▸ Methodist Central Hall, The Green, Billingham, Teeside. 1932

Norman T. Rider
- St Peter, Highfield Rd, Hall Green, Birmingham. 1964

E.H. Rimmer
- Anglican church, Llanwygm. 1927
- St Whatley, Clayshott, Surrey. 1936–7

Frank Rimmington
- St Mark, Edge Lane, Edge Hill, Liverpool. 1925–7

Giuseppe Rinvolucri
- RC St Teresa of Lisieux, Dundonald Ave, Abergele, Denbighshire. 1934. Altered 1971 by Bowen, Dann, Davies. II
- RC St Peter, Henley Rd, Ludlow, Shropshire. 1936
- RC St Teresa of the Child Jesus, Aylesbury Rd, Princes Risborough, Bucks. 1937–8

E.C. Roberts
- Thornhill Crematorium, Thornhill Rd, Llanishen, Cardiff. 1954

Francis B. Roberts
- RC St Mary Magdalen, Penwortham, Lancs. 1987
- St Christopher, Blackpool, Lancs. 1990–1
- St Jude, Blackburn, Lancs. 1993

Hugh D. Roberts
- St Philip and St James, Odd Down, Bath. 1957

John Roberts Associates
- New Life Church, Brumby Wood Lane, Scunthorpe. 1975. David Broughton.

J.J. Robinson
- RC St Colman's College Chapel, Coleraine, Co. Derry. 1937–8. B+

Robert Robinson
- RC Blessed Sacrament, Alexandra Rd, Gorseinon, Swansea. 1968

Thomas Roderick
- RC Church of the Resurrection, Ely, Cardiff. 1934. II

H.S. Rogers
- St Luke, Oxford Rd, Crowley, Oxford. 1937–8

Robert Rogerson and Philip Spence
- Ruchazie Church, Elibank St, Glasgow. 1955. By R.W.K.C. Rogerson.
- Fernhill and Cathkin Church, Neilvaig Drive, Glasgow. 1962
- St Mary Tron, Red Rd, Springburn, Glasgow. 1962–5
- Victoria Park Parish Church, Broomhill Drive, Glasgow. 1968–70

Robert A. Ronchetti
- RC St Mary Immaculate, Rotherham. 1954–5

R.H. Rosner
- German Lutheran Church, Cottingham Rd, Hull. 1967–8

Alexander Ross and Son
- Episcopal. St Paul, Kinlochleven, Highland. 1954

David J.A. Ross, Archibald M. Doak and Alexander R. Whitelaw
- Moncrieff Church, East Kilbride, S. Lanarkshire. 1964
- See also Doak and Whitelaw

Launcelot H. Ross
- Drumchapel Old Church, Drumchapel Rd, Glasgow. 1936–43. C
- Drumry St Mary, Drumry Rd East, Glasgow. 1955–7. Ross, Doak and Whitelaw.

W.A. Ross (War Office)
- St Wilfrid, Towthorpe, N. Yorks. 1933
- St Alban, Larkhill, Wilts. 1937

Anthony J. Rossi
- RC St Patrick, Victoria Rd, Consett, Co. Durham. 1959
- RC St Pius, Sussex Rd, Moorside, Consett, Co. Durham. 1959
- RC St Joseph, Church Lane, Murton, Co. Durham. 1965
- RC Our Lady Queen of Peace, Penshaw, Co. Durham. 1965
- RC St Bede, New Rd, Usworth, Washington, Co. Durham. 1965
- RC Holy Rosary, Horsley Hill Square, S. Shields. 1967–8
- RC St Patrick, Stanley, Co. Durham. 1968
- RC Holy Family, Gardiner Rd, Grindon, Sunderland. 1968
- RC St Laban, Queen Victoria St, Pelaw, Gateshead. 1972 (Rossi, McCann and Partners)
- RC St Patrick, Fairfield Rd, Stockton-on-Tees. 1973 (Rossi, McCann and Partners)
- RC St Anne, Rokeby View, Harlow Green, Gateshead. 1976 (Rossi, McCann and Partners)

E. Vernon Royle
- St Mark, Laceby Rd, Grimsby. 1959–61

B.A. Rush and Associates
- RC St Joseph, Whitnash, Warks. 1971–2
- RC Our Lady of the Wayside, Shirley, Birmingham. 1971–2

H.T. Rushton
- Holy Cross, Skellingthorpe Rd, Boultham, Lincoln. 1939–40

A.H. Ryan-Tennyson
- St Paul, Pixmore Way, Letchworth, Herts. 1924

Vyvyan Salisbury
- RC Abbey of St Mary and St Petroc, Bodmin, Cornwall. 1965

Sandy and Norris
- RC English Martyrs, Evelyn Rd, Sparkhill, Birmingham. 1923
- RC St Joseph, Grange Park Rd, LB Waltham Forest. 1924
- RC Sacred Heart, Victoria Rd, Tipton, Sandwell, W. Mids. 1940
- RC Ratcliffe College, Ratcliffe-on-the-Wreake, Leics. 1958–62
- RC St Mary, Loughborough, Leics. 1959
- See also Norris and Reynolds.

Raphael Martin Sargent
- RC Holy family, Farnham, Surrey. 1956–7

A.E.F. Saunders
- Methodist church, Woodbridge Rd, Guildford, Surrey. 1966
- Congregational church, Portsmouth Rd, Guildford, Surrey. 1967

W.H. Saunders and Son
- RC Immaculate Conception, Portswood Rd, Portswood, Southampton. 1955
- Baptist church, Kent St, Portsmouth. 1956–7

Saxon and Smith
- RC St Aloysius, Huyton, Liverpool. 1953

William Peel Schofield
- Christian Science, First Church, Headingley Lane, Leeds. 1912–32

Alfred Schildt (of Frankfurt)
- German Lutheran Church, Chalmers Crescent, Edinburgh. 1967. With Reiach and Hall.

Scoles and Raymond
- RC St Joseph, Queen St, Newton Abbot, Devon. 1915

Hugh Segar (Sam) Scorer
- See Clarke Hall, Scorer and Bright.

Adrian Gilbert Scott
- RC Mount St Mary Chapel, Chesterfield, Derbys. 1923
- RC Christ the King, The Crescent, Wimbledon, LB Merton. 1928
- RC St Joseph, High St, Wealdstone, LB Harrow. 1931
- RC St Aidan, Chipstead Valley Rd, Coulsdon, LB Croydon. 1931. Completed in 1966 by Burles, Newton and Partners.
- RC Holy Name, Manchester. Tower 1932
- RC Convent chapel, Farnborough Hill, Farnborough, Hants. 1933. II. Additions
- RC St Teresa, Warwick Rd, Beaconsfield, Bucks. Walsingham Chapel, west end and English Martyrs Chapel, 1934 adds to church by A.S.G. Butler (q.v.)
- RC SS Mary and Joseph, New North St, Lansbury, LB Tower Hamlets. 1951–4
- RC St Joseph, Moreton Rd, Upton, Birkenhead. 1953–4
- RC Our Lady of Victories, High St, RB Kensington and Chelsea. 1955–8
- RC Our Lady and St Rose, Gregory Ave, Weoley Castle, Birmingham. 1959

Sir Giles Gilbert Scott
- Cathedral Church of Christ, Liverpool. 1904–78. I
- RC Annunciation, Charminster Rd, Bournemouth. 1906, 1960. II*
- RC St Joseph, Cromer Rd, Sheringham, Norfolk. 1908–9, 1934. II
- RC Our Lady Star of the Sea and St Maughold, Ramsey, Isle of Man. 1909.
- RC Our Lady of the Assumption, The Hill, Northfleet, Kent. 1913–16. II
- St Paul, Derby Lane, Stoneycroft, Liverpool. 1916. II*
- Charterhouse School Chapel, Godalming, Surrey. 1922–7. II*
- RC Ampleforth Abbey and College, N. Yorks. Additions, 1922–61. II
- Abbey Church, Downside Abbey Church of St Gregory the Great, Stratton-on-the-Fosse, Somerset. nave c.1923–5. I
- RC St Alphege, Oldfield Lane, Bath. 1925–54. II
- St Michael, Fordbridge Rd, Ashford, Surrey. 1927–8
- All Saints, Hose Side Rd, Wallasey, Wirral. 1927–39
- The Whittall Chantry, St Mary and All Saints, Church St, Kidderminster, Worcs. 1928. I
- Salvation Army. William Booth Memorial Training College, with hall. 1928–32. With Gordon and Viner. II
- RC St Ninian, Marionville Rd, Restalrig, Edinburgh. 1929
- St Francis of Assisi, Terriers, High Wycombe. 1929–30. B
- RC Our Lady Star of the Sea, Broadstairs Rd, Broadstairs, Kent. 1930–1. II
- St Andrew, Blenheim Crescent, Luton, Beds. 1931–2. II
- St Alban, West Heath Drive, Golders Green, LB Barnet. 1932. II
- RC Cathedral Church of St Columba, Oban. 1935, 1952. A
- St Leonard, St Leonards, E. Sussex. 1953–61. With Adrian Gilbert Scott.
- RC Our Lady of Mount Carmel, Kensington Church St, RB Kensington and Chelsea. 1954–9
- St Alban, Brooke St, Holborn, LB Camden. 1961 rebuilding of William Butterfield church incorporating his west end. With Adrian Gilbert Scott.
- RC Christ the King, Armada Way, Plymouth. 1961–2

Richard Gilbert Scott (Sir Giles Gilbert Scott, Son and Partner)
- St Mark, Biggin Hill, LB Bromley. 1955–9
- RC Our Lady Help of Christians, Tile Cross, Birmingham. 1966 (with Robert Brandt)
- RC St Thomas More, Horse Shoes Lane, Sheldon, Birmingham. 1969–70 (with Robert Brandt)

Scott and Williamson
- RC Our Lady of Perpetual Succour, Stephendale Rd, Fulham, LB Hammersmith and Fulham. 1922
- RC Holy Cross, Ashington Rd, Fulham. 1924, extended by T.B. Scott, 1955–6

Thomas H.B. Scott
- RC St Bonaventure, Parkway, Welwyn Garden City, Herts. 1926
- RC St Agnes, Cricklewood, LB Barnet. 1930
- RC St Thomas of Canterbury, Fulham. 1932
- RC St Lawrence, The Green, Feltham, LB Hounslow. 1933–4, 1936–40
- RC Our Lady of Muswell, Muswell Hill, LB Haringey. 1940
- RC Our Lady of Mount Carmel, Lampeter, Ceredigion. 1940
- RC Our Lady of Peace, Southbourne, Bowlem, 1940

Monsignor Bruno Scott-James
- RC Slipper Chapel, Houghton St Giles, Norfolk. Additions 1938, to medieval chapel restored by Thomas Garner 1904–. I

Henry Seaver
- Church in Ireland. St Colman, Newcastle, Co. Down. 1927. B
- Church in Ireland. St Christopher, Mersey St, Belfast. B. With R.H. Gibson.
- Church in Ireland. St Martin, Kenilworth St, Belfast. 1933. B
- Church in Ireland. St Patrick's Memorial Church, Saul, Co. Down. 1933. B+

John Seeds
- Congregational church, Donegal St, Belfast. 1932–3

Hon. John Seely (Lord Mottistone) and Paul Paget
- St Faith, Lee-on-the-Solent, Hants. 1933, extended 1936. II
- St George, Six Mile Bottom, Cambs. 1933
- St John, Island Rd, Barrow-in-Furness, Cumbria. 1935
- Holy Rood, Findon, Sussex. 1935
- St John, Newtown, Carlisle. 1936
- St Barnabas, Brookside, Carlisle. 1936. II
- All Saints Mission Church and hall, Heston, LB Hounslow. 1937
- St John the Baptist, Great Cambridge Rd, Tottenham, LB Haringey. 1937
- Ascension, Hanger Hill, LB Ealing. 1938–9
- St Bede's Chapel, College of St Hilda and St Bede, University of Durham. 1939–40
- All Hallows, Barking, Great Tower St, City of London. Reconstruction of Saxon and medieval church, 1949–57, with vestry 1931–2. I

- St Michael and St George, White City Estate, LB Hammersmith. 1952–3. Demolished.
- St Nicholas and All Hallows, Aberfeldy St, LB Tower Hamlets. 1954
- All Saints, Gosforth Lane, Oxhey, Herts. 1954
- Congregational. City Temple, Holborn Viaduct, City of London. Rebuilding behind facade of 1873–4 by H.F. Lockwood. 1954–5
- St Luke, Leagrave, Luton, Beds. 1956
- St Mary, Upper St, LB Islington. Replacement of bombed church, with 1751–4 tower by Launcelot Dowbiggin. II
- St George, Stevenage, Herts. 1956–60
- Methodist. Westminster College Chapel, Oxford. 1957–60
- St Mary, Hammersmith Rd, Fulham. 1960–1
- St Francis, Duston, Northampton. 1967
- St Mark, Gabalfa, Cardiff. 1967–8.

Seth-Smith, W.E. Monroe and Alexander Matthew
- St John the Evangelist, The Meads, Eastbourne, E. Sussex. 1957

Philip N. Shaffrey
- St Mary, Swanlinbar, 1958–9

D.A. Shanks
- Church in Ireland. St Ignatius, Carryduff, Co. Down. 1964–5. B

Stewart Michael Shaw, John E. Baikie and Frank Perry
- Old St Paul's Episcopal Church, Edinburgh. Additions 1962

Patrick J. Sheahan
- RC Our Lady Help of Christians, Hollow Way, Oxford. 1961

E.C. Shearman
- St Barnabas, Pitshanger Lane, LB Ealing. 1914–15. II. With Ernest A. Tyler.
- St Gabriel, Noel Rd, Acton, LB Ealing. 1929–31
- St Francis, Great West Rd, Osterley, LB Hounslow. 1933–5. II
- St Barnabas, Temple Fortune, LB Barnet. 1935–65

A. Ernest Shennan
- RC Our Lady of the Assumpton, Liverpool. 1950

Peter Shepheard
- Bishop Otter College (Chichester Institute of Higher Education) Chapel. 1963

Richard Sheppard, Robson and Partners
- Churchill College Chapel, Madingley Rd, Cambridge. 1965–8. II

J.G.R. Sheridan (E. Kirby and Sons)
- St Giles, Aintree Lane, Aintree, Liverpool. 1955–6

Colin Shewring
- St Luke, Halifax Drive, Leicester. Interior of church 1960–6 by David Boddington.
- Holy Family, Blackbird Leys Rd, Oxford. 1964–5

Thomas Shine, Bishop of Middlesborough
- RC Corpus Christi, Spring Bank West, Hull. 1932
- RC Holy Name, Hall Rd, Hull. 1933
- RC St Joseph, Marton Rd, Middlesborough. 1934

Godfrey B. Shipp
- Baptist church, Bilborough, Nottingham. 1959

C. Evelyn Simmons
- RC St Ninian, Victory Ave, Gretna, Dumfries and Galloway. 1917. B

Ronald G. Sims
- St Paul, Heslington, Hull. Extensions and remodelling 1971–3. II
- Anglican church, Bessacar, Doncaster. 1975
- St Paul, St Paul St, Hull. 1977–8
- St Mary, Putney Bridge, LB Wandsworth. Remodelling after fire damage, 1980–1. I

Ronald H. Sims and Patrick J. Coles
- Methodist. Punshon Memorial Church, Bournemouth. 1955–9

Peter Sinclair
- Denbeath Church, Buckhaven, Fife. 1931
- Wemyss Parish Church, E. Wemyss, Fife. 1936–7
- St Margaret, Woodside Rd, Glenrothes, Fife. 1953–4. B

W. Braxton Sinclair
- Christian Science. First Church, Southport, Sefton. 1924–33. Demolished.
- Christian Science. First Church, Widmore Rd, LB Bromley. 1927–32. II
- Christian Science. First Church, Sheen Rd, LB Richmond. 1939–53

Eric H. Skipper
- St Michael, Waddington, Lincs. 1955–6

Smart, Stewart and Mitchell
- Episcopal. St Finnian, Lumphinnans Rd, Lochgelly, Fife. 1937–8

Smee and Houchin
- Methodist church, Shirley, LB Croydon. 1936
- Trinity Methodist Church, E. Grinstead, Sussex. 1939
- See also H.R. Houchin

A. Llewellyn Smith
- Presbyterian. St Mark, Greenwich. 1955
- St Stephen, Canonbury, LB Islington. 1956–9, rebuilding behind Inwood and Clifton facade, 1839
- St Mary, Kennington Park Rd, Newington, LB Southwark. 1957–8, behind tower of 1876 by J. Fowler of Louth.

Frederick W. Beresford Smith
- St Francis, Keynsham, Bath. 1959

G. Smith
- Congregational church, Oxford Rd, Cowley, Oxford. 1929–30

John Joseph Martin Smith
- Baptist church, Mark's Gate, Ilford, LB Redbridge. 1957–8
- Baptist church, Harewood Drive, Claybury Park, Ilford, LB Redbridge. 1958
- Baptist church, Chingford, LB Waltham Forest. 1959

M. Purdon Smith
- Lincluden Parish Church, Margaret Walk, Dumfries. 1953
- See also John Sutherland

Peter F. Smith
- St Martin, Higher Poynton, Stockport. 1965.

Thomas Smith, William Wilson and Stanley H. Cox
- All Saints, Cyncoed, Merthyr Tydfil. 1959

Smith and Outhwaite
- Trinity Methodist Church, Royland Rd, Loughborough, Leics. 1964–6

Elkington Smithers and Bent Jorgen Jorgenson
- Swedish (Lutheran) Seamen's Church, Lower Rd, Rotherhithe, LB Southwark. 1967

J.C.S. Soutar
- Chapel, Mill Hill School, LB Barnet. 1926. II
- Chapel, Belmont Boarding School, Hereford. 1928

Spalding, Myers and Attenbrow
- Baptist Tabernacle, Greenleaf Rd, Walthamstow, LB Waltham Forest. 1949–50

Sir Basil Spence
- Cathedral Church of St Michael, Coventry. 1954–62. I
- St John, Willenhall, Coventry. 1955–7
- St Chad, Bell Green, Coventry. 1955–7
- St Oswald, Jardine Crescent, Tile Hill, Coventry. 1955–7.
- Trinity College Chapel, Glenmorgan, Scotland
- Church of Scotland. St Andrew, Clermiston View, Edinburgh. 1957–9
- Edinburgh University Chapel. 1958–60
- St Paul, Wordsworth Ave, Sheffield. 1958–9.
- St Hugh, Sturdee Rd, Eyres Monsell, Leicester. 1957–9
- St Aidan, New Parks Boulevard, Leicester. 1957–9
- St Francis, Greenbrow, Wythenshawe, Manchester. 1959–61
- St Catherine of Siena, Richmond Rd, Sheffield. 1958–62. II
- Meeting House, University of Sussex, Falmer, Brighton. 1965–6. II*
- Mortonhall Crematorium Chapel, Edinburgh. 1964–6. A. (Basil Spence, Glover and Ferguson.)
- St Matthew, Reading. 1967

H.R. Spencer
- St George, Marfleet Lane, Hull. 1955 in shell of 1938
- St Thomas, Hotham Rd, Hull. 1957
- Holy Apostles, Walker St, Hull. 1960

Spiers Ltd.
- Scottish Episcopal. Holy Cross, Great Western Rd, Knightswood, Glasgow. 1937–9. Remodelled by Whyte and Nicol, 1947

Charles Spooner
- St Paul, Burges Rd, East Ham, LB Newham. 1933

J.G. Stark
- RC church, Wool, Dorset. 1971

A.P. Starkey
- Christian Science Church, Watford, Herts. 1930–1

E.F. Starling

▸ St Peter, Dover's Green, Reigate, Surrey. 1955
▸ St Barnabas, Rushet Rd, St Paul's Cray, LB Bromley. 1962–4
▸ St Luke, Cell Barnes Lane, St Albans, Herts. 1968

Stellmacs Ltd, Designers and Builders

▸ RC Our Lady of Lourdes, Lourdes Ave, Glasgow. 1937–9

John E. Sterrett

▸ RC St Joseph, Gardenia Ave, Luton, Beds. 1958–60
▸ RC Our Lady and St George, London Road, LB Enfield. 1959

Stevenage Development Corporation

▸ St Andrew dual-purpose church and hall, Stevenage. 1953

Stevens, Scanlon and Co.

▸ Methodist church, Romford Rd, LB Newham. 1964

Samuel Stevenson

▸ Dromore First Presbyterian Church, Co. Down. 1915. B
▸ Ulsterville Presbyterian Church, Lisburn Rd, Belfast. 1923. B
▸ Congregational church, Donegall St, Belfast. 1952 reconstruction of church of 1932 and earlier.

W. Stevenson

▸ Church of Christ, Blair Ave, Glenrothes, Fife. 1975–6

Stevenson and Dunsworth

▸ Episcopal. St Donnan, Nostie, Lochalsh, Highland. 1962–4
▸ Episcopal. St Hilda, Oxgangs Rd North, Edinburgh. 1965. By Frederick R. Stevenson.

John Stewart and Patterson

▸ Helensburgh West Parish Church, Dunbarton, W. Dunbartonshire. 1923
▸ Netherlee church, Glasgow. 1934–5
▸ Balornock North Church, Northgate Rd, Glasgow. 1949–52

Stewart and Paterson

▸ Giffnock South Church, Greenhill Ave, Giffnock. 1927. B
▸ Baptist church, Inverness, Highland. 1932

Pascal J. Stienlet and J.C. Maxwell

▸ RC St Edward, Whitley Bay, N. Tyneside. 1928
▸ RC St Joseph, Armstrong Rd, Benwell, Newcastle upon Tyne. 1929

Pascal J. Stienlet and Son

▸ RC St Patrick, Owton Manor Lane, W. Hartlepool. 1961
▸ RC Our Lady and St Columba, Wallsend upon Tyne. 1961–2
▸ RC St Oswald, Gainsborough Ave, Whiteleas, S. Shields. 1965

Walter Stirrup and Son

▸ RC St Mary, Duke St, Denton, Greater Manchester. 1962

Stocks Bros. Buildings

▸ Danleigh and Bona Church, St Mary's Avenue, Inverness, Highland. 1979
▸ RC St Augustine of Canterbury, Whitecross St, Barton-upon-Humber. 1987, incorporating presbytery by Beart Foss, 1938

David Stokes

▸ RC Our Lady of the Visitation, Greenford, LB Ealing. 1956–9
▸ RC Our Lady of Walsingham, Haseldine Rd, London Colney, Herts. 1959

P.D. Stonham and Son

▸ St Elisabeth, Victoria Drive, Eastbourne. II. With A.R.G. Fenning, S.J. Tatchell and G.C. Wilson.

David Stratton-Davis

▸ St John, Churchdown, Glos. 1957
▸ St Michael, Whaddon Rd, Lynworth, Cheltenham, Glos. 1965–6

Harold Stratton-Davis and Charles W. Yates

▸ Holy Trinity, Longlevens, Glos. 1935
▸ St Mary, Birdlip, Glos. 1957

Granville Streatfield

▸ Chapel, Oakham School, Oakham, Rutland. 1924–5

Sutcliffe, Brandt and Partners

▸ St James, Bernard St, Southampton. 1956

E.A. Sutherland

▸ Methodist. Anniesland Church, Bearsden Rd, Glasgow. 1927

John Sutherland

▸ RC St Teresa, Glasgow St, Dumfries. 1956–8
▸ RC St Andrew, Shakespeare St, Dumfries. 1963–4. (Sutherland and Dickie)
▸ RC Church of the Resurrection, Riverbank, Gatehouse of Fleet, Dumfries and Galloway. 1971. (Sutherland, Dickie and Copland)

F.B. Swainson, J.V. Wilson and D.A. Shields

▸ Rockcliffe Park Church, Hurworth, Co. Durham. 1971

Edward A. Swan

▸ St Philip, Marksbury Ave, N. Sheen, Richmond. 1928–9 with C16 interior from Woodhall Farm, Oxted, Surrey.
▸ St Alban, Gander Green Lane, Cheam, Sutton. 1930, with barns from Cheam Court Farm. With A.J. Marshall.

James Swan

▸ Archbishop Benson Church Hall, Austin Rd, Handsworth, Birmingham. 1936. (Now United Church of God)

T. Aikman Swan

▸ Stenhouse Saughton Church, Gorgie Rd, Edinburgh. 1935. B
▸ Ormiston Parish Church, E. Lothian, 1938. B

Victor J. Syborn

▸ Methodist. Miller Memorial Church, Tottenham, LB Haringey. 1957–8

Charles Sykes

▸ Christ Church, Beckenham, LB Bromley. 1949. With Leslie T. Moore.

Elsworthy Sykes

▸ Methodist. Yaddlethorpe Church, Moorwell Rd, Scunthorpe. 1966–7
▸ St Nicholas, Hessle Rd, Hull. 1969–70, replacing John Bilson church of 1915, demolished 1968, from which some fittings incorporated.
▸ Methodist. Centenary Church, Frodingham Rd, Scunthorpe. 1971–2

Keith Symmons

▸ RC St Anne, Brixington Lane, Exmouth, Devon. 1968

Dragomir Tadic

▸ Serbian Orthodox. St Lazar, Cob Lane, Bournville, Birmingham. 1968

W.D.R. Taggart

▸ Church in Ireland. St Bartholomew, Stranmillis Rd, Belfast. B
▸ Church in Ireland. St Finnian, Cregagh, Belfast. B

Thomas S. Tait

▸ Christian Science. Second Church, Palace Gardens Terrace, RB Kensington and Chelsea. 1926, as Sir John Burnet, Tait and Son. II

Talbot Brown, Panter and Partners

▸ St Barnabas, Wellingborough, Northants. 1951–3

Michael Tapper

▸ College of the Order of the Resurrection, Mirfield, W. Yorks. Nave and aisles 1937. II

Sir Walter Tapper

▸ Annunciation, Old Quebec St, St Marylebone, City of Westminster. 1912–14. II*
▸ St Michael, Little Coates, Grimsby. 1913–14 adds to earlier church. B
▸ College of the Order of the Resurrection, Mirfield, W. Yorks. 1911–37. Completed by Michael Tapper. II
▸ St Mary, W. Cliffe Grove, Harrogate, N. Yorks. 1916–23
▸ St Columba, Liverpool. 1923
▸ Lower Chapel, Eton College, Eton, Berks. 1924
▸ Our Lady with St Thomas of Canterbury, Mount Rd, Gorton, Manchester. 1924–7
▸ Ascension, Malvern Link, Worcs. 1927–8
▸ St Stephen, Grimsby. 1927–9
▸ Hengrave Hall Chapel, Suffolk. 1929
▸ St Oswald, Harewood St, Deepdale, Preston, Lancs. 1934. Demolished

Harold O. Tarbolton

▸ RC Our Lady, Bangour Village Hospital, W. Lothian. 1924–30
▸ Episcopal. Church of the Ascension, Mosspark Drive, Glasgow. 1925–6
▸ Episcopal. St David of Scotland, Boswall Parkway, Edinburgh. 1939
▸ Episcopal. St Salvador, Saughton Mains Street, Edinburgh. 1939–42. With Matthew M. Ochterlony

S. Tatchell

▸ Chapel, Sir Robert Geffrye's Ironmongers' Almshouses, Mottingham, LB Bromley. 1935–7

A.J. Taylor

▸ Christian Science Church, N. View, Bristol. 1939

A.P. Taylor

▸ United Reformed Church, Clifford Ave, Hull. 1953

Harry Taylor

▸ Gracemount Church, Edinburgh. 1961
▸ Muirhouse Parish Church, Pennywell Gardens, Edinburgh. 1963

Isaac Taylor and W.C. Young

▸ St Matthew and St Aidan, Roundthorn Rd, Oldham. 1932–3. II
▸ St Paul, Victoria Ave, Blackley, Manchester. 1933
▸ St Gabriel, Bishop's Rd, Prestwich, Manchester. 1933–4
▸ St Luke the Physician, Benchill Rd, Wythenshawe, Manchester. 1938–9. II
▸ St Andrew, Cheadle Rd, Cheadle Hulme, Cheshire. 1957–9

Taylor, Roberts and Bowman

▸ St Saviour, Denton Lane, Chadderton, Greater Manchester. 1960–2

J.A. Teather

▸ Holy Trinity, Millhouses, Sheffield. 1939–40

Clifford Tee and Gale

▸ Friends' Meeting House, Watford Rd, King's Norton, Birmingham. 1964

F.W. Tempest

▸ Methodist church, Blidworth, Notts. 1932

Edwin James Tench

▸ Rayne Church, Essex. 1915–16

Herbert Theale

▸ RC St Athanasius, Fountains Rd, Kirkdale, Liverpool. 1954–7

C. Theobald and D. Skinray

▸ Somerville College Chapel, Oxford. 1934. II

Dewi Prys Thomas

▸ Friends' Meeting House, Telegraph Rd, Heswall, Cheshire. 1961–2. With Gerald Beech.

John Leslie Thomas

▸ Prefabricated church, Ebbw Vale, Blaenau Gwent, 1960

P. Hartland Thomas

▸ St Oswald, Cheddar Grove, Bedminster Down, Bristol. 1927. II
▸ St Mary, High St, Shirehampton, Bristol. 1929. II
▸ St Cuthbert, Sandy Park Rd, Brislington, Bristol. 1933
▸ All Saints, Southbrook, Swindon, Wilts. 1937

Sir Percy Thomas and Son (Percy Thomas Partnership from 1971)

- ▶ Methodist. King St Church, The Crescent, Plymouth. 1957
- ▶ Methodist. St Andrew, Cardiff. 1959
- ▶ RC Our Lady Help of Christians, Machynlleth, Montgomeryshire. 1965
- ▶ RC Cathedral of SS Peter and Paul, Clifton, Bristol. 1969–73

R.P. Thomas

- ▶ St John the Evangelist, Redlands Lane, Fareham, Hants. 1961–3

Bruce D. Thompson

- ▶ Methodist. St Paul, Dronfield, Derbys. 1959

Charles Clayton Thompson

- ▶ See Currey and Thompson

G.L. Thompson

- ▶ St Richard's Chapel, Selby, N. Yorkshire. 1965

Thompson and Whitehead

- ▶ St Cedd, Lodge Ave, LB Barking and Dagenham. 1963–4

Thoms and Nairn

- ▶ RC St Vincent de Paul, Tain, Ross and Cromarty. 1985–6. By Trevor Black.

Frank Thomson

- ▶ Craigiebank Church, Craigie Ave, W. Ferry, Dundee. 1937. B

James Taylor Thomson

- ▶ United Free Church. New Bridgegate Church, Dixon Rd, Govanhill, Glasgow. 1923. Thomson, Sandilands and Macleod.
- ▶ Mosspark Parish Church, Ashkirk Drive, Glasgow. 1925–9. Thomson, Sandilands and MacLeod.
- ▶ Scottish Presbyterian. St John Renfield, Beaconsfield Rd, Kelvinside, Glasgow. 1929–31. B
- ▶ High Carntyne Church, Carntynehall Rd, Glasgow. 1931–2. B

Leslie Grahame Thomson

- ▶ Reid Memorial Church, W. Savile Terrace, Blackford, Edinburgh. 1929–33. A
- ▶ Fairmilehead Parish Church, Frogston Rd West, Edinburgh. 1937–8. B
- ▶ Moncur Memorial Church, Stronsay, Orkney. 1950–5
- ▶ Longstone Parish Church, Kingsknowe Rd North, Edinburgh. 1954
- ▶ Christ Church, Dunoline, Corran Esplanade, Oban. 1957. B

Thomson, Sandilands and MacLeod

- ▶ New Bridgegate Church, Dixon Rd, Warren St, Glasgow. 1922–3. B
- ▶ Mosspark Parish Church, Ashkirk Rd, Glasgow. 1927. B

Philip Tilden

- ▶ Chapel for the Order of the Salesian of St John Bosco, Shrigley Hall, Pott Shrigley, Cheshire. 1936–8. II

W.W. Todd

- ▶ St George, Biggin Hill, LB Bromley. 1947. For RAF

J.B.L. Tolhurst

- ▶ St Luke, Well Hall, Eltham, LB Greenwich. S. aisle added to church by Temple Moore, 1933.

Tulloch and Fitzsimons

- ▶ Lowe Memorial Presbyterian Church, Finaghy, Belfast. 1935. B

Tomei and Maxwell

- ▶ RC St Richard, Market Ave, Chichester, W. Sussex. 1958
- ▶ RC All Saints, Queen's Rd, Hersham, Surrey. 1959–60
- ▶ RC St Dominic, Violet Lane, Waddon, LB Croydon. 1961
- ▶ RC St Columba, Queenhill Rd, Selsdon, LB Croydon. 1962
- ▶ RC Good Shepherd, Dunley Drive, New Addington, LB Croydon. 1962
- ▶ RC Sacred Heart, Guy Rd, Wallington, LB Sutton. 1963–5
- ▶ RC St Matthias, Brinkley Rd, Worcester Park, LB Sutton. 1965
- ▶ RC Our Lady and St Peter, Victoria Drive, Putney, LB Wandsworth. 1971 (Tomei, Mackley and Pound).

Peter Tong

- ▶ St Ninian, Harlow Green, Gateshead. 1967

W.J. Walker Todd

- ▶ Episcopal. St Columba, Bathgate, W. Lothian. 1916

H. Tooley and R.C. Foster

- ▶ St Anne, Chingford, LB Waltham Forest. 1953
- ▶ RC St Edmund, Traps Hill, Loughton, Essex. 1958

John F. Torry

- ▶ RC Good Shepherd, Dalmilling, N. Ayrshire. 1957

Henry Bingham Towner

- ▶ St Thomas of Canterbury, Mayfield, E. Sussex. 1957
- ▶ RC Our Lady of Lourdes, Rottingdean, Brighton. 1958
- ▶ Convent of the Holy Family, Norfolk Rd, Littlehampton, W. Sussex. 1960
- ▶ RC Blessed Sacrament, Chelmsford, Essex. 1962
- ▶ St Mark, W. Wickham, LB Bromley. 1962–3

Sidney Toy

- ▶ St Andrew, Redruth, Cornwall. 1924–5

E.J. Toye

- ▶ RC St Patrick, Buncrana Rd, Pennyburn, Londonderry, Co. Derry. 1932. B+. Completed by J.P. McGrath.

J.J. Tracey

- ▶ RC St Mary Queen of Peace, Garrison, Co. Fermanagh. 1973
- ▶ See also Liam McCormick and Partners

Frank Tranmer

- ▶ Christian Science. First Church, Harrogate, Yorks. 1929

Martin Travers

- ▶ St Matthew, New Kent Rd, LB Southwark. 1926–7 internal remodelling of 1855–7 church by Henry Jarvis. II
- ▶ Good Shepherd, Queen Mary's Ave, Carshalton, LB Sutton. 1930. With T.F.W. Grant. II
- ▶ Holy Redeemer, Main Rd, Streatham Vale, LB Lambeth. 1931. With T.F.W. Grant.
- ▶ Emmanuel Church, Lea Bridge Rd, Leyton, LB Waltham Forest. 1934–5. With T.F.W. Grant. II

H.F. Trew

- ▶ RC Chapel of St Thomas More and St John Fisher, Hampton Green, Box, Minchinhampton, Glos. 1930

J.K. Trew and R.M. Dunn

- ▶ Guards Chapel, Wellington Barracks. City of Westminster. II. See also H.S. Goodhart-Rendel.

Matthew Trotter

- ▶ RC SS Peter and Paul, Redhill Rd, Roseworth, Stockton-on-Tees. 1956

F.G. Troup

- ▶ St Richard, Aldwick, W. Sussex. 1933
- ▶ St Andrew, Warninglid, E. Sussex. 1935

Thomas F. Trower

- ▶ Methodist church, Upwell, Isle of Ely, Cambs. 1956

A.E. Tutte

- ▶ Methodist church, Drayton, Hants. 1933

Richard Twentyman (as Lavender and Twentyman; Lavender, Twentyman and Percy from 1942; Twentyman, Percy and Partners from c.1960

- ▶ St Gabriel, Walstead Rd, Fullbrook, Walsall. 1937–9
- ▶ St Martin, Dixon St, Parkfield (Ettingshall), Wolverhampton. 1937–9. II
- ▶ All Saints, Walsall St, Darlaston, W. Mids. 1952
- ▶ Crematorium chapel, Bushbury, Wolverhampton. 1954
- ▶ St Nicholas, Engleton Rd, Radford, Coventry. 1954–5
- ▶ Emmanuel, Queen Elizabeth Avenue, Bentley, Walsall. 1955–7
- ▶ St Chad, New Rd, Rubery, Worcs. 1956–60
- ▶ St Andrew, Hunter St, Whitmore Reans, Wolverhampton. 1965

Twentyman, Percy and Partners

- ▶ St Andrew, Runcorn, Cheshire. 1965
- ▶ Crematorium chapel, Redditch, Worcs. 1973 (John Hares)

J.A. Tynan

- ▶ RC St Joseph, Ederny, Co. Fermanagh. 1954

Cecil Upcher

- ▶ St Alban, Grove Walk, Lakenham, Norwich. 1932–8

Francis Xavier Velarde

- ▶ RC St Matthew, Townsend Ave, Clubmoor, Liverpool. 1930
- ▶ RC St Gabriel, Brownhill Drive, Blackburn. 1932–3
- ▶ RC St Monica, Fernhill Rd, Bootle, Merseyside. 1936. II
- ▶ RC Our Lady of Pity, Greasby, Cheshire. 1952
- ▶ RC English Martyrs, St George's Rd, Wallasey, Wirral. 1952–3
- ▶ RC St Teresa, Upholland College, Lancs. 1952–7
- ▶ RC St Cuthbert, Mouldsworth, Cheshire. 1955
- ▶ RC St Alexander, St John's Rd, Kirkdale, Liverpool. 1955–7. Demolished.
- ▶ RC St Luke, Love Lane, Pinner, LB Harrow. 1957. Church hall 1965 by Grima.
- ▶ RC Holy Cross, Hoylake Rd, Bidston, Birkenhead. 1959
- ▶ RC St Edmund, Nelson Rd, Whitton, LB Richmond. 1961–3. Completed by Richard O'Mahony.
- ▶ RC St Patrick, Loughrigg Ave, Clinkham Wood, St Helens. 1963–4. (F.X. Velarde Partnership)

J. Velarde and Partners

- ▶ RC St Teresa, Borehamwood, Herts. 1962–3

Austin Vernon and Partners

- ▶ Church Army Chapel, Vanbrugh Park, LB Greenwich. 1965

J. Jeffrey Waddell

- ▶ Lockhart Memorial Church, Albion Rd, Edinburgh. 1927. By Waddell and Young. B
- ▶ Kinlochleven Parish Church, Highland. 1930
- ▶ St Bride, Sanquhar, Dumfries and Galloway. 1930–1. Chancel and internal rebuilding of 1822–3 church by James Thomson (Waddell and Young)

F.T. Waddington and H.G. Waddington

- ▶ St Mary, Blackpool, Lancs. 1932

Kenneth Waite

- ▶ St Luke, Folkestone, Kent. 1960

D.J. Walker and Partners

- ▶ Holy Family, Pontefract, W. Yorks. 1965
- ▶ St Benedict, Garforth, W. Yorks. 1969

Walker and Biggin

- ▶ RC Our Lady of Lourdes, Leeds. 1960

Stansfeld T. (Bob) Walker and Graham Winteringham
▸ St Thomas, Garrett's Green Lane, Garrett's Green, Birmingham. 1957–60
▸ St James, Aston, Birmingham. 1969

Charles Walsh (Crendon Concrete Co.)
▸ RC Our Lady of Light, Chearsley Rd, Long Crendon, Bucks. 1971

Joseph E. Walter
▸ RC St Boniface, Lympstone, Devon. 1956
▸ RC St Brannoc, Braunton, Devon. 1958

E.J. Walters
▸ See also below
▸ RC Our Lady and St Petroc, Ashburton, Devon. 1935
▸ RC St John the Baptist, Dale Rd, Purley, LB Croydon. 1939. Completed 1958 by Walters and Kerr Bate.
▸ RC St Pancras, High St, Lewes, E. Sussex. 1939

Walters and Kerr Bate
▸ RC St Benedict (Ealing Abbey), Charlbury Grove, LB Ealing. 1895–7, 1905 (by F.A. Walters), 1962. II
▸ RC St Mary, Canton, Cardiff. 1906–27. (F.A. Walters). II
▸ RC Buckfast Abbey Church, Buckfastleigh, Devon. 1907–32 (F.A. Walters). Blessed Sacrament chapel by Paul Pearn, 1965. II*
▸ RC Our Lady of Lourdes, Station Rd, Ashby-de-la-Zouch, Leics. 1908–15. (F.A. Walters). II
▸ RC St Joseph, Penarth. 1914–15, 1928. II
▸ RC St Wilfrid, Lorrimore Rd, LB Southwark. 1915 (F.A. Walters)
▸ RC Our Lady of Lourdes, Weydown Rd, Haslemere, Surrey. 1924 (F.A. Walters)
▸ RC Cathedral Church of St Peter, Jewry St, Winchester, Hants. 1926 (F.A. Walters). II
▸ RC Our Lady of Lourdes, Rothamsted Ave, Harpenden, Herts. 1928–36. (F.A. Walters)
▸ RC St John the Baptist, Dale Rd, Purley, LB Croydon. 1939 (E.J. Walters), 1958
▸ RC St Joan, Highbury, LB Islington. 1959.
▸ RC St Catherine Labouré, Woolwich Rd, LB Greenwich. 1961
▸ RC Our Lady and St Philip Neri, Sydenham Rd, LB Lewisham. 1964

D. Garbutt Walton
▸ Methodist church, Deal, Kent. 1966

P.J.W. Ware
▸ RC St Cuthbert, Burnham-on-Sea, Somerset. 1966–7

E.P. Warren
▸ Good Shepherd, Preston, Brighton. 1921–2, 1927. Furnishings and organ case by W.H. Randoll Blacking.

Paul Waterhouse
▸ Convent of the Incarnation, Fairacres Rd, Cowley, Oxford. 1922–3

W.G. Watkins
▸ St Giles, Lamb Gardens, Lincoln. 1936

Alexander F. Watson
▸ RC Our Lady of the Rosary, Southlands Rd, Bexhill, E. Sussex. 1954–5

J. Fletcher Watson
▸ All Saints, Bawdeswell, Norfolk. 1953–5

R. Paxton Watson and B. Costin
▸ Christ Church, Blackfriars Rd, LB Southwark. 1960

W. Charles Waymouth
▸ St Andrew, Harrow Rd, Sudbury, LB Brent. 1925–6. II

Stanley J. Wearing and Barry C.C. Hastings
▸ Baptist church. St Mary, Norwich. 1955–6

Aston Webb and Sons
▸ St Leonard, Turners Hill, E. Sussex. Tower and porches, 1923, to church of 1895 by Lacy Ridge
▸ Chapel, Camberwell New Cemetery, LB Southwark. 1930

Maurice Webb
▸ Chapel, Whiteley Village, Surrey. 1912, 1925–6. II
▸ St Lawrence College Chapel, Ramsgate. 1927

W.R. Norman Webster
▸ Baptist Church, Downfield Estate, Cambridge. 1958

Ronald Weeks
▸ See Percy Thomas Partnership

Weightman and Bullen
▸ RC St Mary, Highfield St, Liverpool. 1948–53
▸ RC St William of York, Thornton, Lancs. 1956–7
▸ RC St Catherine, Lane Head, Lowton, Greater Manchester. 1956–9
▸ RC St Mary, St Mary's Rd, Crumpsall, Manchester. 1958
▸ RC Holy Ghost, Bootle, Sefton, Merseyside. 1958
▸ RC St Ambrose, Heathgate Ave, Speke, Liverpool. 1959–61
▸ RC St Mary's Priory Church, Leyland, Lancs. 1962–4
▸ RC St Margaret Mary, Pilch Lane, Knotty Ash, Liverpool. 1962–4
▸ RC St Winefride, Welshpool, Montgomeryshire. 1963
▸ RC St David, St David's Lane, Mold, Flintshire. 1964
▸ RC Sacred Heart, The Highway, Hawarden, Flintshire. 1966–7
▸ RC St David, Llandrindod Wells, Radnorshire. 1971
▸ RC St Mary, Ffynnongroew Rd, Rhyl, Flintshire. 1974–5

Welch and Lander
▸ See also Nugent Francis Cachemaille-Day
▸ See also Felix Lander
▸ Methodist church, Hendon, LB Barnet. 1937–8
▸ St Luke, Mission Church and hall, Watford, Herts. 1938
▸ Barnet Mission Church and hall, LB Barnet. 1938
▸ St Barnabas, Adeyfield, Hemel Hempstead, Herts. 1953
▸ Holy Cross, Balmoral Drive, Boreham Wood, Herts. 1955. By Felix J. Lander.

Wellesley and Wills
▸ SS Mary and George, Dashwood Ave, High Wycombe, Bucks. 1935–8. B

A. Randall Wells
▸ St Wilfrid, Selby Rd, Halton, Leeds. 1937–9. II

Weston, Burnett and Thomas
▸ Evangelical Church, James St, Southampton. 1965

Harold Wharfe
▸ Christ the King, Bowburn, Durham. 1963–78

William B. Wheatley and Holdsworth
▸ Danish Lutheran. St Nicholai, Osborne St, Hull. 1955

Harry A. Wheeler and Frank Sproson
▸ Church of Scotland. St Columba, Church St, Glenrothes, Fife. 1960–1
▸ Torbain Church, Kirkaldy, Fife. 1964–8
▸ Episcopal. St Peter, Townsend Place, Kirkcaldy, Fife. 1976

Peter Whiston
▸ RC St Margaret, Davidson's Mains, Edinburgh. 1950. With Alexander McRobie.
▸ RC Santa Maria Abbey, W. Lothian. 1951–
▸ RC St Ninian, Macbeth Moir Rd, Musselburgh, Midlothian. 1955–7
▸ RC St Mark, Oxgangs Ave, Edinburgh. 1959
▸ RC St Columba, Kirkgate, Cupar, Fife. 1964
▸ RC St Joseph, Linlithgow, W. Lothian. 1965. Conversion of United Secession church of 1827
▸ Church of Scotland. St Anthony, Mar Gardens, High Burnside, Glasgow. 1967–70
▸ RC St Paul, Pennywell Rd, Edinburgh. 1968
▸ RC Corpus Christi, Lincoln Ave, Scotstounhill, Glasgow. 1969–72. C

George F. Whitby
▸ Grange Free Church, Northolt, LB Ealing. 1956–7

Claude Neville White
▸ Solihull School Chapel, Solihull, Birmingham. 1959–62

G.M. White and C.C. Hegarty
▸ RC church, Tamnhern, Co. Derry. 1966–7

K.C. White
▸ Emmanuel, Dudley Drive, Morden, LB Merton. 1962

Patrick M. White
▸ RC St Anne, Prince Charles Rd, Queen's Park, Wrexham. 1960–2

White and Hegarty
▸ RC St Mary, Star of the Sea, Eglinton, Co. Derry. 1960

William White (Building Design Partnership)
▸ Church of Christ the Servant, Digmoor, Lancs. 1972

J.P. Whittle (Halliday, Meesham and Partners)
▸ Presbyterian. St Columba, Wilmslow Rd, Handforth, Cheadle, Cheshire. 1968–9

Whyte and Galloway
▸ St Aidan, Clarkston, Edinburgh. 1924
▸ St Margaret, Newlands, Glasgow. 1924. Demolished
▸ St Serf, Shettleston Rd, Glasgow. 1934–6
▸ Episcopal. St Barnabas, Craigpark, Dennistoun, Glasgow. 1935–6

H.H. Wigglesworth and Marshall Mackenzie
▸ Lutheran. Swedish Sailors Mission, Lower Rd, Rotherhithe, LB Southwark. 1930
▸ See also Elkington Smithers and Bent Jorgen Jorgenson.

M.L. Wilkinson
▸ St Christopher, Blackheath, LB Lewisham. 1946

J.H. Willet
▸ St Barnabas, Emmer Green, Reading. 1924

Desmond Williams and Associates
▸ RC Our Lady Immaculate, Dunstable, Beds. 1961–4
▸ RC St Patrick, Elliot St, Rochdale. 1965–8
▸ RC St Anthony, Farnham Rd, Farnham Royal, Bucks. 1964 completion of church by Arthur Fairbrother (q.v.)
▸ RC St Augustine, Grosvenor Square, Chorlton-on-Medlock, Manchester. 1965–8
▸ RC St Dunstan, Edgbaston, Birmingham. 1965–8. By Jack Edmonson.
▸ See also H. Greenhalgh

Gilbert Williams
▸ Christian Science. First Church, Hendon, LB Barnet. 1961
▸ Christian Science. First Church, Holylake. 1968–9

Harry Williams
▸ St Ninian, Kilmarnock. 1959

Leonard Williams

- RC All Saints, Oxted, Surrey. 1914–22
- RC St George, Harrow Rd, Sudbury, LB Brent. 1926–30, completed by J. Eustace Salisbury. II

Mrs R. Williams

- St John, St James's Rd, Shirley, Southampton. 1960

Williams, Sleight and Co

- RC St Wilfrid, Boulevard, Hull. 1954–6

Williams and Winckley

- RC St Margaret, St Margaret's Rd, Twickenham, LB Richmond-on-Thames. 1968
- RC St Elphege, Stafford Rd, Beddington, LB Sutton. 1971. Replacement of church by J.H. Beart Foss and Fr. Benedict Williamson, 1908, now used as hall.

Clough Williams-Ellis

- Christian Science. First Church, University Ave, Belfast. 1923–37. B+
- Moriah Methodist Chapel, Llanystumdwy, Dwyfor, Gwynedd. 1936. II

Fr. Benedict Williamson

- RC St Ignatius, Stamford Hill, LB Haringey. 1896–1927. II
- RC St Boniface, Mitcham Rd, Tooting, LB Wandsworth. 1907, remodelled with west facade 1927. II (By Williamson and Foss).
- RC Sacred Heart, Southwold, Suffolk. 1914
- St Edmund's College, Chapel, Cambridge. 1916
- RC Chapel, Hare St House, Buntingdon, Herts. 1916
- RC English Martyrs, Royston, Herts. 1916–7
- RC Our Lady of Perpetual Succour, Tynemouth St, Fulham. 1922. With T.H.B. Scott
- RC Sacred Heart and Mary Immaculate, Mill Hill, LB Barnet. 1923. Demolished 1994
- RC Holy Cross, Ashington Rd, Parson's Green, Fulham. 1924

J.H.H. Willman

- St Gregory, Salisbury, Wilts. 1937–8

S. Alex Wilmot and J.R. Armstrong

- Congregational (United Reformed) Church, Chester Rd, Pype Hayes, Birmingham. 1929–30

Willmott and Smith

- St Edward King and Confessor, Westville Rd, Roath, Cardiff. 1921. Nave 1968

James Mollison Wilson

- St Matthew, Thatto Heath, St Helens. 1953–4
- RC St David, Eskdale Ave, Moss Bank, St Helens. 1956–7

John W. Wilson

- Congregational church, Lodge Rd, Knowle, Warks. 1922–3

T.E. Wilson

- RC St Joseph, Uppingham Rd, Leicester. 1967–8
- RC St Joseph, Station Rd, Oakham, Rutland. 1975
- RC St Peter, Hinckley Rd, Leicester. 1978

W.G. Wilson

- St Mary, Thorpeness, Suffolk. 1936–7. II

A.E. Wiseman

- St John the Divine, Goresbrook Rd, Becontree, LB Barking and Dagenham. 1934. Demolished 1997
- St Patrick, Blake Ave, LB Barking. 1940

Edgar Joseph Wood

- Baptist church, Fryerns, Basildon, Essex. 1954
- Baptist church, Crofton Park. 1959
- Baptist chapel, Townley Rd, Bexleyheath, LB Bexley. 1961–2

Kenneth B. Wood

- Emmanuel, Tolworth, LB Kingston. 1957–9

Walter B. Wood

- St Catharine, Wotton, Gloucester. 1915

Wood, Goldstraw and Yorath

- St Werburgh, High Lane, Burslem, Stoke-on-Trent, Staffs, 1952–3
- St John the Baptist, Barlaston, Staffs. 1984

Wood, Kendrick and Williams

- All Saints, Belwell Lane, Four Oaks, Sutton Coldfield. 1955–7 (chancel, baptistery and vestries). see also Edwin F. Reynolds. II*

R.B. Wood-Jones

- St John, Flixton, Manchester. 1968. In association with Marsden and Arshavir.

H.A. Noel Woodall (Richard Owen and Son)

- Welsh Presbyterian church, Stanley Rd, Bootle, Merseyside. 1951
- Baptist church, Kirkby, Merseyside. 1957–8

Woodroofe, Buchanan and Coulter

- St Paul, Lorrimore Square, LB Southwark. 1955–60
- Baptist church, Balham, LB Wandsworth. 1959

E. Glyn Wooley

- St Mary, Merlin St, Johnstown, Rhosllanerchrugog, Denbighshire. 1926–8. Completed by H. Anthony Clark, F.C. Roberts and Partners, 1957

Thomas Worthington and Sons

- St Edward Mission Church and hall, Mottingham, LB Bromley. 1936

Graham Wright Partnership

- Christ Church, Thurncourt Rd, Leicester. 1957
- St Chad, Broad Ave, Leicester. 1968
- St Theodore, Nicklaus Rd, Rushey Mead, Leicester. 1980

Wycliffe Noble and Partners

- Salvation Army Citadel, Brompton Lane, Hendon, LB Barnet. 1962

Wylie, Shanks and Partners

- Colston Milton Church, Egilsay Crescent, Glasgow. 1950–2

S.A.S. Yeo

- Seven Day Adventist church, Holloway Rd, LB Islington. 1928

Yorke, Rosenberg and Mardall (Cyril Mardall, né Sjöström)

- Lutheran. Finnish Seamen's Mission, Albion Rd, Rotherhithe, LB Southwark. 1956–8

Arthur Young

- RC St Richard of Chichester, Station Rd, Buntingford, Herts. 1915. II*
- St Michael and All Angels, S. Lancing, W. Sussex. 1924. With A.D. Reid.
- RC Our Lady and St Peter, Aldeburgh, Suffolk. 1925. With A.D. Reid.
- RC St John the Divine, Earlsfield, LB Wandsworth. 1925. With A.D. Reid.

James Reid Young and Mackenzie

- Rosemary Presbyterian Church, North Circular Rd, Belfast. 1955–6
- Methodist church, Cavehill, Belfast. 1956–7

W.C. Young

- St Luke, Benchill, Manchester. 1938–9

Young and Mackenzie

- First Presbyterian Church, Broughshane, Co. Antrim. 1929–30. B+
- Methodist church, Cavehill Rd, Belfast. 1953

Young and Purves

- German Lutheran. Martin Luther Church, Barton Rd, Stretford, Manchester. 1963. By T.D. Howcroft.

ADDENDA

A.J. Hodsdon Archard and Partners

- St John the Baptist, King Edward's Rd, LB Hackney. 1956, remodelled 1972

John Finlayson and Iain Langlands

- United Reformed Church. St John, Somerset Rd, New Barnet, LB Barnet. 1969

Gunton and Gunton

- Methodist Central Hall, Mare St, LB Hackney. 1926–7

Martin Heine

- United Reformed Church, Rectory Rd, LB Hackney, 1992–3

Alan Hodgson Hope

- Methodist Hall, Belfast. 1934

James B. Kennedy

- RC St Colman, Lambeg, Co. Down. 1989–91
- RC St Brigid, Malone Rd, Belfast. 1994–6

Laurence McConville

- RC church, Holywood, Co. Down. 1995

Wilfrid C. Mangan

- RC Our Lady and St Joseph, Balls Pond Rd, Dalston, LB Hackney, 1962–4

D.F. Martin-Smith

- St George, Britwell, Slough, 1958

Bernard Miller

- St Bertelin, Eccleshall Rd, Stafford. 1955

T.H.B. Scott

- RC Our Lady of Good Counsel, Bouverie Rd, LB Hackney. 1936

Peter F. Smith (Ferguson, Smith and Associates)

- United Reformed Church, Manor Rd, LB Hackney. 1969

Pascal J. Stienlet

- RC St Joseph, Westgate, Wetherby, W. Yorks. 1986

Henry Bingham Towner

- RC St Thomas More, Seaford, E. Sussex. 1935–6

Tracey and Mullarky

- RC church, Dunloy, Co. Antrim. 1990
- RC church, Coagh, Co. Tyrone. 1992